Ambition and Delight

Ambition and Delight

A Life in Experimental Biology

HENRY R. BOURNE

To order additional copies of this book, contact:
Xlibris Corporation
1-888-795-4274
www.Xlibris.com
Orders@Xlibris.com
58711

For my children and grandchildren—Michael,
Randy, Molly, Julia, Henry, and Luke

ACKNOWLEDGMENTS

During this book's long gestation, I received valuable help, advice, and encouragement from many people. Their advice, criticisms, and memories corrected errors and rescued me from potential disasters. These readers include my two sons, Michael Bourne and Randy Bourne, plus many friends and colleagues, including Steve Arkin, Ole Faergeman, Adrian Ferre-D'Amare, Al Gilman, Jane Hirshfield, Taroh Iiri, Matt Lerner, Dyche Mullins, John Nathan, John Newell, Miranda Robertson, Antonina Roll-Mecak, Bill Seaman, Holly Smith, and Keith Yamamoto. I followed their advice in many cases, but not all, and all the book's faults are my own. Elaine Meng's unique blend of esthetic and technical prowess contributed to preparation of the 3D structures of protein molecules depicted in chapter 11 and on the cover. Elizabeth Stark, a remarkable wordsmith and editor, took on the formidable task of teaching me how to craft sentences, organize paragraphs, and shape coherent chapters. She skillfully managed to criticize and encourage at the same time, improving the book immeasurably.

Finally, I want to thank Nancy Bourne, who first had to live through the life of this memoir with me, and then found herself reading the story all over again, in multiple iterations. Her memory for dates and details, along with her gift for nuance, shepherded me through thorny thickets in the writing. For her similarly generous and even more crucial help during the living of the life, I am deeply grateful.

CONTENTS

PROLOGUE

OR

WHY READ THIS BOOK?

"Why do you lab guys claim experiments are more fun than anything you can do with your clothes on?" The associate dean looked puzzled, but gave me no time for an answer. "Makes me wonder if you know what real fun is!" he added, flashing a grin.

I laughed. With his clothes off, this distinguished, white-haired clinician was known to have had more fun than most of his colleagues—and not only in his youth.

It was also true, I reflected, that he had little knowledge of what experimental biologists do in their labs. Like many bright, sophisticated people, he couldn't imagine anything less dreary than the apparently solitary life of a laboratory scientist.

From forty years of working in labs, I know that experimental biologists lead lives that are anything but dreary and solitary. Instead, we feel viscerally engaged for most of our working lives, driven by curiosity, hope, ambition, and delight—and sometimes, to be sure, ravaged by disappointment and despair. Intensely social, we jostle against colleagues and their ideas at every turn. We question or answer, disagree or agree, compete or collaborate—not just now and then, when the spirit moves us, but always, as if our lives depended on it, as in fact they do.

One way to tell people what our lives are really like, I thought, would be to describe the life of a real experimental biologist. The biologist whose life I know best is myself. Would telling my story be worthwhile, considering that successful books about scientists[1] almost invariably depict the lives and discoveries of towering geniuses?

Perhaps, on the other hand, the life of an "ordinary" scientist and his discoveries could offer real advantages. For one thing, stories like mine have not often been told. For another, it may be easier to understand and identify with thoughts and feelings of a non-genius, whether in triumph or in failure. (The associate dean might ask whether the average genius, fully clothed, has more fun than the ordinary scientist in the lab. My best guess is "No," although I'm sure we could find a genius who disagrees.)

Beginning as an ignorant young man from the provinces, I entered science after a series of tortuous switchbacks in other directions and eventually slipped in through the back door, almost inadvertently. I took several wrong paths, and research apprenticeships with a menagerie of mentors taught me how not to do experimental biology. In my thirties, I found a marvelous mentor, and began a career as an independent scientist. Thereafter, I directed a productive research lab, taught students and postdocs and, for almost a decade, chaired an academic department in a first-rate biomedical research institution. I met with both failure and success, but over the long run, amounting to 40 years, experimental biology gave me immense satisfaction, amazing joy, and a full life, in and out of science.

My story is not "representative." No one is a typical experimental biologist. Instead, scientists differ profoundly from one another, and so do their discoveries. Their personalities, virtues, faults, joys, and sorrows shape everything they accomplish, and shape their failures as well. Each brings to a question her or his unique blend of knowledge and ignorance, insight and blind spots, rigorous analysis and wandering imagination. A scientist's life, like anyone else's, is ineluctably contingent and unpredictable, depending on innate character, background, and chance-dependent encounters with a unique set of people and challenges.

At best an unpredictable enterprise, discovery works most efficiently by harnessing every atom of human diversity it can find. Consequently, interactions between individuals drive almost every discovery. Both the exuberant variations among scientists and their fertile conflicts and collaborations are absolutely necessary. Working together, two good minds are almost always more effective than one.[2]

For this reason, the isolated genius of legend has trouble keeping up, and most successful experimental biologists are intensely social creatures.

Among these interactions, the relation between young scientists and their elders plays crucial roles. By bringing two minds together, such relations often furnish the essential element for discovery. They also form the core of experimental biology's social network, an indispensable conduit for its lore, gossip, insights, and values. I know neurobiologists, for example, who trace their heritage to scientific giants of the late 19th and early 20th centuries, like Charles Sherrington and Ramon y Cajal. My own mentors changed the course of my life in science, and my later mentoring of students and postdoctoral fellows has taught them—and me—indispensable lessons.

I'll tell about these individuals and their interactions, focusing mainly on the process of scientific discovery. My stories describe discoveries that affected me (and others) in very different ways. The first discovery, which ultimately won the Nobel Prize, began in several competing labs, including my own. The initial findings confused many of us, but set the stage for one lab (sadly, not my own) to conceive the right strategy and do the right experiments. This discovery framed questions I would ask for three more decades.

The second "discovery," which in fact comprised hundreds of individual discoveries, whirled me in a maelstrom of new ideas and opportunities for new experiments. This was a real scientific revolution, bringing scientists the very grail they always seek—new questions to explore and new experimental tools for asking them. The DNA revolution, triggered by experimenters who learned how to decipher and manipulate sequences of the genetic material, opened new avenues for exploring how cells and organisms work, and in doing so transformed the intellectual foundations and practical conduct of experiments as well as the working lives of thousands of biologists.

The first 40 years of the DNA revolution may have generated the most exciting train of discoveries and challenges experimental biology has seen or is likely to see for many decades. Although I joined the revolution rather late myself, my career in science coincided almost exactly with the rapid explosion of new molecular knowledge that transformed biology in the 20th century. My colleagues and I kept our clothes on, but we also had enormous fun, for many years.

The third kind of discovery is more circumscribed, and brings a great but very different emotional reward—the visceral, immensely satisfying "click" of unraveling a complex puzzle. One click story served as the spark that kindled writing this book. It begins with a rare disease, proceeds through a frustrating effort to resolve a paradox, and ends in a delicious surprise. The story will help non-scientists to feel the transcendent delight of that click, or something very like it. I want to transmit that delight for its own sake, but also because it is critical for sustaining what we call "real life." Between great discoveries and scientific revolutions, scientists live for clicks like this. Minor clicks keep us going for a week or two. The click story I highlight in this book sustained me for years.

———

The twists, turns, and fun of my career are tightly bound to the biological questions I tackled in this period. Those questions formed part of the much broader effort of thousands of scientists, which aimed very high—at nothing less than understanding the molecular mechanisms that give life to the earth's organisms. My particular questions belonged to a new field, "cell signaling," focused on mechanisms cells use to detect and respond to external signals. This field hardly existed when I first entered a lab, but has now become a thriving enterprise in academia and industry. Let me try to convey a sense of what was at stake.

In the 1950s biologists knew that all organisms, even one-celled bacteria, could mount complex responses to external stimuli, like light, heat, or chemical compounds. Physiologists had established that organs and cells of multicellular organisms produce or respond to dozens of distinct chemical stimuli, or "signals" like insulin and other hormones or neurotransmitters like acetylcholine. (Insulin, secreted into the blood from cells in the pancreas, controls the concentration of blood sugar, and acetylcholine is released from nerves to stimulate contraction of muscles.)

As scientists identified hundreds of new intercellular signals, they began to wonder how cells detect them and convert them into responses. Most chemical signals could not penetrate into the cell directly, because they were unable to cross the fatty peripheral membrane around it. Indirect evidence suggested that these signals must associate with distinct sites on the cell's surface. Although no one had ever seen these sites, they came to be called *receptors*.

How receptors initiate responses remained a mystery, partly because so little was known about chemicals inside the cell. Many of these chemicals were proteins, large molecules made up of chains of chemical building blocks. Some proteins, the enzymes, had been extracted from broken-up cells and shown to convert one chemical into another. But none of the enzymes, it seemed, served as a receptor for a chemical signal generated outside the cell.

Although many scientists feared that breaking cells would inevitably abolish responses to external stimuli, Earl Sutherland's lab dared to try—and made a critical breakthrough, by showing how a hormone causes membranes from broken cells to produce a small chemical compound that regulates enzymes found inside the cells. This compound, cyclic AMP, represented the first-discovered biological strategy for transmitting hormonal signals across cell membranes.

I was in college when Sutherland discovered cyclic AMP. It posed appealing questions as I zigzagged through laboratories in the late 1960s, and was to play a major role in my own lab's experiments a decade later. One of my experiments helped to set the stage for a momentous discovery by another lab, which I mentioned above. In the late 1970s, they identified, in exquisite biochemical detail, the signaling relay device cells use to convert external hormone signals into cyclic AMP signals inside the cell.

At the time no one could have imagined the cornucopia of questions and experiments that relay device would generate. It represented the first established molecular machine for transmitting external signals across membranes, and remains today the best understood of such machines. For 20 years it served as the main focus of my own research.

More broadly, this signal relay device, in combination with cyclic AMP itself and other devices soon to be discovered, created the field of cell signaling. Four fertile concepts anchored the new field to the wider enterprise of cell and molecular biology. These concepts, which I describe more fully below, include *signaling pathways* for transmitting information, *molecular recognition* of individual proteins and signals, *activation* of receptors or enzymes, and the pivotal roles played by the *three-dimensional* (3D) *shapes* of signaling molecules (usually proteins) in recognition and activation.

Abstractly, a *signaling pathway* could look something like this:

Initial stimulus $\rightarrow$ A$\rightarrow$ B$\rightarrow$ C$\rightarrow$ D$\rightarrow$ E$\rightarrow$Response

Each letter in the pathway represents a chemical entity of some kind, which may be a protein or a small molecule like cyclic AMP. Arrows represent transfer of a signal, positive or negative, between one entity and the next.[3] Signaling pathways can branch and interconnect to form huge "networks," which allow combinations of signal inputs to evoke a large variety of complex output responses.

Every transfer of information in cells involves at least one *molecular recognition* event. A protein first recognizes a sort of tag or zip code on a second protein or a small molecule, then associates with or modifies it.

Why is molecular recognition so important for transmitting signals? The basic problem is that every cell contains about 10,000 different proteins, each present in thousands of copies. Each of these molecules needs to recognize a subset of other molecules, just as millions of New Yorkers need systems for recognizing their friends and co-workers. Instead of faces, telephone numbers, or uniforms, virtually every protein in a cell is covered with tags and tag-reading devices designed to specify which molecules will recognize each other. Each of these millions of molecules, like an air traveler inspecting luggage at a carousel, inspects the molecules it meets to identify appropriate partners and targets. Molecule A can transmit a signal to molecule B only if it recognizes it first.

How does A actually transfer a signal to B? What does the arrow really represent? Briefly, signals are transmitted in three ways. The first is direct *activation*: A recognizes B, associates with B, and "instructs" B to change its activity—in other words, A "activates" (or inactivates) B. Think of one partner signaling another to pirouette in a dance. Alternatively, A may recognize B and *localize* it to the specific site in the cell where B can accomplish some key function—like a murder in a gangster movie, signaled by "Stay here, fella, and kill anybody who walks in that door!" Rather than commit a murder, B is more likely to convert chemical X into chemical Y enzymatically, but can do so only if A places B in the right place to find X. In a third mode of signal transmission, A may chemically modify B, thereby attaching a new tag (or removing an old one). These metaphorical tags and tag-readers may sound fanciful, but every biotech company or pharmaceutical manufacturer uses exactly this framework to understand and create new ways for modifying signals in bacteria, plants, animals, or patients.

The last fundamental concept you will meet is the idea that the *3D shape* of a molecule crucially determines its function. When I went to medical school, scientists knew the 3D shapes of less than a dozen proteins. Now they know thousands of structures, including those of receptors and signal relay proteins I studied. These shapes show us the crevices and handles signaling proteins use to recognize other molecules, as well as the molecular details of signal transmission.

The notion that these shapes transmit signals seems even more amazing when we consider how small they are. A protein is 1,000-fold smaller than a cell, which is itself pretty tiny—2,000 average cells, lined up in a row, would cover a distance of about one inch. If a cell were the size of a lecture hall big enough to seat 75 people, the average protein molecule would be the size of an electrical socket. Nonetheless, nature machines these minuscule molecules to very close tolerances. In a later chapter, for example, I tell how we traced a devastating inherited disease to a tiny change in a signaling protein, a change that altered the protein's shape by only one part in 3,000.

Scientifically, then, the stakes were high. Outside the lab, they were even higher, and still are. As a society we are constantly pushed and pulled by discoveries made in labs, and we need to understand them well enough to make crucial social decisions about climate, energy resources, medical care, and many other problems. That means young people and adults need to know how science works and who scientists are. Citizens need to feel, in their bones, that science is a very human enterprise—not magical, not diabolical, not unknowable, not conducted in mysterious hidden rites, but instead closely enmeshed in the rough granularity of the real world around us. I hope this book will transmit the message that this human enterprise is conducted by people who are fallible, ambitious, stupid, bright, and sometimes inspired, but always human, as well. And I hope that young people will learn from it that becoming a scientist is a goal normal human beings can aspire to, and one that brings many rewards.

Finally, it's worth noting that the decades from 1970 through the first decade of the 21st century saw profound changes in experimental biology and its practitioners. As our questions probed more deeply and our experimental tools became more powerful, the world in which we lived and worked became transformed in almost every way, from the size and organization of our research labs to training of young biologists, research funding, reward and promotion of professors, and relations between academia and industry. Today's signaling aficionado can hardly imagine the ignorance, mistaken ideas, and technological limitations his predecessors had to deal with in the 1960s. By the same token, a researcher suddenly transplanted from a lab in 1966 into the 21st century would find opportunities, stresses, and even dangers she or he could not have imagined.

Although I did not start writing with the goal of highlighting these transformations, they frame the events and human interactions of every chapter. I touch on them explicitly in the chapter on my experience as chair of an academic department, and return to them again at the end, as possible clues to the equally profound changes future decades will bring.

———

Finally, I must confess a secret. I have found it impossible to describe my life in science without also including dollops of real science. This can be a problem, because science often baffles, bores, or mystifies smart, curious people. They are not usually baffled, I think, because the ideas are so difficult, at least not in experimental biology. (The core concepts of fields like quantum physics or string theory do baffle many ordinarily thoughtful people, me included.)

Instead, my guess is that non-scientists find science mysterious for the same reason scientists spend so much time in close-knit communities of colleagues who care about a narrow set of questions. The problem with science is that there's just too damn much of it. Threatened with blizzards of new facts, both scientists and non-scientists hunker down like penguins, husbanding their attention and hoping the weather will clear. Confronted by the snowballing facts and terminology of an unfamiliar scientific field, even scientists know how it feels to recoil in confusion or shudder with boredom. Such experiences should help us sympathize with non-scientists.

For me, curiosity survives a fact-blizzard most successfully when I remind myself that it's not necessary to master every scientific detail. The going will be smooth in some places, rough in others. For the latter cases, let me offer this advice: when you find yourself puzzled, do your best to relax and take it easy. It is fine to re-read a sentence, but do not trudge back through previous paragraphs or chapters. Instead, walk deliberately through murky passages, without stopping to fumble for your flashlight. Keep moving into the light. Puzzled scientists follow the same strategy, which is practical and effective. Join the club!

The strategy works because each puzzle is likely to recur in a different context, and new contexts furnish new clues. Combining these with clues recalled from the puzzle's earlier appearances often helps. In addition, you may be bothered by an apparent contradiction between two facts or interpretations. Experimental biologists are old hands at juggling mutually incompatible ideas, sometimes for years.[4] When resolution comes, it sometimes reveals that one idea was clearly correct, the other clearly wrong. More often, we find that both ideas are part correct, part wrong. The apparent contradiction vanishes when a new fact appears, or we look at the old findings from a different perspective. This experience will be familiar to anyone who has lived long enough to experience the myriad contradictions and ambiguities of ordinary human interactions.

Finally, I have tried to write for both non-specialist readers and scientists, focusing primarily on the interface between personal feelings and thoughts, on the one hand, and scientific discovery, on the other. In describing the science I often substitute metaphor and simile for technical jargon and acronyms, and relegate details to the notes at the end of the book, which also include references to "scientific" publications. As a result, some scientists may be disappointed by the loss of biochemical precision, but non-specialists will be spared the labor of mastering vast lexicons of mystifying technical language.

CHAPTER 1

Unconscious Decisions

GROWING UP

On a sunny afternoon in late October, I negotiate the tight curves of Route 86, a narrow road in North Carolina. Red-dirt ditches and rail fences flash past our windows, and here and there derelict tobacco barns dot green fields. I am driving Nancy from her college to our home town. We talk quietly about our families and the lazy weekend before us. We are 20 years old. The future is an opaque blur, except that we know we will marry some day.

Then, as we round a grove of trees, a beige Chevrolet crosses the lane in front of us, leaps the roadside ditch, rolls gracefully, and comes to rest in the meadow, front doors open and upside down. Everything is quiet as a silent movie, until suddenly I hear myself yelling, and find myself running, in slow motion. Why did I park so far away?

On her back in the ditch, a fat woman moans softly between snores, a pale, undulating mound of flesh. Near the Chevrolet, a man lies on the grass, arms folded comfortably in front of him. Is he asleep? Grass stains on his shirt. No blood. Hurrying from one to the other, I have no idea what to do.

Nancy runs up. "We'd better call an ambulance!"

We flag a passing truck, whose driver finds a nearby house with a telephone. State police arrive and calmly shoo us back to our car. They say both passengers from the beige car are alive, and ambulances take them away.

Back on the road, I am numb. Nancy and I re-live 30 minutes of helpless ignorance, in broken sentences and long pauses. But by the time we reach home I think I've put the whole scene behind me.

I hadn't put the scene behind me, and still haven't. Instead, that beige car's spiraling trajectory marked the beginning of a new era in my life. Before the next week was out, I would tell Nancy and my parents I had made an important decision. Although no one—least of all myself—imagined that this decision might point toward a career in science, it did intertwine multiple strands of my life in the 20 preceding years. And those strands form patterns that still guide how I think, work, and communicate, in science and in my life.

———

I grew up in Danville, Virginia, a sleepy town of 35,000, with tobacco warehouses and a big cotton mill. My father practiced general surgery in Danville for 40 years. My mother was a housewife and mother, smart, independent, and sharp of tongue. She also cared deeply about social justice. The newspaper in our conservative little town once described her as "a known integrationist." Mama and Daddy were loving, generous, and supportive parents to my two younger brothers and me. Both died more than a decade ago, but every day I catch myself repeating one of Mama's pithy phrases or mimicking Daddy's laugh.

Mama, the daughter of a Methodist preacher, grew up in a close-knit family, awash in words and delighting in word games, foreign accents, arcane vocabulary, puns, ditties, songs, poems, and stories. Her brother became a scholar who specialized in early American literature, and she and her sister taught high school French, German, and Latin. Mama treasured the memory of her beloved Latin professor, so profoundly moved by a passage in Virgil's Aeneid that he had to retire behind a bookcase to cry. That passage—"Sunt lacrymae rerum et mentem mortalia tangunt"—could be translated, she said, as "There are tears of things, and mortal things touch the mind." As a child, I had a hard time understanding what Virgil or anybody else might mean by "tears of things".[1] Sixty years later, his words resonate more clearly.

Slated to follow in his father's steps as a hard-scrabble farmer in western Virginia, Daddy barely managed to escape. He was 18 when a letter from his older sister told him she and her husband would give him room and board in Charlottesville, which meant he could attend the University of Virginia. The letter came while he was plowing. "I left the plow and the mule standing in that field," he told me. "Daddy kept shouting I couldn't leave, the farm needed me. But I left for Charlottesville the next day." With scant schooling and poor grades in college, he barely qualified for medical school. Yet he went on to become Danville's first formally trained, board-qualified surgeon. He told me that hard work and "drive"—a favorite word of his—could achieve almost anything. I believed him, even when I wasn't sure where to find the "drive" in myself.

In my earliest memories, my Grandma reads me stories. Her reading, along with my Mama's love of books, made me a devoted bookworm. I immersed myself in Hardy Boys and Tarzan stories, and progressed to *Treasure Island*, *Huckleberry Finn*, *Robinson Crusoe*, *Haji Baba of Isphahan*, and *Gulliver's Travels*. Eavesdropping on grownups led me to *The Sun Also Rises* and *Light in August*. I read both, cover to cover, understanding almost nothing. A diligently prurient pre-adolescent, I mesmerized myself dredging Salinger for dirty words and my father's gynecology texts for dirty pictures.

Boyhood was a happy time for me, as it was for most white children from well-to-do families in Southern towns. Cap pistols cracking, we played cowboys and Indians in the afternoons after school and ran after fireflies on long summer evenings. I swam the length of the Golf Club pool underwater, and struggled to hit softballs in pickup games. On Saturday afternoons I enjoyed cowboy movies and popcorn. My favorite dinner was fried chicken, corn on the cob, and ice cream.

Picking through memories, I find no hint of any propensity for science in general, or for biology in particular. I seem to have had no ambition in that direction, and found no special delight in nature.

Math puzzles offered opportunities to bring home good grades, but otherwise failed to entice. I liked knowing how car motors, radios, and other machines worked, but felt no desire to tinker with them myself. Birds, bugs, and snakes fascinated young biophiliacs like Charles Darwin and E.O. Wilson, but held little charm for me.

I did learn lessons not taught to many Danville children. My mother's strong feelings about racial injustice led to the most vivid experience of my childhood. One morning, I yelled, "Go away, nigger!" to an old black man shambling by on the sidewalk. My unprovoked cry reflected the vocabulary and prejudice of eight-year-old playmates. Mama's angry rebuke sticks with me even now: "What you did was wrong. Never repeat it. Never. Think how that old man feels! Other boys, even grownups, hurt Negroes every day—you must not."

Mama's idealism left a real mark on me. I would always strive to be "a good boy," and often succeeded. But my yen for virtue would sometimes be matched by an inability to read selfish motives and meanness, both in others and in myself.

Six years later, the Supreme Court would mandate integration of public schools. Mama worked hard to integrate Danville's schools, libraries, and parks. Hers was a brave stand in our town, where most of her friends followed politicians defiantly urging what they called "Massive Resistance" to integration. With a few allies she managed to integrate the local Young Women's Christian Association, but her struggle against the "white power structure" lasted for decades and met with little success. Proud of Mama's stand, Daddy took a practical approach to racial justice. Every week he removed appendices, gall bladders, or uterine fibroid tumors in the dingy operating room at Winslow, the segregated "Negro hospital"—a run-down fire-trap, known to black people as little more than a place to die. A third of the town was black, but Danville had only two black doctors, dozens of white ones. Most of the latter would have nothing to do with Winslow.

Daddy wanted me to become a doctor, but never said so. I kept my own counsel, at first not wanting to think about adult pursuits and then, as a teenager, suspecting that writing books would be more my kind of fun. Still, I've never known anyone more able to enjoy every moment of his life, at work and at home, than he. For sustained happiness and sheer delight in work, his love of medicine was the most powerful model I ever encountered.

I learned a lot from Daddy about medicine. Tagging along on weekend rounds at the hospital, I loved to watch him at the bedside. He was usually funny, but also tender and sympathetic, and on occasion remarkably blunt: "God damn it, Will, that thing's got to come out." He also brought me to the emergency room and even the operating room. Swathed in a green gown, I would be introduced as his "learned colleague from New York," given a stool or chair to stand on, and allowed to watch him suture a wound or remove a gallbladder or an appendix.

I often rode with Daddy on his house calls, although I usually had to wait in the car. "Why did you stand on the steps so long, talking with that old lady?" I asked, after one especially long wait. "Sometimes, son," he told me, "the only thing you can do is listen and talk."

A rather different medical opportunity came when I was about 12. One afternoon, while walking through the hospital on his rounds, Daddy told me about a patient who had died the evening before. Lying in her hospital bed, she was talking with family about her upcoming gallbladder operation, which had been scheduled for today. Suddenly, in the middle of a sentence, she jerked upright, rolled her eyes, and died. "The autopsy is happening right now. A healthy woman with gallstones is not supposed to die, just like that. And we don't know why she died. Would you like to find out?" Daddy asked. With some trepidation, I said I would. (Attending an autopsy was officially forbidden to 12-year-olds, even in the 1950s. Now it would be impossible.)

I remember a clean, brightly lit room. I had met Dr. Hooker, one of the pathologists. He and his associate bent over the gray body of an obese woman, stretched on a metal table. Daddy and I stood, silent and still, at the head of the table, a yard or so from the focus of everyone's attention. Green-garbed, rubber-gloved, the pathologists worked steadily, removing and weighing one organ after another. Now and then one or the other would mention a football score, part of a halting parallel conversation, but they were intent on the job at hand.

Nothing in the abdomen appeared abnormal, so they moved on to the chest. A few minutes later, I heard Dr. Hooker's quiet whistle, followed by "Oh, so that's it." He held up a large and confusing structure, pink, gray, and white—in retrospect, lungs, heart, and their connecting blood vessels—and pointed to a dark-red glob. "A massive pulmonary embolus," he said. The blood clot had moved to a big blood vessel in her chest and cut off blood flow to the lungs. Probably the clot came from a leg vein, although neither leg was swollen or tender before she died, and she had not complained about her legs.

Wide-eyed at the whole procedure, I monitored my own reaction as well. I was proud, but also relieved, to find the autopsy more fascinating than stressful. Mainly, I was struck by the participants' matter-of-fact approach to death. To them death was a puzzle, rather than a source of horror or mystery. Knowing how the body is put together, they took it apart to find out why the patient died. I wryly remembered a lunch after the funeral of my grandmother, a few months earlier—the Grandma who read me so many stories. To my dismay, family members had chatted cheerfully about the old lady's life and laughed about funny events during her gradual descent into senility. Where, I had wondered, was their reverence and awe? Daddy and Dr. Hooker saw death was an integral element of being alive. Now I began to understand.

Looking back over almost six decades, I see that autopsy in a different light, as well. Although no one thought of it as a scientific experiment, for practical purposes it was the first one I ever saw. Like any lab scientist, these doctors had a question to ask, they carefully performed the appropriate experiment, and got a definitive answer to their question. It would be more than a decade before I would see a "real" experiment again—real, I mean, in the sense that the experimenters really needed to know the answer.

———

From first grade on, I made it my business to get good grades. Everything was grist to the mill—reading, math problems, spelling, homonyms and synonyms, Virginia's history, even geography. Innate curiosity may have played a part, but I cared most about pleasing teachers and parents. I did try to suppress my penchant for self-congratulation, both to avoid social ridicule and because Daddy warned me against getting "a bad case of the big head." Still, like most self-involved nerds at that age, I had little idea what others really thought. To me, driven by free-floating ambition, academic success furnished a sense of my own importance and promises of continued future prowess.

I was also preternaturally well-behaved. One dramatic instance occurred after football practice, when I was 11. Complex offensive plays and real uniforms with shiny helmets and cleated shoes had not prevented our neighborhood football team from collecting an abysmal record of losses to tougher teams. We practiced five days a week on the playground of Forest Hills Elementary School. One evening, as we took off our cleats and the coaches drove home, someone called attention to the sun's red reflection in a tall classroom window.

"You could hit that sun with a rock!" exclaimed a team-mate. Anticipating how things might turn out, I slunk away. My friends collected rocks and set methodically to work. They broke every pane in every window of 20 classrooms, including windows three stories above the practice field. Wonderfully satisfying, a friend told me later.

This stunning achievement elicited predictable reactions from school, coaches, and parents. I congratulated myself for my righteous behavior, but had sense enough not to do so out loud. None of my friends reviled me for failing to join their celebration, nor did my parents praise me. In fact, no one seemed surprised at how thoroughly I had adopted law-abiding grownup values. That sixth-grader—praise-seeking, watchful, prudent, and idealistic, with more than a tinge of self-righteousness—is still my core self. Now I can't help regretting that I didn't dare break the traces more often—not only as a youth, but also as a scientist. Prudence was to save me from making many foolish mistakes, but it has also constrained my imagination and willingness to take risks.

In any case, school and I seemed made for each other, to the point that I was allowed to skip from the fourth to the fifth grade, in the middle of the school year. Soon my mother's brother suggested I might profit from a more academically challenging high school. This would be unusual for Danville, where boys ordinarily changed schools only when they got into trouble so bad that only a military school could straighten them out. Touring boarding schools in New England, my parents and I found Andover, with 750 students and a beautiful campus, north of Boston.

In the summer of 1954, just before I was to leave for Andover, something much more important happened—Nancy and I had our first date. We had known each other since we were babies, and her shining brown eyes and ready laugh had attracted me ever since I moved up into the fifth grade. But I was shy and Nancy, more socially adept, had to make the first move. One weekend, when her boyfriend would be out of town, she asked one of her friends to invite me to a party. I was entranced, but my crew-cut hair and conspicuous lack of social grace failed to impress. (I didn't find this out until Nancy told me, years later.) Still, over the next three or four years we managed to become friends, partly because we both loved to talk about people and books, and partly—I have always suspected—because Nancy's mother liked me. But leaving for Andover put me at a real disadvantage for the next three years, because my eloquent letters couldn't compete against boys who shared Nancy's classes.

At Andover I said goodbye to Mama and Daddy at the door to my dorm, a 14-year-old ready for exciting adventure. Everything was new. My roommate bitterly criticized both his parents, who were divorced. No boy in Danville complained about his parents, and divorce was both rare and unmentionable. For the first time I heard people disparage Jews, a group almost unknown in Danville. My Virginia drawl elicited teasing—"You talk like a Southern hick!"—so I promptly suppressed it.

Immersion in a world of adolescent boys was a shocking experience. I was an innocent who trusted people to like and care for me, as my parents did. A ninth-grade year at home had not prepared me for the refinements of casual cruelty teenage boys administer so expertly to one another, nor for my new peers' vast lexicons of sexual behavior and their endless schemes for seducing virgins. I managed to evade most of the cruelty, partly by feigning indifference, partly by learning how to aim sharp barbs at others. But I also managed to make close friends. Five decades later, we still care for one another, our teenage demons long forgiven.

The teaching at Andover was magnificent. With help from the tutoring I'd received for the entrance exams, I landed a position in an advanced math class. Instead of the sedate meander I was used to, math at Andover tumbled pell-mell over rocks and rapids. Relentless as any football coach, Mr. Sides demanded commitment: "Don't sit there telling yourself you don't know. Start with what you do know. Be always on the attack!" He was over the top, but funny, enthusiastic, and crystal-clear. I had to struggle to stay in the middle of the pack, which would have irked me in Danville. But somehow Mr. Sides made the fast pace feel like fun, and different from everything that came before. I loved it.

I thought English would prove easier, but Mr. Hyde soon had my number. Red ink blared: "Each paragraph repeats the same idea. You bore your reader. Every paragraph must say something new!"

Challenged, I set to work. For three years I studied history, English and American literature, French, Latin, and math—algebra, geometry, trigonometry, and calculus. I took only one science course, in physics, but it failed to capture my imagination. (I remember only that the teacher looked and talked like Elmer Fudd. My guess is that the teacher laid the answers out for us clearly, and we just learned them. I got a good grade, but had no sense that it would be fun to know more.) But I worked hard to succeed, and did—out of class as well as in. I was at best a so-so athlete, but wrote news stories for the school's weekly newspaper, and in senior year became its editor. Still pleasing parents and teachers, and beginning to please myself as well.

In 1957, as a graduating senior, I felt good. My grades were excellent, I was editor of the newspaper, and Andover had accomplished its task—I had been admitted to Harvard. Testing out of introductory English, math, and language requirements, I would skip Harvard's freshman year altogether and graduate in three years—not a smart move, but at the time I was proud of it. My ambition was not tethered to a defined goal. Because Daddy found such delight in practicing surgery, I told myself I would take pre-med courses. I also played with the idea of becoming a newspaper reporter, or a writer. Surely I could afford to remain undifferentiated for a few years. In any case, as everyone could see, I was destined for ever-continuing triumph.

——

At Harvard, no matter where I looked, triumph failed to appear. Some of my Harvard classmates had satisfying experiences, but others did not. One friend flunked out after a single semester, two after a year; another took a leave of absence, graduating years later. My own Harvard balloon sprung a leak and drifted, steadily losing altitude.

As my first pre-med course, I chose biology, which proved a disaster. In 1957 the course devoted most of its time to classifying species into endless families, phyla, and genera—one semester for the animal kingdom, one for plants. Dozens of students rustled newspapers as lecturers droned. We hardly touched on genetics. DNA was mentioned once or twice, but its structure, discovered four years earlier, was omitted altogether. (James Watson, co-discoverer of DNA's 3D structure, had joined the Department of Biology the year before, and would be promoted to tenure a year afterward, but his presence and ideas had not yet trickled down to the freshman course.) Instead, supervised by bored graduate students, we cut up dead animals or plants. At first I read the assigned material, but memorizing for tests was more work than I was prepared to do. So I perused dozens of chapters the night before each exam, and dozed over multiple choice questions the next day. I scraped through with a C+, a more than generous grade.

I tried to rationalize this disaster by telling myself that medicine was not right for me, but other courses led to similar disappointments. In my major, American "history and lit," a few courses really did engage my interest, but I treaded water through others, sometimes narrowly escaping failure. My tutor assigned me to write a paper on the nine volumes of Henry Adams's *History of the United States 1801-1817*. I had six weeks to complete the job, but put it off until the last available weekend. My reading was cursory and the resulting essay, as my tutor gently put it, "thin." This performance embarrassed me, but I was too apathetic to care.

At Harvard I could no longer pretend to be the academic hotshot I had been in Danville and at Andover. The competition was smarter, to be sure, but the critical problem was lack of motivation. Called on to grapple hard with gritty material, I lacked the necessary *sitzfleisch* to do so. I didn't care enough. To my bewildered surprise, I became discouraged and depressed, although I refused to admit it. Harvard provided none of the academic praise I had enjoyed so comfortably in Danville and at Andover. Instead Harvard was telling me that I could no longer expect to slide effortlessly over the smooth surface of every subject, but must get to work. I stubbornly refused to listen.

I wonder at the unexamined life I led in those college years. Confused lack of self-awareness even kept me from recognizing that I was depressed. Nancy was the only bright star in my firmament, but she was at Duke, in North Carolina, and I was in snowy, slushy Massachusetts. My letters told Nancy about papers I was writing (one, I remember, on *Middlemarch*) and how I looked forward to seeing her when I came home—but not a word about how I really felt at Harvard. I invited her to visit, and we had a marvelous weekend, but Nancy was also dating boys at Duke and an old flame from Danville. She kept saying she liked me as a good friend, and seemed to mean it. But I wanted more.

Then, one blazing summer day in 1959, we were sitting by a lake outside Danville. Nancy looked me in the eye and said, "I am going to marry you." No preamble, no preparation, just those words. Completely speechless, I felt as if I were ascending to heaven. I could hardly believe my luck. I still feel the same way, 50 years later.

I've never understood precisely what changed Nancy's mind. My persistence and the deluge of letters over many years played their parts, and perhaps I was beginning to grow out of my clumsy, eager nerdiness. In addition, Nancy says, she heard I was dating a bombshell in Richmond (a woman, I knew, who didn't come close to matching Nancy). This news may have helped persuade Nancy to agree with her mother's opinion of me.

I would have to endure my next and last year at Harvard, and Nancy would spend it in England as an exchange student. We knew we would marry sometime after that, though we didn't tell the world. I had said nothing to my parents about how unhappy I was in college, but they had somehow figured it out. Delighted to see me more cheerful, they somehow guessed that Nancy had rescued my drifting balloon and guided it to a safe landing.

In June 1960, I graduated from Harvard and Nancy returned from England for her last year at Duke. After graduation, I moved to Richmond, Virginia, near Danville, where I had landed a job as a reporter for the *News Leader*, the afternoon newspaper. I was still learning the ropes, shadowing regular reporters on their beats and writing features and some news stories on my own. The other reporters were bright, energetic, fun to work with, and good teachers, but my own reporting was not satisfying. The *News Leader* was not a good newspaper, and many of my colleagues seemed to be marking time. We singled out the managing editor for special ridicule. Most of the time he slept in his glass cubicle, but would occasionally trail through the newsroom a plume of cigar smoke as he performed his only apparent function, the collection and disposal of empty Coca-Cola bottles. After work, and any weekend I didn't drive to Duke to meet Nancy, I was supposed to be writing—fiction, I claimed. On several occasions I even rolled paper into the typewriter, and waited for a short story to appear. In vain.

Then, in October, came the surreal spiral of that beige Chevrolet across Route 86. When Nancy and I reached Danville, we related our adventure to everyone, and promptly put it out of mind. Perhaps I didn't really forget it, though—at least, so I suspect from the telephone calls I made four days later. Proudly, I told Nancy and my parents I had decided to leave the newspaper job and go to medical school.

Welcome to everyone, my decision still seemed to come out of nowhere. Mama and Daddy knew that years earlier I had briefly entertained, and then discarded, the idea of becoming a doctor. Nancy and I had not discussed it. It surprised even me, because I was too unaware of my own subterranean feelings to connect the dots between Route 86 and medical school.

It is not the case that those unconscious passengers in the meadow somehow triggered a latent urge to handle medical emergencies. Instead, the accident provoked compelling but inarticulate feelings. For one thing, my abject fecklessness at the accident scene must have called to mind the more disturbing, if less dramatic, fecklessness I felt in Richmond. Later I connected this to a notorious headline in the *News Leader*, a month before the accident. Huge type at the top of page one announced that

PROMISED RAIN FAILS TO FALL

In the newsroom we derided this sentence, crafted by our redoubtable managing editor, as 1960's least newsworthy headline. At the time I didn't recognize how precisely the headline summarized my career in Richmond, because it would have hurt too much.

Other submerged feelings triggered by the accident probably related to the fact that Nancy and I witnessed it together. I didn't articulate it this way, but our marriage plans commanded me to stop drifting and take some decisive action, much as the accident demanded that we try to do something. Certainly I couldn't afford to remain so feckless about the direction of my life. At the same time, Nancy's love, support, and encouragement had already helped me recover some of the old sense that I was "special," regardless of my academic performance at Harvard. She had restored my confidence, and I knew she would help me now. Amazingly, I communicated nothing about any of these feelings, even to Nancy, partly owing to my engrained habit of keeping doubts to myself, but mainly because my blithe lack of self-awareness prevented me from recognizing my own desperation, and even from clearly realizing how her love rescued me from it. I wonder how many other 20-year-olds are as clueless.

Why did I decide to go into medicine? Through the fog of unexamined feelings, it's not easy to be sure, but it seems likely that I understood that neither journalism nor literature would work for me. It was not that I saw medicine as a route into biology, because I vividly recalled that awful biology course and knew little about medicine's intellectual underpinnings. But I did know that practicing medicine gave my Daddy endless satisfaction and delight. Perhaps I was aware enough to guess that my life needed, in addition to Nancy, precisely that kind of delight.

Chapter 2

Asking Questions

Medicine, the Tutor of Biology[1]

I'll begin with one of my most vivid memories from medical school.

I had finished the pre-clinical courses, including pathology, and was just starting the most exciting course for second-year medical students, "physical diagnosis." Now I was to interview and examine a hospitalized patient, and then write up my findings and present them to an attending physician and an audience of other students.

My first patient, Mrs. Green, was a friendly, voluble housewife and mother, 40 years old. Her diagnosis was straightforward, even for me, because she was receiving an intravenous antibiotic to treat a *Staphylococcus aureus* infection on one of her heart valves. I was embarrassed to ask her to talk to me, considering she could derive no possible benefit from conversation with an ignorant medical student. Somehow Mrs. Green made me feel more comfortable, so I could be as thorough as I needed to be—which meant spending several hours taking her medical history and practicing my rudimentary skills in physical examination.

The next day, at the bedside, I described Mrs. Green's case to Philip Tumulty, a rosy-faced professor. Because I had painstakingly memorized all my findings, I was able to relate her story at breakneck speed, finishing with a triumphal diagnosis of acute bacterial endocarditis. I was proud to have packed such a voluminous list of questions and physical signs into 10 minutes.

Tumulty listened carefully and thanked me. Then he asked the patient how she was feeling, and put her immediately at ease. (His secret was simple—he genuinely wanted to know how she felt.)

Next he asked her his first "medical" question. "Tell me, "did you have any boils on your body in the last month? Or pimples? Red? White? Sore? On your legs, your bottom? Your neck? Nose? Scalp? Cheeks? Arms? Hands? Anywhere?"

I knew the answer to this question, which I had stated clearly in my list of positive and negative findings: "The patient denies any history of skin or other infections prior to the present illness."

Still, Mrs. Green gave the question a few moments' thought, and replied: "Well, I did have a tiny little boil right here"—pointing to a site near the last joint of her left index finger—"but it came to a head, I popped it, and it went away. That was a couple of weeks before I got sick."

I had asked an abstract, general question, and gotten a negative answer. It is frequently hard to pinpoint the original source of bacteria that colonize a heart valve, and that little pustule could well have been the source. Tumulty didn't need to underline the message, one I have re-learned many times since. When you ask a question, you must ask it in the right way. In this case, if I had asked the question in as many ways as possible, I would have gotten a positive answer. (If, to the contrary, Mrs. Green had given persistently negative answers, I could have been much more certain that the negative was correct.)

My mistake meant a great deal to me, but was not earthshaking for the patient. Later medical training gave me opportunities to witness more important consequences of failing to ask the right question. There was a truckdriver with the diagnosis of "fever of unknown origin," who was hospitalized for two weeks before someone reminded the intern to do a rectal exam. It revealed a peri-rectal abscess, which was eventually cured (along with the fever) by surgery. A sadder story was that of an old lady with low-grade fever, anemia, and very low numbers of white blood cells. Examination of her bone marrow suggested she might have a bizarre blood disorder, perhaps an atypical leukemia. She died a few weeks later, and the autopsy showed she had disseminated tuberculosis. The right antibiotics could have helped her, but no one had thought to look for TB bacilli, under the microscope or by culturing the bone marrow.

Neither of these people was my patient, but their cases taught us all the crucial importance of asking good questions. I didn't realize it then, but Tumulty and the patients who trained us as doctors were also teaching one of the most essential lessons every scientist has to learn. Medicine would teach me many other useful lessons, about biology, and about myself.

———

In the fall of 1960, when I decided to go to medical school, I knew very little about medicine or medical training. I soon found that admission to a medical school required science courses I had not taken, plus the Medical College Admission Tests (MCATs). It was already October, so I had to move fast. Leaving the newspaper, I found a retired professor in Richmond to tutor me in chemistry, through mid-December. The University of Virginia generously allowed me to take premed courses in Charlottesville, beginning in January. During that first half year I took the first and second semesters of both chemistry and physics, plus a chemistry lab course. I spent the summer completing the last requirement, organic chemistry.

To my surprise, total immersion in science courses was fun. I worked hard, and more efficiently than many undergraduates, who seemed almost as young and undirected as I had been in that disastrous biology course, four years earlier. Now I worked with a purpose, and enjoyed it thoroughly. As a result, I got good grades and in May did well in the MCATs.

In the meantime, I had to apply to medical schools. The University of Virginia, my Daddy's school, readily gave me an interview and admitted me. In June 1961, an admissions officer at Harvard suggested that I apply for admission in 1962 instead, because their class was filled for the coming September. I also applied to Johns Hopkins, in Baltimore. Getting into medical school then was not the daunting obstacle course it has become,[2] but Hopkins was an outstanding school, and classes would begin in a few weeks. Fortunately, Hopkins invited me for an interview, in early July.

In Baltimore, my interviewer was a gentlemanly Southerner named Vernon Mountcastle. He invited me into his book-lined office, offered coffee, and sat me down for a chat. Calm and friendly, he gently explored my education, my family, and how I had not decided to become a doctor until I was already graduated from college. I tried to give candid answers, but my account of that decision cannot have been informative, because I didn't understand it myself.

Then Mountcastle asked an unexpected question: "How does it feel to move from one intellectual world to another? You spent college studying qualitative, language-intensive humanities, and now you've been exposed to the quantitative, analytical world of chemistry and physics. How are they different?"

Without thinking, I quickly replied that the two worlds seemed much the same to me. "In both you take a hard look at things and try to connect them with one another. And the strong connections satisfy you the most, in both."

Mountcastle listened to whatever additional wisdom I had to offer, but was not convinced. He was polite, but firm. "I think you'll find that's not the whole story," he said. "Making connections in science requires very different skills. And for me the results are much more satisfying."

This little story shows how ignorant I was. Who was I to express any opinion whatever? What little I knew about science came from textbooks, not experience. At the time I had no idea who Mountcastle was. I didn't know it, but he was in fact the first real scientist I had met, and already a renowned neurobiologist,[3] superbly qualified to think and talk about how the brain works and how it feels to do science. Mountcastle's question was a good one. The answer I gave was correct, for me at least, and still is, but that is because my kind of intelligence works best in making connections among ideas and judging them qualitatively. Unlike many of my colleagues (and Mountcastle himself), I'm not as good at applying rigorous quantitative analysis to complex data or logical sequences of causation.

More immediately crucial for me, in August Mountcastle saw
fit to admit me to medical school at Hopkins, a gift for which I shall
always be grateful. In September, 1961, I moved to Baltimore.

At the time I assumed that admission into medical school reflected
my intrinsic worth, but now I appreciate more clearly the crucial roles
of luck and privilege. I had the inordinate good fortune of belonging
to a family rich enough to send me to Andover, a step that gave me
a ticket to Harvard. My father smoothed the way into those pre-med
courses in Charlottesville and, of course, paid the tuition, then and
later. And the Harvard degree persuaded Hopkins to give me an
interview and accept me late in the season. Opportunities like these
were closed to most young Americans in 1961, and remain so still.

———

After the chagrin of Harvard and Richmond, converging
influences made the following four years brim with energy and
delight. First, Nancy and I married in 1962, in the summer after
my first year in Baltimore. She taught school to pay the rent on
our tiny apartment, two blocks from the hospital. Marrying Nancy
was the luckiest event in my very lucky life. Second, drifting was
finally over, and I felt sure that hard work would make me into a
doctor. Third, Hopkins in the 1960s was a magnificent place for
medical students to learn, and not only in the required formal
courses. Respecting and even cherishing medical students, the
faculty welcomed us to take electives in their labs and clinics for
one unassigned quarter every year. Students had only to ask.

Though praise-seeking was still hard-wired, the raw substance
of human biology grabbed my attention and held it. Our first course
was biochemistry. Ten weeks of morning lectures and afternoon labs
focused on metabolism—the body's conversion of foodstuffs and
oxygen into fat, carbohydrate, protein, and the energy necessary to
keep the corporeal enterprise humming.

It was thrilling to learn how enzymes create and use the body's
energy currency, a small chemical called ATP. In the 21st century
metabolism is old-hat, but then it appeared luminous, at least to

me. It seemed as if biochemists had toiled for years to construct this magnificent edifice for my own pleasure. I marveled at how my liver and muscles coordinate all these chemical reactions without conscious effort on my part, but under the tight control of hormones like insulin. By contrast, if I were diabetic, lack of insulin would cause my liver to make too much sugar and prevent my muscles from using it efficiently—so the blood sugar would rise. Gradually I began to catch hints of how the whole unlikely shebang of the body hangs together, and how it can go awry.

By 1961 I had found a school that seemed to have heard of DNA. We even had a short course on bacterial genetics, in which we learned that bacteria have sex (that is, how they exchange genetic material) and can increase the amount of particular enzymes in response to extracellular stimuli.

I was amazed to learn how tiny proteins really are. Five weeks into the biochemistry course, I was assigned to tell my small group of 10 students about the 3D structure of hemoglobin,[4] the red protein in blood cells that carries oxygen from lungs to tissues. The structure, solved two years earlier, revealed four sites for binding oxygen, each on a separately folded chain of amino acids. To show the shape to my classmates, I made a crude hemoglobin model out of flexible copper tubing, scrounged from a biochemistry lab. About 18 inches in diameter, it was 500 million times larger than the real thing.

Later courses that year offered new revelations, almost daily. In physiology I learned how Walter Cannon had identified the "fight or flight" response, which increases heart rate, redistributes blood flow to muscles, and increases release of sugar from the liver into the blood. My sprint to the auto accident in 1960 must have elicited each of those responses. Cannon prevented these cardiovascular responses in animals by surgically removing two small glands located just above the kidneys, plus most of the nerves that make up the so-called sympathetic nervous system. In a different course, microbiologists showed us how a few bacteria, called pneumococci, can cause fatal pneumonia in a mouse, and how their virulence depends on a distinctive sugar molecule in the bacterium's coat. Almost 20 years earlier, the pneumococcus's ability to make this coat had allowed Oswald Avery and his colleagues to establish that DNA is the genetic material. To do so, they incubated mutant pneumococci, which were unable to make this coat or cause pneumonia, with pure DNA extracted from normally virulent bacteria. During the incubation, one or two mutant bacteria would absorb the DNA, incorporate it into their genetic material, and gain the ability to kill a mouse by inducing pneumonia.[5]

The anatomy course required endless memorization of names for muscles, nerves, and bones, but offered ample opportunity for faculty and students, mostly male, to guffaw at ribald jokes. We saw one professor's notorious collection of the penis bones of dozens of animals and heard him describe the Dartos muscle (surrounding the scrotum, it tightens when males are exposed to cold). To our chortling delight, on one occasion Professor Strange (as I'll call him) was hoist by his own petard. In anatomy class, he paused at a dissecting table. One of the class's few female students was carefully separating the cadaver's testicle from its thick fibrous coat. Unable to restrain himself, Strange slyly inquired, "And aren't *you* having fun?"

The young woman's reply was immediate: "It's a tough nut to crack." For once, Strange was unable to frame a reply.

My first research experience came in the summer after that first year. The day after Nancy and I moved into our Baltimore apartment, I learned how to perform external cardiac massage on dogs. Three years earlier, a Hopkins surgeon, James Jude, had applied external cardiac massage to the first human patients. It was already becoming the standard procedure for resuscitating patients after sudden death. I worked with Guy Knickerbocker, a bright, friendly PhD in electrical engineering.

Guy's sharp eye had captured the first hint that external cardiac massage might work. He was working with Professor William Kouwenhoven, an electrical engineer, devising ways to treat electrical linemen who died from cardiac arrest after being electrocuted. In their dog experiments, electrocuting shocks caused a fatal heart rhythm, called ventricular fibrillation, which they could convert back to a normal rhythm by "defibrillating" the heart with a specially designed second shock. The delay between electrocution and defibrillating shock had to be short, however. Dogs recovered nicely after a two-minute delay, but waiting longer than four minutes caused irreversible brain damage—as it also does in people.

One day during the cardiac-arrest phase of such an experiment, Guy was bored. He propped his elbow on the dog's chest, he told me, and much to his surprise a blip immediately appeared on the device he used to monitor the dog's blood pressure. Lifting the elbow and propping it again produced another blip. Perhaps pressure on the chest was pushing blood out of the heart into the arteries, and raising blood pressure. If so, he thought, applying regular "beats" of chest pressure might maintain normal blood flow, enough to keep the brain alive until the defibrillating electrodes arrived.

And it worked. Guy made external cardiac massage work in dogs, and Jude then applied it successfully to human patients. Now Guy enlisted me to help with experiments designed to measure actual blood flow to the dog's brain during cardiac massage. He carefully showed me how to do every step. First the animal would be anesthetized, put on a respirator, and connected to the blood pressure monitor. Guy taught me how to insert a tube into a blood vessel leading to the brain, inject into it a special radioactive chemical (an isotope of either xenon or krypton), and record how fast normal blood flow washed radioactivity out of the brain. After washout, and 30 seconds after a second radioactive injection, I would stop the dog's heart with an electrocuting shock, wait another 30 seconds, and then apply manual pressure to the dog's chest, once every second, while the recorder measured radioactive washout again. After four minutes of this massage, I would deliver the defibrillating shock, wait 30 minutes, and repeat the whole procedure, measuring brain blood flow during the dog's normal heart beat and during massage.

Comparing washout rates during massage to those produced by the normal heartbeat would reflect relative rates of brain blood flow under the two conditions. More repetitions were needed only to make the answer more precise. When all the results were in, external cardiac massage turned out to work about a third as well as the normally functioning heart. This sufficed, apparently, to keep the dog's brain alive.

After a few weeks, Guy would help me set up the dog and then let me complete the experiment by myself. I enjoyed the work, not so much because of the actual results, but because I worked hard, mastered the procedure, and felt my contribution was useful. Perhaps it really was, because my generous co-workers listed me as first author of the paper reporting our results.[6] "Your first chance to see your name in lights," they said.

It never occurred to me to wonder whether these experiments were "real" science, although I did vaguely wonder what real "question" we were asking. We never had the slightest doubt, of course, that external massage would preserve blood flow to the brain. After all, dogs and people showed normal brain function after one or more cycles of cardiac arrest, massage, and defibrillation. Moreover, Guy had completed a couple of blood flow measurements before I arrived, so we already knew how they would come out. Now I know that it may not be exciting to get more precise results by doing repeated experiments, but such experiments are often necessary, just like a routine rectal examination, culturing bone marrow, or careful questions about boils for a patient with endocarditis.

———

After the first two years of medical school, I spent the rest of my medical training with live human patients. This included two years of rotating through hospital wards at Hopkins, plus a year of medical internship and a year of medical residency at Columbia, in New York City. (The Columbia years were interrupted by an ostensibly "scientific" interlude, which I'll reserve for the next chapter.)

Patients on the ward taught me how very hard it can be to predict responses to disease and treatment. In one case we (the intern, that is, along with me, the medical student) made a mistake in treating a fragile old woman for her gastric hemorrhage: giving her too much blood pushed her into overt heart failure. I was glad but surprised when a small dose of diuretic and reducing her fluid intake led to her prompt recovery and discharge home, much improved. On the other hand, I can't forget another patient, a healthy-appearing 65-year-old man recovering from a small heart attack. We told him to rest in his hospital bed for two weeks—routine treatment in those days. Hating the regimen, he took to wandering at night, and eventually fell and broke his hip. This kept him immobile for a long period, and he ultimately died from a pulmonary embolus, like the woman whose autopsy I remembered from childhood. Patients can show either robust resistance or hyper-susceptibility to change, and neither is easy to predict. (The same is true of other complex systems, including cells, animals, experiments, universities, faculty, and students.)

Patient care taught me its hardest lessons when I became an intern at Columbia. No longer a student watching someone else bow under the pressure of 120-hour weeks, now I myself was on duty all night, every other night. I'd get home at 8 or 9 p.m. on my night off, and start work again at 7 a.m. Lack of sleep was not the only problem. I worried more about my patients and spent more time at the hospital than my fellow interns did. They left for home at 5 p.m., but their patients inexplicably fared as well as mine. Worse, many of my colleagues seemed to love every minute of their internships. One bright-eyed young fellow kept exclaiming, over and over, "I just love working on the wards." I could cheerfully have murdered him, but instead kept my misery to myself and pretended to enjoy the hospital as he did.

The first seven or eight months of that internship year were the worst. By February, the stress had almost pushed me over the edge, but didn't quite succeed. Then, slowly and gradually, things got better. I remember very well one event during my slow recovery. Around midnight, the interns would try to find a moment to get together for a sandwich and coffee. I sat talking to a man I'll call Randy, who had been an intern the year before me and was on duty that night to supervise me and the other interns on duty.

Delicately and indirectly, Randy talked about the psychological hardships of internship, and how different interns deal with them.

He stuck to generalities and examples from previous interns he had known, never intimating for a moment that I might be undergoing similar difficulties myself.

"These guys have all been super-successful before they came here, so now they push themselves constantly," Randy said. "Watch them struggle to get every last thing done, especially the crap tasks that can wait. Instead, they need to focus on the really crucial jobs—there aren't so many of those. Then on their night off they can get away early and re-charge batteries for the next day."

Randy's point was not profound, but he had precisely diagnosed my trouble. I wasn't sure he was trying to help me until I discovered, years later, that he had suffered a "nervous breakdown" during his own internship and had to take a leave of absence. Now I am deeply grateful for the kind, skilled help Randy gave me. His indirect advice was correct. I had to learn to pay most attention to critical problems and winnow the less important ones, devoting less time to them. It worked—not perfectly, but well enough.

At home I told Nancy my troubles. She would give birth to our oldest son that year, and had plenty to cope with on her own, but gave me all the support she could. I gave her very little in return during that period, because the pressures of internship and desire for sleep captured all my attention.

One episode has become a legend in our family. On November 9, 1965, a power failure blacked out much of the northeastern U.S., including New York City. Five months into my internship, I called Nancy from the hospital. Sitting in our eighth-floor apartment, she told me that the lights were off and the elevator dead in our apartment building. Our first baby was due that very week. To my retrospective shame and amazement, I said I thought I ought to stay at the hospital, because the blackout would bring lots of emergency patients.

Nancy minced no words. "Get yourself home right now. I need you more."

Our son Michael was born four days later, on a night I was off duty and able to take Nancy to the hospital. My response to the blackout was nothing to be proud of, and I'm lucky Nancy didn't turn me out on the street. The story reveals Nancy's clear thinking and determination, but also shows how she helped me learn about priorities. I was in danger of letting internship drive me crazy, but Nancy reminded me what was really important. Not, I confess, for the last time.

These experiences had little direct relevance to a scientific career, but were necessary steps in the much more difficult task of growing up.

———

After the scientific interlude I describe in the next chapter, Nancy and I returned to New York for my second year of post-MD clinical training. This time I worked only once every three nights, and supervised the activities of interns and medical students. This year, unlike the internship year, I enjoyed myself thoroughly. Part of the difference was that I now got more sleep. I was also better organized, more able to focus on critical issues rather than petty details.

The most crucial difference was that I could now devote much of my time and effort to activities I had most liked about medical school—that is, posing questions and looking for answers. I found that I loved solving clinical puzzles. I proudly identified unsuspected rare diseases in several patients, and set up a system for surveying patients' clinical charts for evidence of possible therapeutic misadventures or harmful interactions between drugs. I especially liked seeing sick people in the emergency room, where their diagnoses had to be based on whatever information we could glean by taking a history and examining the patient. By contrast, ward patients usually carried obvious diagnostic "labels." Their diseases were well documented and understood, so that our job was often little more than to set up a few extra tests and administer drug therapies appropriate for this or that disorder.

Hindsight leads me to suspect that I was beginning to glimpse a fundamental difference between medical practitioners and scientists in the lab. Stated succinctly, it is this: doctors seek answers, while scientists seek questions. This is precisely as it should be. To do the right thing for their patients, doctors correctly focus on determining the correct diagnosis and identifying the very best possible treatment.

For lab scientists, however, once it is known every answer becomes profoundly uninteresting, except as a potential tool or stimulus for posing new questions. It's the questions that turn us on.

Medical training gave me the first hint of this distinction, but it would take more years to discern it clearly, or to discover which side of the divide was right for me.

CHAPTER 3

A Not So Artful Dodger

Two Years at the NIH

The internship at Columbia was sleep-deprived and stressful, but that year brought an additional worry, just as urgent—that I would have to serve in the Vietnam War. In 1965, the word was out: all young MDs were to be drafted as soon as they finished residency training.

Soon after internship started, I received a letter ordering me to report for an army physical examination in lower Manhattan. Before the exam, we filled out forms in an ancient brownstone mansion, and an intimidating sergeant told us to take off our clothes. Doctors, he announced, would retain their underpants, signifying that it was OK to go to the front of every line. This would allow us to return quickly to our patients. On leaving the orientation room, we should turn left and climb the stairs.

The broad stairway offered an extraordinary sight: the bare buttocks of more than a hundred young men, a dozen arrayed on every stair, climbing to examining rooms in the sky. The surreal vision of all those buttocks sealed my determination to avoid Vietnam. The underpants privilege failed to reassure me.

Unfortunately, though, I passed the physical exam, didn't want to move to Sweden, and was not a conscientious objector. (It would take two more years for me to realize how stupid the Vietnam War really was.) I had heard of an alternative: in lieu of military service, a small number of MDs was allowed to serve for two years as researchers at the NIH, outside Washington. Science could serve as a convenient way to dodge the draft.

I knew no one at the NIH, but was advised to make an official application. The selection committee offered me a day of interviews, based on good grades and authorship of a scientific paper in medical school. (This was the paper on blood flow to the brain in dogs treated with external cardiac massage.) The competition was tough, but I thought I was well qualified.

Clad in a dark suit and conservative tie, I traveled to the National Institutes of Health (NIH) in Bethesda, Maryland, and found Building 10, an ugly but imposing brick behemoth, said to be the biggest biomedical research building in the world. The first interviewer was Robert Berliner, a well-known scientist and chair of the committee. To his question about my paper, I responded with a crisp summary, trying to sound thoughtful about pressing on a dog's chest and measuring brain blood flow.

Berliner gave me a cool, appraising look. "Hmmm. Did your blood flow measurements depend on assumptions? What are they?" I hadn't a ghost of an idea, and stumbled and stuttered. Finally, Berliner told me the answer—something about whether the radioactive tracer substance we used was distributed through the brain in the same fashion when blood flow was driven by external cardiac massage *vs.* the dog's normal heartbeat.[1] I had not given the question a single thought, and missed it, cold. Failure to understand the basis of my experiments probably wouldn't help me qualify for further scientific training.

In the day's last interview, I discussed kidney diseases with an affable physiologist. I thought I was holding my own, until he announced his verdict, just as I prepared to say thank you and goodbye: "Yesterday, Dr. Bourne, I wanted you to work in my lab. Now, after talking with you, I don't." I was mystified, but too shocked to ask how I had offended. I still don't know. Perhaps he felt this cocky youngster needed a comeuppance. I barely got away without crying.

Downcast and sorely disappointed, I returned to the stress of internship. Nancy listened to my tale of woe, and was supportive when I received the expected turndown letter from the NIH. I was sure Vietnam could not be avoided. Near the end of internship year, however, ward rounds were interrupted by a summons to answer a long-distance call. I heard a secretary announce Dr. Bernard Brodie, from the NIH. "I like your resumé," Brodie said. "Maybe you'd like to work in my lab. Could you come down here to talk with me?" He didn't say so, but I could tell he needed hands in the lab and had found me by trolling through files of rejected candidates. I couldn't afford to be proud: sure, I would come to Bethesda.

I asked people at Columbia who Brodie was, but no one could tell me anything. This man had it in his power to change my life, and I knew nothing about him. What might I be getting into? Apprehensive, I took two days off from my internship and returned to Building 10 for the interview. Trudging through endless corridors, I eventually found Brodie's lab. Bored and formidable, his secretary gave me a skeptical look and told me to wait in Brodie's office. This was a nondescript room with a gray desk, blackboard, three padded metal chairs, and bookshelves crammed with dusty books and scientific journals. Uneasy, I surveyed the room and tried to imagine Brodie. The piles of paper on every horizontal surface were not very helpful. I saw manuscript drafts, forms to be signed, letters, reprints from journals, and multiple pads of lined notepaper covered with illegible scrawls.

Suddenly, here was the man himself, smiling wide and shaking my hand. Elegant suit, tie askew, gray hair, craggy nose and chin, and deep-set eyes. He was cordial, with a broad smile that alternated with a look of intense determination. I began to feel confident that this was going to work out. Brodie posed a few perfunctory questions, and then took charge, offering to tell me about his lab.

"Wouldn't you like to discover how the brain works?" The question introduced a non-stop monologue, apparently impromptu but also coherent and detailed. In memory I hear it like a dramatic, soul-wrenching aria, sung in a foreign language. I can recollect a few words, but most of the substance eludes me. I must have assented to Brodie's offer to discover how the brain works, because he stepped to the blackboard and wrote the names of two neurotransmitters, one at top right, the other at top left. I knew these were chemicals released from the endings of nerves to regulate the next cell (a muscle, a cell in some organ, or another nerve cell) in multiple different signal relay systems that communicate messages from one part of the body or brain to another. Then he began to cover the blackboard with names, arrows, and question marks.

First Brodie concentrated on the left side of the board. He reminded me that this transmitter, chemically related to adrenaline, was responsible for life-saving "fight-or-flight" responses to danger. "In the old days you were running from a tiger. Now it kicks in when you run to catch the bus," he said. Just as I had learned in medical school, the brain tells a specialized set of nerves to release the transmitter onto target organs throughout the body, making the heart beat faster, dilating the pupils, and diverting blood flow from tissues like the gut to the muscles we need to run or confront the danger.

Neurons within the brain release this same transmitter, Brodie said. He drew a picture of one of these neurons, showing where certain drugs act to stimulate transmitter release. Activating these neurons, he said, turns on neural pathways that promote increased activity and expenditure of energy—including but not limited to fight-or-flight. One drug that releases this transmitter, he pointed out, is amphetamine—a well known "upper," which excites patients and elevates their mood.

Brodie announced that a second transmitter, spelled out at the board's upper right-hand corner, acts in the brain as a downer. He inferred this notion from experiments in his lab showing a big effect of a drug on this neurotransmitter in rat brains. I had used the same drug to reduce high blood pressure in patients, and knew its most dangerous side effect was mental depression, severe enough to make patients want to kill themselves.

Other labs disagreed with him about the action of this transmitter, Brodie said, "but they just haven't got it right." I wondered briefly why this news had not filtered down to medical students, but soon learned that this was the theory he and I would prove, working together. Woven through details I no longer remember was Brodie's favorite refrain, an oracular fragment of Euclidean rhetoric: "We first make the assumption, which we later prove, that . . . ."

Somehow, I gathered, we would establish the proper role of this transmitter in the brain, and show definitively that it and the transmitter on the left oppose one another's actions. We would do this by giving drugs to rats and measuring their effects on behavior and brain chemicals. The details don't matter, because in retrospect Brodie's grand theory was woefully premature. (With the right twist, the grand theory might seem to predict effects of Prozac, a widely used anti-depressant drug that was developed much later.[2]) His opponents didn't have it right, either. The brain has turned out to be much more complicated, and more interesting. But nobody knew enough to guess right in 1966.

I wasn't about to argue with Brodie's passion for simple explanation. I couldn't follow everything he said, but he was brilliant, charismatic, and persuasive. He had talked for more than two hours when I dared to interrupt. "I would like to work in your lab, very much. Could I begin in July?"

The answer, fortunately, was yes.

———

Before going to the NIH, I had spent a few compulsory hours in the lab portion of a biochemistry course and worked for four months in a smelly dog surgery lab. Brodie's lab was unlike either, just as Brodie was unlike anyone I had known.

The day I arrived, Brodie's secretary introduced me to a young man named Jim Davis. "Dr. Brodie is out of town. He says you are both MDs, and you'll work on the project together." Jim, like me, had left his residency program to dodge the draft. He was bright, friendly, and headed for a career in academic neurology. Brodie's lecture on how the brain works, combined with Jim's inexhaustible enthusiasm, had made him an eager convert. Pacing restlessly back and forth, Jim told me that Brodie's favorite neurotransmitters would not only explain how the brain works, but would also reveal causes of brain diseases.

Impressed by his apparent confidence, I made a quiet confession. "You know, Jim, I don't really understand exactly how Brodie's experiments will prove his theory. Can you explain how?"

Jim first launched into an explanation, but quickly backtracked. "Actually, I can't keep it straight either."

Getting the theory right, we agreed, would be tough. Then we each confessed something more disturbing. Neither Jim nor I had ever done a real experiment.

After our first talk, learning that Brodie would not return until the next day, Jim and I decided to explore the lab. Occupying two floors in a wing of Building 10, it housed at least 40 scientists. The central corridor on our floor was lined, from one end to the other, by shelves containing hundreds of small horizontal compartments. The compartments, arrayed in chronological order, contained reprints of Brodie's published papers, each tagged with a small white card listing authors, title, and year. Brodie's lab, we were to learn, was immensely prolific. Rumor had it that he had founded a new scientific journal, just to get everything published. For the scientists, the lab's high productivity had its down side. Manuscripts languished on Brodie's desk for months, sometimes even years. Laboring lovingly over every paper, he found it hard to keep up with the scientists. Some manuscripts, it was rumored, never saw the light of day at all. When Brodie retired, after I left the lab, several unpublished manuscripts were found under his secretary's desk. According to the story, the primary authors—mostly visiting scientists from other countries—had returned home before Brodie could get to their manuscripts. (An alternative theory was that the visiting scientists had incurred the arbitrary enmity of the boss's secretary, a forbidding woman who terrified us and was rumored to frighten Brodie himself.)

Walking down the long corridor, I heard machines emit menacing sounds on every side. Busy scientists in white coats emerged briefly into hallways and swiftly returned to their labs, intent on mysterious pursuits. Doors off the corridor opened into more than a dozen small rooms. Jim and I explored them all. Most were "wet labs," with a large sink and three or four "benches"—hard tables from whose surfaces sprouted spigots for hot and cold water and valves for vacuum lines, air at high pressure, or gas for Bunsen burners. Bench tops were littered with test tubes, small centrifuges, and small plastic rat cages (some containing rats), often accompanied by cigarette butts and soft-drink bottles. In those days, eating and smoking in the lab were not forbidden. Each wet lab housed one or two scientists, to whom we introduced ourselves. Everyone was friendly, but busy and used to meeting newcomers.

Other rooms contained large pieces of equipment instead of work benches: plastic tanks connected by tangled wires to boxes bristling with knobs and dials; huge freezers; insulated boxes of dry ice; multiple whirring centrifuges; glass columns filled with a substance that looked like sand.

One especially forbidding contraption was a glass box, three feet square and eight feet high, which enclosed two stacks of circular plastic trays. Holes distributed around each tray's periphery held small glass vials. Less timid than I, and more curious, Jim began to push random buttons on the control panel. Sure enough, some trays rotated; others rose or descended. Soon he pushed too many buttons. Smooth motion came to a halt, trays began to shake, and the device emitted a low grinding noise, then an ear-splitting alarm. A white-coated scientist quickly appeared, pushed more buttons, and silenced the alarm. He told us off, in no uncertain terms. In our ignorance, he said, we had come close to destroying a newly purchased and fantastically expensive scintillation counter.

I knew what a scintilla was, and had heard of scintillating conversation, but couldn't imagine why scientists would want to count scintillations. I learned that scintillations are used to measure radioactivity: when a radioactive atom in one of the vials decays, it releases energy that is converted into (scintillating) light detectable by the scintillation counter. Later I would use scintillation counters every day—but not the one Jim had nearly destroyed. Within two weeks that device deconstructed itself, mysteriously but definitively, with no help from either of us.

Because Brodie was to supervise us directly, Jim and I occupied a lab all by ourselves, full of pipets, glass beakers, and unidentifiable glass-and-metal objects of unknown use and provenance. Except for the fact that he was every bit as ignorant as I, Jim was a good person to share the lab. Always immensely enthusiastic, he was less given to doubt and discouragement than I, and more willing to tackle an experiment or procedure, even when he wasn't sure what it was supposed to show. He loved to talk, but walked back and forth during conversations, fiddled unconsciously with everything that came to hand, and often transferred it to the breast pocket of his white lab coat. Within a month, all my pens and pencils migrated to Jim's desk drawer.

Other scientists on our floor, almost all male, were divided into small groups of three to six individuals, each headed by a senior scientist who reported directly to Brodie. Most were quiet and hard-working, but approachable and generally similar to people we already knew. Some were less ordinary. One fellow suffered from intractable constipation, caused by paregoric, an opiate drug to which he had become addicted. Another, a biochemist from India, infuriated lawn-proud neighbors by planting rows of corn in place of the neatly tonsured grass in his suburban front yard. And an orotund cigar smoker, housed in the corridor upstairs, descended often to our floor, where he collared unfortunate souls to share his wisdom on every subject, even science; he probably did experiments, but we never found out what they were.

One pale, cadaverous fellow magically appeared at two o'clock every day. He would usually spend less than an hour in the lab, giving instructions to his postdoctoral fellow, a female scientist from Finland. She, unlike her adviser, worked like a demon. Sporting a dirty blue parka, she huddled four hours every day in the "cold room" built inside her lab. (This room, with thickly insulated metal walls, was correctly named. To slow decay of biological samples, it was maintained at a temperature just above freezing, 24 hours a day.) There she was said to be purifying something, but I didn't ask what it was. Tall, bespectacled, and taciturn, she seemed intimidating but was probably just shy. We dubbed her The Dorsal Finn.

A dark, handsome Italian came to the lab for a sabbatical year to explore how the brain controls sexual behavior in rats. He conducted his experiments at night, in near-darkness, because rats sleep in the daytime. Every night he would sit for hours, counting copulations of animals treated with drugs that altered brain neurotransmitters. In the morning he delightedly regaled anyone who would listen with lurid accounts of nocturnal love among the rodents.

Of all the people in the lab, only the cigar smoker and the connoisseur of copulation showed much interest in talking with us, or indeed with the scientists around us. Most people kept to themselves, interacting almost exclusively with people in their own separate wet labs. Later I discovered that this uncommunicative style differed from that of most labs, but Jim and I didn't know enough to question it. Clearly we were supposed to work pretty much on our own.

No denizen of the lab was stranger than Brodie himself. Jim and I didn't see much of him, because he traveled a lot and—when he was in town—rarely appeared in the lab before four in the afternoon. Meeting with him for an hour or two, at long intervals, Jim and I would briefly report results of our experiments. Sometimes we received marching orders for the next set of experiments, but often Brodie's attention was directed elsewhere, and he would launch into another hypnotic monologue. We listened as his mind roamed restlessly across trackless wildernesses of biology and chemistry. For months I hung on his words.

Even after I realized that Brodie didn't know everything, the bold sweep of his mental forays dazzled me. His own ignorance never fazed him. In an elevator one evening, I overheard him impart a new theory to two of his senior scientists. The theory, he said, explained how insulin works. I was intrigued, because it was then a great mystery how insulin induces sugar in the blood stream to enter cells, and explaining the mechanism might offer clues to understanding diabetes. In the middle of an unusually persuasive riff, Brodie suddenly interrupted himself. "Remind me," he asked, "does insulin make the blood sugar go up, or down?"

We learned more about Brodie from rare gossip sessions in the lab. Many stories expressed awe for his past scientific prowess. Others were tinged with amusement and even derision, directed toward his behavior and current ideas. Every lab gossips about its senior figure, and some of the gossip is even true. Our information came from individuals who had known Brodie only a few years longer than Jim and I had. More senior people, who knew Brodie better, had little time to spend with us. For more reliable information, I would have to wait for Robert Kanigel's remarkable book, *Apprentice to Genius*,[3] published in 1986.

In Kanigel's account, between 1941 and 1955 Brodie transformed the science of pharmacology. Applying his training as a chemist, he devised novel methods for measuring concentrations of drugs in blood and other tissues. These methods led to a series of extraordinary discoveries. During World War II, he and his colleagues converted a nearly worthless antimalarial drug into an effective treatment. Later they invented drugs still used today, including acetominophen, the analgesic now known as Tylenol.[4] In the process they invented the new field of drug metabolism. Finally, in the mid-1950s, they discovered a new class of drug-metabolizing enzymes.[5] Together, these discoveries revealed basic principles that are still applied, 50 years later, by drug companies to discover new drugs and by physicians to optimize drug therapy in patients.

Reading Kanigel, I learned that in those years Brodie's lab was an exciting place to do science. His colleagues found him enormously energetic, brilliant, hard-driving, and totally fearless in his determination to solve any problem he chose to tackle. He involved himself in every project and every experiment, constantly questioning assumptions and thinking outside the box. Supreme self-confidence told him that hard thinking and the right experiment would furnish the answer—as in fact it did, over and over. He repeatedly urged his colleagues to perform imaginative experiments, saying: "Let's take a flyer." Invariably, his people became caught up in every project Brodie undertook, driven to think better and work harder. The only negative note, according to Kanigel, was Brodie's penchant for controlling every detail of the project himself. Sometimes, when his charm and persuasive powers did not produce the desired effect, he could become overbearing and demand too much of his colleagues.

Brodie moved his lab from New York City to the new NIH campus in Bethesda, Maryland, in 1949. Several scientists in his lab moved to Bethesda with him, including his technician, a brilliant young man named Julius Axelrod. Together, Axelrod and Brodie had discovered Tylenol in New York. And at the NIH, in 1954, Axelrod's experiments discovered the liver enzymes that proved to be responsible for metabolizing almost all known drugs. He felt that Brodie unfairly claimed credit for this discovery,[5] and decided to leave the lab. After a year of graduate classes, Axelrod got a PhD degree from George Washington University, and was allowed to start a small lab at NIH on his own.

Our labmates intimated that Brodie and Axelrod had not been on speaking terms since Axelrod left. If we talked to Axelrod, they warned, we should be careful not to let Brodie know. I did visit the Axelrod lab once. Although both labs were housed in Building 10, the two were as different as their chiefs. Between 1954 and 1966, Brodie's lab grew to occupy two floors, housing 40 scientists. Axelrod's lab, with its half-dozen scientists, remained the same size during this entire period. We addressed our lab chief as "Dr. Brodie." To his postdocs, Axelrod was simply "Julie".

Kanigel shows how Axelrod inherited Brodie's let's-take-a-flyer style and passed it on to his own scientific progeny, but Brodie never revealed any residue of that style to Jim and me. We were tiny blips on his radar screen, and I had the impression that even group leaders also saw him rarely. As his lab expanded, Brodie's scientific style had changed. More and more, I suspect, lieutenants took charge of squads of scientists focused on different projects. Just a few years before our arrival, Jim and I heard, one lieutenant had regularly corralled unlucky scientists in the lab to attend after-dinner discussion sessions with Brodie. At these sessions, held once or twice a week, six or eight bleary-eyed individuals would sit in Brodie's living room until well past midnight, talking about a project that wasn't working or hearing the latest idea on his mind. When that lieutenant took a position elsewhere, Brodie had to recruit participants for these sessions on his own, and night time sessions came less often. During my time in the lab, in fact, I don't remember one.

By the late 1960s, most lab members—including, after a few months, me—saw one exposure to a Brodie monologue as an adventure, but repeated exposure as an unwelcome chore. Brodie still tried to recruit listeners, but we didn't make it easy. Taking advantage of his habitually tardy appearance in the lab, we arranged a warning system to alert the entire corridor when Brodie arrived. Before he could prowl about to round up a quorum, many of us would scuttle quickly out the other end of the corridor and go home. If caught, we could usually manage to beg off by citing a previous engagement. Some members of the lab claimed to have discovered a fail-safe method, useful in a real pinch. They would keep a rat in a cage near the lab bench. Regularly supplied with food and water, the rat led a quiet life—until Brodie walked in. Then the lab scientist would remove the rat from its cage and carry it to a guillotine used to sacrifice animals: "Excuse me a moment, Dr. Brodie. I have to take a time point." Unable to stand the sight of blood, Brodie invariably ducked out. Unharmed, the rat returned to its cage.

———

At first I found experiments just as unfamiliar and strange as the most peculiar characters in the lab. Like every beginner, I had trouble accomplishing the simplest maneuvers without mishap. Brodie himself didn't perform experiments, and was never easy to reach, so we learned experimental procedures from other scientists in the lab. At first I couldn't even use a pipet to transfer a given amount of liquid from one tube to another tube. Sometimes I would suck too hard on the rubber tube connected to the top of the pipet, and find myself spitting out radioactivity or vile-tasting chemicals. It was not easy, either, to poke a rat's tail vein with a fine needle to inject a drug. And I always hated "sacrificing" rats. The word seemed a bizarre euphemism for transforming a warm creature into an inanimate object.

With practice, these tasks became easier. When I mastered the simple procedures, the real trouble emerged. Sometimes the experiment Brodie designed was impossible. Once, for instance, Jim and I were instructed to treat rats simultaneously with three different drugs. The combination rapidly induced convulsions, and animals died within minutes, before we could detect the predicted changes in concentrations of chemicals in their brains. Disappointment rapidly turned into black comedy. Drawing on his medical experience, Jim decided that the animals died because their blood sugar was low. The obvious remedy was to place them in what he called the Intensive Care Unit, a cage in which every animal received an injection of sugar solution every five minutes. I objected that we had no evidence that the blood sugar was low, or even that the drugs we gave would lower blood sugar, especially so quickly. Unquenchably confident, Jim forged stubbornly ahead. The rats died even faster.

Even when an experiment was practically feasible, the result rarely conformed to Brodie's theory. "Jim, this result is just what those guys in Sweden would predict," I would say. The Swedish lab's view of brain neurotransmitters differed dramatically from Brodie's.

"Oh, you're always pessimistic," Jim would reply. But eventually he would admit he too was baffled. We pored over Brodie's published papers and those of other labs, trying to reconcile his theory with previous findings. It plain didn't work. Perhaps the rival labs he disparaged were doing better experiments and getting more consistent results.

"Maybe Brodie's idea just isn't right. Can that be?" we asked one another.

In retrospect, our frustrations resulted from a lethal combination of defects. First, ignorant beginners need feedback and advice, but these were hard to come by. We saw Brodie infrequently, and the lab's organization promoted intellectual isolation. Formal lab meetings were non-existent. Each scientist in the lab belonged to a small group, focused on its own problem. Groups didn't talk to one another. Jim and I were the only members of our group; no one else worked on our project or seemed to care about it.

Then we began to realize that Brodie himself was a problem.

"Henry," Jim would say, "you're always critical of the experiments he wants us to do, but you don't tell Dr. Brodie."

"Yeah, but how can I argue with an old testament prophet?" I'd reply. "He always says we didn't do the experiment right—and maybe he's right. And then he comes up with another new experiment, and the whole damn cycle repeats itself. To hell with Brodie's theory!"

The underlying problem was our woeful lack of experience. We didn't know enough—or thought we didn't—to imagine alternative ideas, troubleshoot failed experiments, or discard one approach and try another. As MDs and newcomers with little knowledge of basic biology and chemistry, how could we question our leader? Unquenchable self-confidence appears innate in some scientists. While a few such lucky people appear later in this book, neither Jim nor I belonged among them. Instead, acutely aware of our own ignorance, we were afraid to contradict Brodie. That didn't keep me from deeply resenting the prospect of 18 more months of failure and bewilderment.

My stories told Nancy I was undergoing a painful conversion from admiring disciple to resentful, brooding rebel, but most of the time we could ignore the lab because the rest of our lives were so much fun. Michael was becoming a lovely, charming three-year-old, we were meeting couples who shared our interests, I was successfully dodging the draft, and—best of all—internship was over.

At this point, Brodie somehow got wind of Jim's and my discouragement. He called me into his office and announced, "It's time for you to start a different project. You and Jim will join different groups in the lab.

"You'll work with Gopal Krishna," he said, referring to the suburban corn farmer. "He's very smart, and he'll teach you a nifty new method. Best of all, you'll study the most exciting new molecule in biology!"

The new molecule, called cyclic AMP, had gotten a mention in my medical biochemistry course, and I knew a bit more about it from an informal course for young researchers Jim and I had taken at the NIH. I hadn't known Gopal worked on it, so it was clearly not one of the lab's mainstream projects. But I didn't need any persuading. I just hoped the new project would preserve my sanity until I could return to clinical medicine. Certainly I had no inkling of the pivotal role the new molecule would play in my own career.

Ira Pastan, who taught the informal course, was smart but low-key and reserved, tingeing every subject with subtle irony. So his almost evangelical reverence for cyclic AMP proved a real surprise.

"Let me tell you why cyclic AMP is so important," Ira began. "This molecule represents the very first answer to a profound biological question. Right now it's the only available answer to that question, which is: how does a cell detect an external stimulus and transform it into a chemical message that elicits the appropriate response inside the cell?" Although stimuli like hormones and neurotransmitters tell the cell to make profound changes in its behavior, these external chemicals themselves can't penetrate the cell's peripheral membrane.

On the board, Ira drew the first "signaling pathway" I had ever seen.

$$\text{Hormone}_{\text{(outside)}} \rightarrow A \rightarrow B_{\text{(inside)}} \rightarrow C_{\text{(inside)}} \rightarrow \text{Response}$$

Then he erased the pathway and amended it, as follows.

$$\text{Hormone}_{\text{(outside)}} \rightarrow \text{Adenylyl cyclase} \rightarrow \text{cyclic AMP}_{\text{(inside)}} \rightarrow$$
$$C_{\text{(inside)}} \rightarrow \text{Response}$$

Located in the cell's peripheral membrane, adenylyl cyclase is the enzyme that makes cyclic AMP. It does so by modifying a small precursor molecule, ATP, which is abundant in every cell.[6] (An enzyme is a protein that converts one chemical substance into another, without changing its own composition or behavior in the process. This enzyme's product, cyclic AMP, is call "cyclic" because three parts of its chemical structure form a triangle—or, in biochemistry jargon, a "cycle.")

Ira reminded us that Earl Sutherland and his colleagues had discovered cyclic AMP in 1957. They were trying to explain how adrenaline, the "fight-or-flight" hormone, causes liver cells to release sugar from their internal stores. (When I ran toward that car wreck in 1960, my liver was pouring sugar into the blood to provide quick energy to my muscles.) They discovered that an adrenaline-stimulated enzyme in liver membranes, called adenylyl cyclase, makes cyclic AMP, and that cyclic AMP in turn triggers a cascade of enzymes that leads to production of sugar for export into the blood.[7]

Then they and other labs went on to discover that cyclic AMP is also responsible for remarkably different (and physiologically important) effects of many other hormones on other tissues (heart, fat, endocrine glands, and the kidney). Ira predicted that cyclic AMP would turn out to transmit signals from many additional hormones, but that future research would reveal that many other hormonal signals depend on mechanisms unrelated to cyclic AMP. With hindsight, we know Ira was right on both counts.

Still, to the eye of a 21st-century biologist it looks strange that so little was known about cyclic AMP, a full nine years after its discovery. The problem—according to Ira Pastan, and confirmed by Gopal—was that cyclic AMP was biochemically difficult to measure. Measurement was tedious, requiring some of the same painstaking biochemical manipulations[7] Sutherland's lab used to discover cyclic AMP in the first place.

This is where Gopal's new method came in. Brodie had bragged about it because the new "cyclase assay" made it convenient to measure effects of any hormones on adenylyl cyclase in the membrane of any cell. Gopal's method only required the enzyme to make radioactive cyclic AMP from its precursor, ATP,[6] which had been tagged in the right place with a highly radioactive phosphate atom. The time was ripe for such an assay. In 1971, four years after I worked with Gopal, Sutherland's discovery would merit a Nobel prize. In 1967 Gopal was climbing onto the cyclic AMP bandwagon, and Brodie invited me to join him.

At first I found Gopal abrupt, formal, and stern. He suggested I apply his new assay to cells isolated from fatty tissues of rats, to confirm previous evidence that adrenaline uses cyclic AMP to cause release of fatty acids from fat cells. Remarkably, it proved easy to adapt another lab's procedure for preparing fat cells and their membranes—I had finally learned to use the pipet! Soon I was able to repeat Gopal's initial findings: adrenaline really did induce fat cell membranes to produce cyclic AMP. I began to see Gopal as shy and taciturn, rather than dour. Then, delighted that one experiment worked exactly as predicted, I departed for a vacation. Nancy and I would spend a week in Florida, leaving Michael with the grandparents—our first separation from our son since he was born.

On my return I found Gopal a very different person, with a beaming smile. He could barely suppress his excitement.

"Look at this!" he exclaimed, showing me a graph. "Adrenaline stimulates adenylyl cyclase in the fat cell membrane, as you found before you left. Treating the cells with thyroid hormone for two hours does nothing to the cyclase, by itself. But pre-treating with thyroid hormone makes the effect of adrenaline twice as strong!"

It was unexpected to see one hormone indirectly increase the effect of another in the test tube, and especially exciting that the effect involved cyclic AMP. From my medical training, I knew that too much thyroid hormone in Graves' disease (thyrotoxicosis) induces a rapid heartbeat and other effects that mimic responses to adrenaline. Thus Gopal's new result might explain symptoms of a human endocrine disease.

But that wasn't all.

"I have submitted this as an abstract for Atlantic City," said Gopal, adding in a quiet voice, "and I listed you as the first author. You'll give the presentation." This was an even bigger surprise. I would present the results to hundreds of biologists at the national scientific meeting in April, in Atlantic City, New Jersey.

"But Gopal," I sputtered, "This is your work, not mine. It wouldn't be right for me talk about it."

"Don't worry!" Gopal replied. "You'll work out the details between now and then, and it will be our work. And very exciting work, too." Grateful to Gopal for his generosity, which was genuine, I easily conquered my scruples and set to work.

My first experiment, however, was a disappointment. Incubating fat cells with thyroid hormone had no effect on the response to adrenaline. Perhaps I was not doing it right. Gopal suggested changing doses and treatment times. The result didn't change. We tried to change other variables—all to no avail. Finally, he repeated the experiment himself—and tried again. Still, no effect.

April was fast approaching, and I was scheduled to give a talk about a result that wasn't true.

"Gopal, what shall we do?" I asked.

"No problem," he answered, with a calming smile. "I'll go to the meeting myself and tell what happened."

The night before the actual talk, I telephoned Gopal from Atlantic City. He was still in Washington. "I'll drive up there early tomorrow morning, and get there at least an hour early," he assured me.

The next day four speakers told their stories to an audience of more than 500 scientists, while I waited anxiously outside the hall. No Gopal. When my talk was announced, I didn't appear. Instead, I pocketed my name-tag and skulked home.

That was the end of my collaboration with Gopal. We barely spoke to one another the rest of my time at the NIH. Brodie reprimanded him for making the lab look bad in public, but I am sorry I didn't confront him myself. I hated such scenes, and still do. I didn't tell Gopal how angry I was, partly because I was ashamed to have wanted a share in real scientific discovery so badly that I allowed my name to stay on the abstract in the first place. In addition, a part of me knew that Gopal genuinely intended to do me a favor. Our real mistake was to trust a one-off experiment enough to present it to scientists at an important meeting. This stupid mistake taught me a hard-earned lesson.

In any case, the NIH years were nearly over. Jim was almost as disillusioned as I. We conjectured that two trained monkeys, given the same reagents and equipment, would have produced exactly the same results. The monkeys might have broken more glassware, or sacrificed more rats. So what? we thought. We'll soon be out of here.

At the goodbye party, my lab-mates gave me a cartoon. In it a man, viewed from the rear, stood on a chair to urinate on the desk before him. The caption: "I quit!" My feelings, exactly—abject failure and bitter disappointment, mixed with scorn for Brodie and his ilk. I was relieved at the prospect of returning to clinical medicine.

———

The future didn't work out that way. Forty years later, I see the story and its characters in a different light.

Now I know, for instance, that failure in the lab happens all the time, and can be salutary, even necessary. I have watched dozens of beginning scientists deal with their own failures, and learn from them how to do better experiments. My failure at the NIH taught me no such thing. I learned only that using research to avoid the draft was not much fun. I had avoided Vietnam, to be sure, but still had a lot to learn how to think about experiments.

I did learn how *not* to teach young scientists how to do science. Fledglings need continuing advice, direction, and encouragement from senior scientists and their fellows, who must not only teach ideas, techniques, and the "culture" of lab investigation, but also bolster determination, cheer success, and console when failure strikes. If Brodie had fostered a close-knit lab, the Atlantic City fiasco would not have happened.

A callow youth caught up in my own troubles, I paid little attention to the more poignant drama before my eyes, the inexorable decline of an immensely gifted senior scientist. Once disappointment and anger began to fade, I began to wonder how Brodie's extraordinarily productive lab of the early 1950s became the dysfunctional organization Jim and I found in 1966. What happened to all that razor-edged verve and imagination?

The relentless growth of Brodie's lab probably interfered with his style of research. In addition, he must have been devastated by the acrimonious break with Axelrod, followed by his former technician's brilliant discoveries. In the late 1950s, Axelrod and his colleagues discovered that the sympathetic neurons which release the adrenaline-like transmitter of the fight-or-flight response also take the transmitter back up after it has acted on key target organs, such as the heart and blood vessels[8]. Their explanation of this mechanism revolutionized understanding of normal cardiovascular regulation, as well as the fight-or-flight response, and set the stage for exciting new treatments of hypertension, heart disease, and psychiatric disorders. In 1970, two years after I left the NIH, Axelrod received the Nobel Prize for this work.

According to Kanigel[3], this Nobel award dealt Brodie a serious blow. From an observation I made in 1967, I know Brodie felt he deserved the prize himself. The boss was out of town, but his secretary said he wanted me to look at a manuscript she had just typed. Retrieving it from the boss's desk, I saw another document, typed on the same machine—a letter nominating Brodie for the Nobel prize. Penciled revisions, in his distinctive scrawl, covered every page.

I scorned Brodie for stooping so low, but now I see his self-nomination as a poignant plea for recognition. He felt his earlier discoveries merited a Nobel, and its award to Axelrod must have broken Brodie's heart. In this light, Jim's and my comical attempts to prove his grand neurotransmitter theory emerge as a failure to create a fitting last hurrah for Brodie. In his heyday, he lavished his time, energy, and imagination on smart, well-trained scientists, driving them to important discoveries. By 1966, he could barely scrounge up a couple of rank novices like Jim and me to take on a project he hoped would overshadow Axelrod's success. Inevitably, the project came to nothing. At the time, I imagined the sad tale was my own, but the real sadness was Brodie's.

A year after Axelrod's Nobel, medical problems forced Brodie to retire from the NIH and move to Arizona, never to direct a lab again. After a series of debilitating strokes, he died in 1989.

CHAPTER 4

Vaulting Ambition

LEARNING A NEW GAME

From the NIH I returned to New York for a year of medical residency, sure I would never enter a laboratory again.

One obvious alternative was a career in academic medicine. I thought it would be fun to treat patients, teach, and do a bit of clinical research on the side. I would need training in a subspecialty—perhaps endocrinology, but I had also heard good things about a new specialty field, called clinical pharmacology. For the sake of adventure, Nancy and I decided I should look at training programs on the west coast. I scheduled interviews with Robert Williams, the head of endocrinology in Seattle, and Kenneth Melmon, the head of clinical pharmacology at the University of California, San Francisco (UCSF).

In the Seattle interviews, I talked a good medical game. No one had any inkling of what a debacle the NIH years had been, and I was careful not to reveal it myself. Williams, a charming senior statesman, introduced me to bright young endocrine researchers and to the chair of his Department. Williams offered me a job, but the chair, to my surprise, told me I should train for a couple of years with Melmon in San Francisco and return to Seattle for a faculty position. I was impressed—mentioning Melmon's name, before I even met him, got me an apparent invitation to a faculty position.

Seattle had been characteristically rainy, but the April weather in San Francisco was glorious. I spent a brilliant Sunday before the interview sauntering through the beautiful city and enjoying an exhilarating ride on a cable car. Even before my Monday interview, I was sure San Francisco was the place for me.

Then I met Ken Melmon. He was a short, muscular fellow, with hands, head, nose, and eyes too big for the rest of him, and taut with energy and ambition. After a crushing handshake, he offered me a chair in his tiny office, then leaned back in his own. I could smell his shoeless feet, propped on the desk right next to me—a reassuring antidote, I hoped, to the risk of being fooled by another accomplished charisma-generator like Brodie. I kept trying to detect the whiff of a charlatan, but couldn't. Ultimately his charisma proved more pungent and insistent than Brodie's, and drowned out the aroma of those feet.

Like Brodie, Ken began our first conversation with an evangelical riff. "Here's what clinical pharmacology means: we want to make drugs more effective—not just in experiments, not just in theory, but when real doctors give them to real patients." Emphasizing each point by extending successive fingers of his right hand, Ken continued. "First, we have to teach doctors how their drugs work, and how the body handles them, so they can prescribe drugs based on real scientific evidence. We have to teach them to be critical about clinical trials of drugs, and design truly objective trials ourselves.

"In this fellowship you'll have a lot to learn," he went on. "It's not enough to be a good internist. You have to become a superb pharmacologist. But your NIH training makes you just the right man for the job." He smiled. I nodded, convinced.

I spent most of the day talking to scientists Ken had recruited to join his clinical pharmacology program. Bright and enthusiastic, most of them studied effects of drugs in animals. At the end of the day I returned to Ken's office.

"What did you learn?" he asked. I told him I understood the rationale of most of the experiments his people described, but thought one project, on blood pressure in monkeys, was poorly thought out. I expected Ken to defend the project, but instead he heartily agreed. "I'm glad you saw that. The guy doing those experiments doesn't understand the big picture." I was flattered that he appreciated my scientific acumen, but he changed the subject.

"You should come to this training program," Ken said. "Here's the only question—what kind of research should you do?" I muttered something about wanting to learn about drug trials and clinical pharmacology in real patients, but he assured me I would learn that in the clinical part of the program. For me he had a different agenda.

"Listen, fella, for a career in academic medicine you've got to do first-rate research. And you've got a gold mine, right in front of your eyes." Ken took his feet off the desk, leaned forward, and gave me a penetrating look. "At the NIH you learned to measure adenylyl cyclase. You can be the only researcher west of the Mississippi River who knows how to do that. For real impact, you should measure it in a clinically relevant human tissue. We'll think about that."

It didn't seem the right time to tell Ken the NIH had completely dashed my enthusiasm for lab research. Instead, I said I liked the program a lot, and would think about it a few days and get back to him, soon.

In truth I was dazzled. This brilliant young scientist in San Francisco saw me as someone with real potential! Working with him promised to be exciting and very different from Hopkins, the NIH, or Columbia.

Back in New York, I told Nancy I had met a brilliant and charismatic academic leader, destined for great things and unlike anyone we knew. She remained faintly skeptical about Ken, but was enthusiastic about moving to San Francisco. A day later I wrote Ken saying I would start the fellowship in July.

———

Once I started work in San Francisco, I found Ken even more impressive. Immensely self-assured, he knew everything and was never at a loss for words. For every question he had a prompt, thorough, unassailable answer. He told me he had received the highest grade in the nation on the Internal Medicine Board Examination. Tireless and fantastically energetic, he traveled constantly, proselytizing for clinical pharmacology. Only six years older than I, Ken had already published dozens of scientific papers—on clinical therapeutics, endocrine disorders, and inflammation. On ward rounds he dazzled smart young doctors and attending physicians. Skillfully diplomatic with older faculty, he was tough and aggressive with younger ones.

One of these was a young nephrologist who disagreed with Ken one day about how to treat a patient. Like Clark Kent in the old Superman comics, the nephrologist was tall and handsome, with broad shoulders and a serious, straight-arrow demeanor. He even wore glasses, a blue suit, and a conservative tie. I can't remember the disease or the therapeutic question, but I'll never forget the body language. He stood up straight and blinked as Ken, at least a head shorter, ticked off on his fingers the reasons his opponent's argument wouldn't hold water. Now and then Ken emphasized a point, speaking slower and louder and pointing his index finger directly at his opponent's chest. As the confrontation proceeded, in front of an audience of students and residents, I saw that the young man was bright, determined, and persistent—and, I thought, probably right. Still, Ken's inexorable determination gradually wore him down, and he eventually wilted. Ken had won. To my surprise, I admired Ken even more than before, even though I had always hated bullies and sided with the underdog.

Ken's approach to luring me into laboratory research was more subtle. Early on, he showed me a paper recently published in *Science* by researchers at Johns Hopkins. It suggested that cyclic AMP acted in human white blood cells to damp allergic reactions. It did this, the paper said by preventing the cells from releasing histamine, a substance that plays a big role in allergies and causes the stuffy nose of hay fever—hence treatment with antihistamines. The evidence was indirect. Two drugs prevented the disease-causing antigen of hay fever from inducing the blood cells to release histamine. Both drugs were known to elevate cyclic AMP in other tissues, so the authors inferred that cyclic AMP itself inhibits allergic release of histamine. But they didn't measure either cyclic AMP or adenylyl cyclase.

Ken didn't say why he thought the *Science* paper might interest me, because he knew I could extract the moral myself. That is, cyclic AMP, a ubiquitous "second messenger" for hormones, was the most exciting new molecule in town, and measuring cyclic AMP production in human white blood cells would be just the ticket for success in academic medicine. I took the lure enthusiastically, listing a host of experiments I could do to extend the findings.

My turnaround was so quick I hardly knew it was happening. What happened to my staunch resolve to stay out of the laboratory? I still don't know for sure. It seemed more a reflex than a conscious decision. Ken used the adenylyl cyclase assay to lure me back into the lab, just as Brodie had used it as a lure to work with Gopal, but I didn't notice the parallel.

One reason for the turnaround, to be sure, was that adenylyl cyclase could be used to solve puzzles and explain mysteries, a process I had always loved—in *Moby Dick*, in suspense novels, in biochemistry and pathology courses, in diagnosing disease, and even in Brodie's office. ("Wouldn't you like to know how the brain works?") But an equally attractive lure was Ken's argument that adenylyl cyclase would open doors to a successful career in academia—that is, I was moved as much by opportunism as by curiosity. Free-floating ambition easily trumped shameful memories of the NIH. So I grabbed adenylyl cyclase, and cyclic AMP grabbed me.

Once the hook was set, Ken reeled me in. "It's a slam-dunk, fella," he pointed out. "White blood cells are the obvious target tissue in humans. They're easy to get, and the only tissue you can take out of a person without hurting him." Besides, these cells were medically relevant because they both fight and cause disease. They normally defend us against infections and tissue injury, but their products also contribute to autoimmune disorders by damaging joints, kidneys, and other tissues.

Ken suggested I learn to work with white cells by tapping the expertise of Bob Lehrer, a bright young faculty member in the Department of Medicine. Bob was trying to understand how white cells defend the body against infections. Specifically, he was asking how white cells kill *Candida albicans*, the fungus responsible for thrush. (Oral thrush—overgrowth of *Candida* in the mouth and throat—can cause serious pain and discomfort in normal individuals. *Candida* infection frequently afflicts patients with other disorders that impair white cells' ability to fight infection, including AIDS, a disease that would be discovered ten years later.)

Bob and I hit it off immediately. He began by showing me how to separate white blood cells from red blood cells. From a friend or colleague, I would draw a couple of ounces of blood into a syringe containing heparin, which prevented it from clotting. Then I diluted the blood into a sugar solution and let it sit a while in a plastic tube. Most of the red cells were denser than the sugar solution, and settled into the bottom half of the tube. I would then suck the top half of the solution, containing most of the white cells, into a pipet, transfer it to a test tube, and spin the cells down in a slow centrifuge. This produced a "button" of cells at the bottom of the tube, which contained a few contaminating red cells. I got rid of these by briefly diluting them into a solution that caused red cells to pop open. The white cells remained intact, so I could centrifuge them down into another pellet and then suspend them in a salt solution appropriate for experiments. Often I would break up the cells (in a device that bombarded them with sonic vibrations) and measure adenylyl cyclase in the resulting cell fragments. It was tedious, but it worked.

To my delight, the cyclase assay itself also worked. As the findings from Hopkins would predict, fragments of white blood cells made lots of cyclic AMP when exposed to isoproterenol (hereafter I'll call it ISO), a chemical relative of adrenaline, the fight-or-flight hormone. Another class of stimulators was the prostaglandins, substances thought to regulate inflammation. So, human white cells could make cyclic AMP. Bob and I wondered what that elevated cyclic AMP might actually be doing in white cells. "Let's see whether it affects the cells' ability to kill *Candida*," Bob suggested.

Quickly we found that prostaglandins prevented human white cells from killing the fungus, and got the same effect by treating cells directly with a chemical analog of cyclic AMP. (The analog was a drug chemically similar to cyclic AMP, but chemically modified so it could more easily cross the cell membrane to enter cells.) Combined with cyclase assays showing that prostaglandins stimulate white cell adenylyl cyclase, these findings made a publishable story. The Hopkins group had suggested, from indirect evidence, that cyclic AMP might turn off an allergic response in white cells. Now we had the first biochemical evidence for cyclic AMP as a regulator in a human cell. Bob and I congratulated ourselves.

Looking back, our paper seems thoroughly pedestrian. It was no real surprise that white cells make cyclic AMP, because it was already known that almost every mammalian tissue does the same. Worse, we discovered no clue as to how cyclic AMP prevents white cells from killing *Candida*, or why this effect might be biologically useful. Nonetheless, this success was the stimulus I needed. Now it was time to ask how cyclic AMP affects other functions of white cells.

———

The first step in this direction seemed an unexpected stroke of luck. Sometime in 1970, Ken had intimated that I might be able to move from the fellowship into a faculty job at UCSF. Beginning to feel more confident in the lab, I was intrigued. In addition, out of the blue, I received a letter inviting me for a job interview at Johns Hopkins, my medical alma mater, in Baltimore. The job sounded perfect. I would be an assistant professor in a group investigating immunity and inflammation—exactly what white cells do. Even better, a research star in that group, Larry Lichtenstein, had written the paper implicating cyclic AMP as a regulator of allergic histamine release. Delighted, I accepted the invitation.

In Baltimore, I met Larry for the first time. A warm, welcoming fellow, he was unassuming and very smart. We talked about the next set of experiments to explore his prediction that cyclic AMP inhibits histamine release. By this time his lab had already shown that a cell-permeating cyclic AMP analog blocked release of histamine.

"Here's another idea, Larry," I said. "I just found that histamine itself stimulates white cells to make cyclic AMP, just like ISO and prostaglandins do. Maybe histamine outside the cells inhibits the antigen from triggering release of more histamine stores. What do you think?"

"I love it," said Larry. "Allergic responses can damp their own intensity. We'll do the experiment next week." (He did have to figure out, of course, how to discriminate between the histamine used to treat the cells and the histamine they released in response to the allergic stimulus. But it turned out that wasn't hard.[1])

When I returned home, Ken was pleased to hear that Hopkins would probably offer me a job, but still hoped I would decide to stay at UCSF. By way of persuasion, he invited Nancy and me to his house for a fine dinner. Nancy and I pondered our decision carefully. We both preferred the Bay Area to Baltimore as a place to live and raise children. By now we had a second son, Randy, who had been six months old when we drove from New York to California, and a daughter, Molly, who was born at UCSF in 1970. "Larry is a really smart scientist, and I like him," I told her, "but I can still work with him long-distance. Besides, Ken has been good to me, UCSF is an exciting place, and I can have a lot of fun here." After a few days, we decided to stay. I wrote Hopkins a long letter saying so, but also expressing delight at the prospect of a trans-continental collaboration with Larry. I asked Ken's secretary to mail the letter.

An hour later, Ken stalked into the lab, red-faced and angry. He had scribbled black ink all over my letter. "If you don't want to go to Hopkins, that's fine!" he barked. Then he crushed the letter into a ball, threw it in the trash basket, and stalked out. Dumbfounded, I wondered what the hell was going on. He made his point, I guess, because I didn't re-type the letter to send it. But I puzzled over that conversation, unable to decipher the message behind it.

Calmer the next day, Ken said I shouldn't say no to Hopkins now, but instead should wait until they formally offered me a job. "You want to get the best possible deal from our department chair, don't you? Well, you'll certainly get a better deal if Hopkins makes you an offer."

"But Ken, why were you so angry?" I asked.

"How do you think Hopkins found out about you?" I didn't answer, ashamed to reveal that I thought my fame had wafted its way to Baltimore on its own.

"I gave Larry your name, and suggested they invite you for an interview," Ken went on. "An offer from Hopkins will do you a huge favor, but your letter almost destroyed it. Listen, Dad: it's time for you to learn how the game is played."

I was miffed to discover how easily I had been fooled, and the subterfuge bothered me. But Ken's ploy worked, and my faint pang of conscience quickly subsided. Hopkins mailed me a formal job offer, and UCSF matched it with a faculty position in the coveted "tenure track," a better offer than I could have bargained for on my own.

Meeting Larry proved the luckiest consequence of Ken's machinations. In the first of a series of experiments, Larry and I followed up the question that came up in our first conversation: histamine really did inhibit histamine release by elevating cyclic AMP in histamine-containing cells. By this time I had adopted a new assay for measuring cyclic AMP itself, extracted from intact white cells. The assay, developed by a rising young scientist called Al Gilman, gave us another tool, in addition to measuring adenylyl cyclase, to assess cyclic AMP's role.

Attracting the interest of other scientists in the cyclic AMP field, our new findings brought Larry and me invitations to the first Gordon Research Conference I attended. Dozens of such Gordon Conferences meet every summer in New England. Each focuses on a different topic and attracts approximately 100 attendees. Conferences are held for a week at private boarding schools, emptied of students for the summer. Attendees sleep in student dormitories, eat in the school dining room, and in the morning and evening hear scientific talks. In the afternoons, they sail, bicycle, hike, gossip, and talk about experiments.

Larry and I shared a speaking slot in the program. He described allergic histamine release and I detailed our cyclic AMP measurements. I was scared and excited, because this was my first scientific talk outside UCSF. Mercifully, it went well. Meeting scientists who cared about the same questions, and every bit as intensely as I, was a heady experience. I was thrilled to meet Al Gilman and other leading cyclic AMP researchers, people I had never seen, although I had read their papers. At dinner, or over a beer after the evening session, they reminisced or speculated about future developments in the field. I listened avidly, and got up courage enough to buttonhole several famous scientists (famous, at least, to me), in order to learn how to do an assay, where to get a hard-to-find lab reagent, or who would be most likely to know the answer to additional questions. Almost everyone was friendly and helpful.

Best of all was the response of Ted Rall, an older, highly respected scientist whose hands had performed the experiments that earned a

Nobel for Earl Sutherland, awarded for discovery of cyclic AMP. "You guys did all the right things," Ted said. "You found hormones that regulate the function, you showed the cyclic AMP analog regulated the function in the same direction, and then you measured cyclic AMP itself. Congratulations!" Now a grizzled veteran of dozens of Gordon Conferences, I understand that one of their essential functions is to initiate youngsters into the tribe. Ted was welcoming me into the community, and I was thrilled.

Larry and I worked together closely for about five years. In addition to ISO, prostaglandins, and histamine, we found another agent that elevated cyclic AMP in white blood cells. This agent—which later proved a useful tool for my lab—was the toxin that causes cholera, by elevating cyclic AMP in cells lining the gut. The cholera bacterium stays in the gut itself, never invading tissues; instead, its toxin elevates cyclic AMP in gut cells, causing transport of salt and water into the intestine. The result is choleric diarrhea, with fluid loss that can prove lethal. Cholera toxin elevated cyclic AMP in white cells and caused the same functional changes we saw with ISO and the other agents. Later we would realize that several unusual aspects of the toxin's action hinted strongly at its biochemical mechanism, which at the time was quite mysterious.[2]

The collaboration with Larry and his colleagues also revealed a role for cyclic AMP in a second kind of white blood cell, called a T lymphocyte. In test tube experiments, cyclic AMP prevents T lymphocytes, obtained from one individual, from killing cells of another individual. This kind of killing normally plays a key role in the body's rejection of transplanted organs. In 1974 Larry and I wrote a long review article, suggesting key roles for cyclic AMP in controlling inflammation, allergy, and immune responses to antigens. That publication expedited my promotion to tenure at UCSF—another benefit of Ken's indirect way of introducing me to Larry.

———

After the NIH, I was seeking mentors, and lucky to find Bob Lehrer and Larry Lichtenstein. Like most scientists, Bob and Larry knew much more science than I did, but they were the first who seemed to take real pleasure in talking about science. Focused and thoughtful, they loved explaining and asking questions.

Ken was a different character altogether. His force of personality and charisma vastly overshadowed anyone I knew. I marveled at the variety and magnetic force of his ideas, and became a devoutly convinced adherent of the new doctrine of clinical pharmacology.

To me, Ken was always—with the brief exception of his response to my almost spoiling his scheme to get me a faculty appointment at UCSF—friendly, encouraging, and even flattering. I owe him a great deal, beginning with his advice that I work on cyclic AMP in white blood cells. I also owe him my appointment to the UCSF faculty, the wonderfully fruitful collaboration with Larry, and my promotion to tenure, in 1975. For a long time I was less aware of another benefit of working for Ken—that he freed me from having to worry about obtaining money for my experiments. I posed the questions, did the experiments, and wrote the papers as well as the detailed proposals for experiments in grant applications to the NIH. But the grants were awarded to Ken, who used the money to pay my postdocs and technicians and buy the lab supplies and technical equipment I needed. On each grant he was listed as—in NIH jargon—the "Principal Investigator," or "PI."

In those days, young faculty in clinical departments often worked "for" a senior faculty member: that is, they occupied the senior person's lab space and spent money from his (never her) grant. The arrangement was comfortable for Ken, because the grants and putting his name on my papers gave him necessary credentials for becoming a mover and shaker in the world of academic medicine. As a bonus, he could feel good about helping a bright young man do science. Still, I wonder how I could have been so naïve. I was 29 when I first came to San Francisco, plenty old enough to have read the signals sooner. But I was too delighted with success in the lab to worry about who was paying the bills.

I enjoyed the gravy train for about five years, but gradually became aware of a cloud on the horizon—Ken's scant interest in the actual experiments. The cloud was easier to see after 1972, my first year as an assistant professor, when I began devoting part of my time to experiments in collaboration with a second faculty member, Gordon Tomkins. I'll tell the Gordon story in the next chapter, but for now it's enough to say that his style and personality contrasted sharply with Ken's.

Ken, in fact, almost never talked about science, and barely found time to give a cursory once-over to manuscripts I was about to submit for publication (with his name listed as a co-author). Instead, he was busy with myriad projects—heading a large NIH grant, with many investigators in several departments; consulting with the Food and Drug Administration in Washington; setting up the country's first institutional committee to review experiments involving human subjects; giving honorary lectures at other medical schools; and authoring the first textbook of clinical pharmacology.

Then the cloud grew larger. I discovered that Ken felt entitled to a substantial share in ownership of my scientific papers. For my two years as a postdoctoral fellow and the next three as an assistant professor at UCSF, Ken was a co-author on almost every paper. Worse than sharing authorship, Ken was giving talks about my work at other universities, I soon learned. What bothered me the most was that his talks invariably got the ideas wrong.

Eventually push came to shove. The first hint was indirect. Attending a conference in Vancouver, I was called by one of Ken's postdocs, who told me I was in serious trouble. Ken was furious that I had not listed him as an author of the manuscript that was to be published in a "Proceedings" volume after this meeting. Without intending to take a stand, I had omitted Ken as an author because the manuscript described experiments I did with Gordon—experiments in which Ken had never shown any interest. I didn't know what to do.

A day after I returned home, Ken held a lab party at his house. At the party, Ken's wife made an off-hand remark: "I just can't understand why young people who work with Ken can't see all he is doing for them." She didn't name me as one of the ungrateful wretches, and may not even have known that I was the chief offender. Still, I took this second hint, and sheepishly added Ken to the list of authors. (Other chapters of this book show that fights over authorship are not confined to faculty protégés and their patrons. This is because authorship is the real coin of the realm in science.)

Finally I began to understand how Ken played the game. I felt he was manipulating and exploiting me, and struggled to disentangle myself from his control. By 1977, with help from other senior faculty at UCSF, I got a lab of my own and was able to apply for my own research grants.

Late in that year, lunching with another faculty member in the cafeteria, I heard intriguing news. "Did you hear the latest grapevine story?" my friend asked. "Ken is talking with Stanford about taking the chair of the Department of Medicine down there." I was quietly pleased, partly because Ken would be immensely pleased to ascend so close to the pinnacle of academic medicine in the U.S., but also because his departure would free me from further involvement with him.

Ken downplayed the story, partly to allay worries of UCSF faculty whose grant support depended on him and his clinical pharmacology program. Nine faculty, including me, were especially concerned about a grant that partly funded our research. This was UCSF's "Program Project Grant" in clinical pharmacology, a large joint grant from the NIH. Ken was the PI of this project. We had recently submitted to the NIH a long written proposal to renew funding of the project, containing individual research proposals from each of our labs. Visiting experts in our fields had reviewed our written proposal and listened for two days to our oral presentations. Their review document would determine our fate. Although Ken expressed unreserved optimism, we awaited the outcome anxiously.

Then Ken received the review in the mail, and gave us good news. Almost certainly, he assured us, the NIH would fund our project. In addition to a detailed written critique, NIH review committees issue a quantitative "priority score" for every grant, based on the mean of scores awarded by individual committee members. The worst possible grade is 500, and a grade of 100 is perfect. In those days, we heard, NIH grants with scores as high as 175 were being funded. Ken said our project's overall score was 140, well within funding range.

For us to receive the money, the grant would also have to be approved by a second, higher committee, the Council of the National Institute of General Medical Sciences (NIGMS). We were not worried, because Council approval almost always reflected the review committee's recommendation. The Council would meet in a couple of months. In the meantime, Ken occasionally traveled the 30 miles to Stanford. Presumably negotiations continued, but to us he remained appropriately silent about their progress.

Then two bombs detonated, on successive days. First, Ken announced that he would take the Stanford position. The very next day, the NIGMS Council met and decided not to fund our project. Everyone in clinical pharmacology was puzzled and dismayed. I congratulated Ken on the Stanford job, but couldn't resist asking why the Council had turned down our proposal, despite a priority score of 140. "I don't know," he replied. "Probably they heard I was going to Stanford."

With Ken soon to depart for Stanford, we were forced to re-group. I was given the task of winding down the project grant, which had a few months still to run. Faculty members funded by the dying grant had to re-apply individually for NIH funds to continue the projects they had proposed. Most of us would eventually be granted money for the projects we had thought the grant renewal would pay for, but only after suffering funding gaps for several months.

A few weeks later, I called an NIH official to discuss details of the project grant's demise. In the course of our conversation, I posed the question I had asked Ken. After a moment of silence came this reply: "What did you say the score was? 140? No, the overall score was 240, clearly out of funding range." The discrepancy surprised both of us, but the official would have no more to do with it. "Dr. Melmon is a very powerful figure. I won't say anything about it, to anybody."

This news troubled and confounded me. What was going on? Immediately I sought out a friend who had applied for support through the same project grant.

"It's not surprising," said my friend, who was more sophisticated than I. "Now I see why the written review was so much more critical and negative than the score was. The real score, 240, fits better with the criticisms those guys made." I had read the review also, but missed the discrepancy.

"Fine," I asked, "but why would Ken tell us the score was 140?"

"It's obvious. Ken was negotiating with Stanford. He counted on news of a good priority score spreading quickly to the guys he was negotiating with," he said. "His bargaining position would be stronger if Stanford thought he would be glad to remain at UCSF as PI of a big, well-funded NIH Program Project Grant. That way, he could keep on raising the ante with Stanford. Why do you think his negotiations continued right up to the day before the Council met?"

Again, I had let myself be duped. I was furious with myself for playing the fool and with Ken for fooling me. Ever cautious, despite the anger, I made an appointment to talk with a high official at UCSF, who knew both Ken and me. I told him the whole story, including the speculation that Ken had used the falsely elevated priority score to support him in negotiating with Stanford.

Unsurprised, the official grinned. "He did that, huh?"

"Yes. And what shall we do about it?" I asked.

The official thought for a moment. "Well, Henry, I think we would do best to do nothing at all.

"Here's why," he continued. "First, we're dealing with a highly respected figure—respected here and even more respected at our sister school, Stanford. Saying anything about this would embarrass him, embarrass Stanford, and embarrass us." He paused a moment, then continued.

"And that's not the only thing. This comes at a delicate time. If we say anything now, we'll have to keep him. I say, let him go."

Seeing that I looked perplexed by his straightforward advice, the official went on. "This kind of thing happens. Every day, walking through the halls, I see someone I know this kind of story about. I say hello, and hide the information in my heart."

And that was that. Ken did go to Stanford. Knowing he wouldn't have another chance to fool me, I was delighted to see him go.

Six years later, in 1984, Ken finally got caught. Perusing a chapter Ken had written for a leading endocrinology text, an expert on the subject suddenly recognized his own phrases, sentences, and even whole paragraphs—which the expert had written for a different textbook. Subsequent investigation showed that about a quarter of Ken's chapter was taken from chapters originally written, by this expert and several others, for a pharmacology text. Ken was one of the editors of that text. The publisher of the cited material threatened to sue, but Ken denied responsibility, claiming that he had instructed his secretary to make sure the endocrinology chapter specifically acknowledged the borrowed material. According to newspaper accounts and articles in *Science* magazine, this proved not to be the case.[3]

Ken resigned from his chairmanship after a Stanford ethics committee judged him guilty of "grossly negligent scholarship." The university censured him, but absolved him of conscious intent to plagiarize. He remained on the Stanford faculty, and later became an Associate Dean. He died in 2002.

My white-hot anger against Ken took a long time to cool. It was not only that I despised him for not turning out to be the hero I thought he was. What I really could not forgive was how he revealed to me my own ignorance. I never expressed that anger to Ken, just as I had not after the earlier botch-up with Gopal.

Perhaps that is just as well, because Ken might not have taken my anger seriously. But I do regret not speaking more directly when he tried later to make friends. Sometime in the early 1990s, Ken invited me to dinner with him at a fine Italian restaurant in San Francisco. I was still angry, and wondered what we could find to talk about, but I was also too timid to say no. In the restaurant we reminisced and joked uncomfortably about the old days, concentrating on our early years together at UCSF.

"I hope we can get together more often from now on," Ken remarked at one point. I mumbled something, but was too much of a coward to say a word about his deception 15 years earlier. So many years after the incident, I should have been honest with him, if only to give us a chance to talk about it directly.

Now, after an additional 15 years, I wonder at the infinite misery we can inflict on ourselves. Despite his intelligence, drive, and extraordinary ability, ambition eventually did Ken in. He wanted badly to move and shake the world, as a scientist, scholar, medical reformer, and academic leader. His hunger for recognition kept him from immersing himself in the real business of learning how nature works.

And then Ken fell. For a long time I thought Stanford's punishment too lenient for the act that provoked it, but for him the pain inflicted may have felt unbearable. From feasting richly on his own success, Ken was reduced to gathering crumbs from under the tables of others.

Macbeth might have diagnosed Ken's problem very much as he did his own:

> . . . I have no spur
> To prick the sides of my intent, but only
> Vaulting ambition, which o'erleaps itself . . . .

The Scottish usurper experienced moments of real insight into his own motivation, but I have no clue whether Ken could do so. Instead, he seemed to believe his actions were genuinely blameless. Perhaps Stanford was correct to absolve him of direct intent to deceive when he borrowed material from other authors, at least in a sense. The possibility that he was committing culpable deception may never have crossed Ken's mind in relation to the false priority score or the borrowed textbook material, any more than it did when he maneuvered to get me a faculty appointment at UCSF. Ambition, I suspect, blinded him.

———

Hindsight has its pitfalls, of course, but I think I understand what those first years at UCSF did for me. My mistakes and false starts proved extremely useful, and may have been necessary.

Cyclic AMP in white blood cells, for instance. Now we know that cyclic AMP is only one of the ways nature uses to limit the extent and intensity of inflammation and immune responses. I thought that vein of semi-precious ore was played out by the mid-1970s, when I took my miner's hat and pick elsewhere. And yet, and yet—*Candida albicans*, histamine release, and adenylyl cyclase may have been easy pickings, but without them I would have left science altogether, and the rest of my life would have brought me much less joy.

The Ken story is similarly mixed. While he was surely not a hero to emulate, I owe much to his generosity. He pointed out the right problem to tackle, schemed to get me appointed a faculty member, shepherded my promotion to tenure, and in the process showed me how to harness my free-floating ambition to a career in science.

In the end Ken's example drove home a much harder lesson—that vaulting ambition by itself is never enough. Instead, I needed a mentor who would teach me how to find and savor the delight of probing nature's secrets.

That story comes next.

CHAPTER 5

Lessons in Delight

NEW WAYS TO THINK ABOUT EXPERIMENTS

In 1972, Nancy urged me to join the recently formed UCSF Commute Club, which runs buses to and from work, across the Golden Gate Bridge. It wasn't so much that a car was expensive—rather, when I drove to work I was tempted to stay late in the lab, and often missed having dinner with our children.

One morning, a couple of weeks after I joined, I climbed into the bus, found the only empty seat, and sat down to read a newspaper. Looking sideways at the man sitting beside me, I saw tousled gray hair, a sharp nose, and glasses. The guy must be 15 years older than I, I thought. I didn't recognize him at first, but he did look like a professor, and was intently perusing a copy of *Nature*. Slowly I realized that a friend had pointed this man out to me a year earlier, and told me his name. This was Gordon Tomkins, a famous biochemist who came to UCSF from the NIH three years earlier, about the same time I did. I felt a shiver of anxiety. I was only a beginning faculty member in the Department of Medicine, and biochemists, notorious intellectual snobs, were said to doubt whether faculty in clinical departments were truly human.

I managed to conquer trepidation and introduce myself. To my surprise, Gordon was friendly and curious. He asked what I did at UCSF, and I told him about cyclic AMP in white blood cells. Gordon too was interested in cyclic AMP, and said his lab used a genetic approach to figure out how cyclic AMP works.

Figure 5-1. Gordon Tomkins

The idea of a "genetic approach" was news to me. I knew little enough about biochemistry, which I vaguely imagined as a more sophisticated version of what I was already doing—that is, taking a biological sample, manipulating it in some way, and then measuring something to assess what the manipulation did. I guessed that "real" biochemists like Gordon purified enzymes and studied how they worked in test tubes. My knowledge of genetics was even slimmer, confined to medical school lectures on bacterial exchange of genetic material and a handful of inherited human diseases. I knew that each gene occupied a separate stretch of the genetic material, DNA, in our cells, and that the sequence of small chemical links that comprise any gene in the DNA chain determines the sequence of amino acid building blocks in the protein that corresponds to that gene. That was it.

This level of ignorance didn't seem an egregious defect in 1972, even in a medical school. Disparate tribes conducted the rites of medicine and biochemistry in different dialects, and genetics was almost a separate language. From the time I entered Brodie's lab, right up to meeting Gordon, I cannot remember a single scientific conversation that touched on genes, DNA, or evolution. Certainly I had never imagined using genetics to ask a biological question.

In contrast, Gordon—like many other biologists—had switched his focus from biochemistry to genetics because genetics seemed to offer sharper tools for dissecting the biological mysteries that fascinated him most. Gordon had made himself a pioneer in applying genetic approaches to ask questions about regulation in animal cells. At that time the favorite targets of genetic analysis were smaller organisms like bacteria. Taking advantage of the simpler organization of bacteria and their faster rate of multiplication, labs everywhere were busily isolating instructive bacterial "mutants". Each mutant bacterium, and all its progeny, differed from the parental bacterial line. The mutant might, for instance, resist killing by a particular antibiotic or fail to prosper without a normally unnecessary nutrient. Such new properties were determined by changes in the sequence of a gene in the bacterium's DNA, changes called "mutations."

"It's very simple," Gordon said, as he launched into explaining how to use genetics to understand how cyclic AMP works. Like many geneticists and molecular biologists, Gordon rarely introduced an idea without saying how simple it was.

"It's like bacterial genetics, except we use cells from a mouse lymphoma, a tumor cell line called S49. Cyclic AMP kills S49 cells, which makes them quite special. We get mutant cells by killing the un-mutated normal cells with cyclic AMP. In practice, we expose normal S49 cells to a chemical analog of cyclic AMP." (This was the same analog Bob Lehrer had used to regulate function of white blood cells, as I described in the previous chapter.)

"We start with a low dose, and gradually increase it," Gordon continued. "The normal cells slowly die off, because they are killed by cyclic AMP, but cyclic AMP-resistant cells multiply and take over the culture. It's as if the cell population 'learns' how to survive and multiply despite cyclic AMP. So I call it a 'training experiment'."

This didn't sound like a powerful "genetic approach" to me. What good is it to kill the normal cells? Answering the question I was too shy to ask, Gordon went on. "We think the cyclic AMP-resistant cells carry a gene mutation that makes them ignore the cyclic AMP treatment. The normal version of the mutated gene must specify a protein that's necessary for cyclic AMP to kill normal S49 cells. So a mutation that inactivates that gene creates a cell that doesn't know cyclic AMP is even there.

"And in fact," Gordon added, "we just found that the cyclic AMP-resistant cells lack a key protein that all normal cells have. So the genetic approach has identified the protein that cyclic AMP uses to kill S49 cells."

Gordon was talking about the regulatory pathway I had learned about in Brodie's lab. In an earlier chapter, the pathway looked like this:

Hormone → adenylyl cyclase → cyclic AMP→ C→ Response

Gordon was telling me that his genetic approach had identified the protein symbolized by "C" in the pathway—that is, the protein responsible for the function that elicits cell death (the "response") in cyclic AMP-treated S49 cells.

The results were nearly as simple as Gordon advertised. Violet Daniel, a postdoc in his lab, found that S49 cells resistant to killing by cyclic AMP contained little or no activity of a known enzyme, which is normally stimulated by cyclic AMP. The enzyme was designated by the acronym, PKA.[1] So for S49 cells the latter part of the pathway should be amended by substituting PKA for C, to read like this:

cyclic AMP → PKA→ Cell death

Gordon was certain that cyclic AMP killed S49 cells by stimulating this enzyme, but quickly admitted that this wasn't much of a surprise. In fact, he said, Violet had hoped PKA would prove to be missing in the resistant cells, because it was the only enzyme regulated by cyclic AMP in any tissue. Indeed, the increase in PKA activity induced by cyclic AMP caused release of sugar from liver cells treated with adrenaline. This was the hormone response, I remembered, that Sutherland's lab used to discover cyclic AMP in the first place.

Timidly, I objected. "Why does nature use this enzyme to kill one kind of cell, when in other cells it does something very different? Do you mean that death of an S49 cell and the fight-or-flight response in a liver cell both depend on the same chemical messenger, cyclic AMP, and the same target enzyme, PKA? Those are very different responses. It sounds pretty bizarre."

Well, Gordon replied, some people thought Violet's result must be wrong, because PKA should exert "natural" effects of cyclic AMP, and cell death hardly seems natural. So, they say, the PKA result must be a side-effect. Gordon took a dim view of this notion. "Do they seriously imagine that evolution evolved a different way for cyclic AMP to work in every tissue and cell? What a *throcking* great coincidence that would be! This enzyme just happens to be absent from the same cells cyclic AMP can't kill? And present in cyclic AMP-sensitive parental cells? How likely is that?" In fact, Gordon and many others thought PKA might be responsible for all or most responses to cyclic AMP in animal cells.

Three decades later we still don't know "why evolution wanted S49 cells to keel over when they see cyclic AMP," as Gordon put it. We do know, though, that cell death is often natural, and even necessary—for instance, in regulating the immune system or in embryonic development.[2]

Hindsight, more than 30 years later, also tells us that Gordon was right about the widespread roles of PKA. Now cyclic AMP is known to act as the chemical messenger for many hormones in animal cells, and in most cases it transmits the message by stimulating PKA, just as Gordon suspected. Responses differ in different cells, of course, but that is because PKA acts on a specific and distinctly different set of targets in each kind of cell. The human body contains many dozens of such targets, designated "X" in the pathway below.

Hormone → adenylyl cyclase → cyclic AMP →
PKA → X → Response

In this way, one kind of X in a particular cell produces the response to cyclic AMP seen in that cell, while a different X, in a different cell, can elicit a quite different response.

Back in 1972, Gordon cannot possibly have known for sure that PKA really does carry most of the messages cyclic AMP initiates in animal cells. The narrower inference, that PKA transmits cyclic AMP's lethal message in S49 cells, rested on firmer ground. It would have been a "throcking" coincidence indeed if the only known target of cyclic AMP was present in normal S49 cells but just happened to be specifically lacking in the S49 cells that survived exposure to cyclic AMP.

Like scientists and everyone else, Gordon and Violet tested the simplest possibility first. If a particular enzyme was known to carry out one effect of cyclic AMP, it was the obvious potential choice to carry out cyclic AMP's death sentence for S49 cells as well. And the simple possibility turned out to be correct.

Although I didn't appreciate it clearly at the time, Gordon's extension of PKA to explain all actions of cyclic AMP was teaching me the extraordinary power of genetics. First, genetic reasoning applies a straightforward syllogism to establish a narrow conclusion: if the mutation that changes the function of a cell or organism affects a single gene and alters its corresponding protein, then that protein must play a key role in the function that is changed. Gordon knew very well that the syllogism applies, strictly speaking, only to the cell or organism tested. But then he proceeded to the next essential step, daring to stretch a limited conclusion to apply—at least tentatively—to the widest possible spectrum of biology. The stretching step is useful for generating new sets of questions. (Many biochemists at the time favored this particular extrapolation to other cells and other responses. They were already beginning to find PKA in multiple tissues and to show it acts on proteins responsible for cyclic AMP-regulated functions.)

In any case, Gordon's interest in cyclic AMP was not confined to the biochemical and cellular events this chemical messenger induces. He was also interested in how hormones might act to stimulate production of cyclic AMP in cells. As the bus reached UCSF, he asked if I would like to look for hormones that increase cyclic AMP in S49 cells. I jumped at the chance. Waiting for the bus, 40 minutes earlier, I knew how to measure cyclic AMP. Now Gordon was about to show me a new way to do science.

———

I was already measuring production of cyclic AMP in white blood cells, so it was easy to extend the experiments to S49 cells, testing the same stimulators of adenylyl cyclase, including ISO, an adrenaline-like drug, plus prostaglandins and cholera toxin. All three robustly increased cyclic AMP in normal S49 cells, just as they had in white blood cells. Like the cyclic AMP analog, they also killed normal S49 cells but did not kill the cells Violet had "trained" to resist killing by cyclic AMP. This was no big surprise, but it did show that the normal S49 cells were susceptible to killing by excess "real" cyclic AMP—that is, by the chemical made in the cells themselves, not just a chemical analog.

At this point, I compared cyclic AMP in the normal cells and in the cyclic AMP-resistant cells. Amazingly, ISO and other stimulators increased cyclic AMP much more effectively in the PKA-deficient cells. The difference was large—at least six-fold. We had expected identical cyclic AMP responses in the two types of cells. Instead, loss of PKA *enhanced* the cells' ability to accumulate their own cyclic AMP.

I rushed to tell Gordon this new result. We saw it implied a surprising paradox. Perhaps hormones use PKA not only to kill normal S49 cells, but also to limit their accumulation of PKA's regulator, cyclic AMP. "Somehow cyclic AMP has found a way to decrease its own accumulation. That really *is* exciting," Gordon said.

I asked Gordon why he found the paradox so exciting. "Look, Henry, it's a surprise. And we always crave surprise, because explaining a surprise will tell us something new about how nature works. We don't really *want* to find exactly what we suspect beforehand, because that just confirms prevailing wisdom."

Part of the power of genetics, to be sure, lies in its ability to test and prove inferences. Thus the "throcking coincidence" of cyclic AMP resistance associated with loss of PKA strongly supports the idea that cyclic AMP kills S49 cells by stimulating PKA. But Gordon knew, as I was discovering, that the power of genetic experiments extends much further. Indeed, for generating real surprise, nothing beats genetics. Greater elevation of cyclic AMP in PKA-deficient cells was exciting precisely because we did not imagine the result before doing the experiment.

I should stop here for a moment, to confess that I had never heard anybody talk this way about science. Certainly I had not seriously entertained the notion that scientists conduct their experiments in quest of surprise. To the contrary, I had assumed, and consistently observed, that science consisted for the most part of doing experiments to show that one's idea about a mechanism in nature was right. Guy Knickerbocker and I had known that cardiac massage would supply blood flow to the brain—and indeed it did. My NIH experience was a painful disaster because Jim Davis and I failed miserably to confirm Brodie's notions about brain neurotransmitters. The one real "surprise" of those years, Gopal's result with thyroid hormone in fat cells, turned out to be wrong, and added a public failure to my record in science. And in San Francisco my experiments with cyclic AMP in white blood cells were coming out pretty much as everyone expected, which pleased us and pleased the journals to which we submitted our papers.

Now, at long last, I learned something truly new—it is not only permissible, but often in fact essential, to do experiments whose results you can't predict beforehand. Indeed, if you are certain what an experiment will show, it may not be worth doing. This new lesson changed everything.

I have been shy about confessing this part of the story to fellow scientists, who tend to find it incredible. "How could you have thought this way at the ripe age of 32?" they ask. Looking back, however, I suspect that even today many bright non-scientists, many beginners in the lab, and perhaps even a few mature scientists, still think science works pretty much as I thought it did back in 1972. Bob Lehrer and Larry Lichtenstein didn't think this way, I'm sure, but they had no opportunity to correct my naïve view because I didn't share it with them.

Exploring the surprising excess of cyclic AMP in cyclic AMP-resistant cells, we wondered how cyclic AMP reduces its own accumulation. The answer involved new twists—new to me at the time, at least—on the simple regulatory pathway we saw earlier. In the new scheme (Figure 5-2), cyclic AMP stimulates PKA, as before.

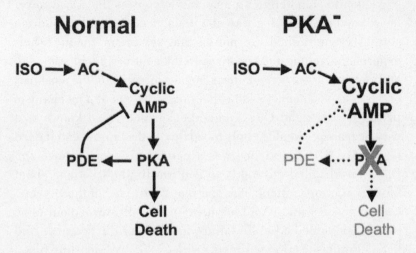

Figure 5-2. Why the PKA⁻ mutant accumulates more cyclic AMP in response to ISO. In normal cells (left) the arrows indicate that ISO causes adenylyl cyclase (AC) to produce cyclic AMP, which in turn activates PKA. Increased PKA activity causes the cell to increase its complement of phosphodiesterase (PDE). The increased PDE activity degrades cyclic AMP. (By convention, a line terminated by a bar signifies a decrease or inhibition, just as a line with an arrowhead signifies an increase or stimulation.) In PKA⁻ cells (right), however, cyclic AMP cannot increase PDE, and therefore cannot act to decrease its own concentration. Consequently, ISO stimulates greater cyclic AMP accumulation in PKA⁻ cells than in wild-type. Note also that in the normal cell PKA stimulates two separate responses, increased PDE and cell death.

Now, however, in addition to causing cell death, we found that increased PKA activity also induces normal S49 cells to make more of an enzyme that degrades cyclic AMP. (The degrading enzyme, classified biochemically as a phosphodiesterase, is abbreviated PDE; its degrading effect on cyclic AMP is symbolized by a bar at the end of a line, as described in the legend beneath the Figure.) PKA-deficient cells contain less of the degrading enzyme, and accumulate more cyclic AMP because they degrade it more slowly.

Our evidence for this scheme was that pretreating normal S49 cells with ISO or with the cyclic AMP analog substantially increased the amount of degrading enzyme, so that later exposure to ISO or prostaglandins induced less of an increase in cyclic AMP. The increase in degrading enzyme did not occur in PKA-deficient cells.[3] Thus cyclic AMP acted through PKA to decrease its own accumulation. Nowadays biologists are used to finding signals that damp their own intensity. They call it negative feedback.[4] (Another example of negative feedback is the ability of histamine to inhibit release of histamine from white blood cells, which I described in the last chapter.)

The scheme's second twist, in addition to feedback regulation, is that the pathway is branched—that is, PKA produces two *separate* effects. As discussed above, in this case separate effects probably depend on separate targets for PKA itself. At the time we published this result, our evidence for branching of the downstream pathway was weak—in essence, PDE activity went up rapidly, in a couple of hours, while death required much longer. Later evidence showed clearly that the two responses in S49 cells really are separate.[5] The whole idea of intracellular pathways of regulation was in its infancy, but it was already clear to many that branches and feedback circuits could combine to produce complex effects in response to very simple input signals. Like most of what I was learning, this idea also was new to me.

As we wrote the paper describing these findings, Gordon taught me another important lesson. Into one sentence, Gordon suggested we insert a simple phrase: "If . . . , *as we imagined*, then . . . ." Those three words were electrifying. I had thought science was all facts, but Gordon dared to unlock closed doors, freeing imagination from its intellectual boudoir to gambol in full public view.

The three years after I met Gordon were enormous fun.[3] Each day I learned something new. We organized a small group of cyclic AMP afficionados who worked with S49 cells, including two brilliant postdocs—Phil Coffino, in Gordon's lab, and Paul Insel, in Ken's lab. Early on, Phil showed us how to grow single S49 cells to create large "clonal" populations, each descended from one mutant cellular ancestor. It was no longer necessary to "train" S49 cells. Now we could "select" multiple "clones," each resistant to killing by the "selective agent" (a cyclic AMP analog, a hormone, or cholera toxin, for instance). As a consequence, the different clones could carry different mutations.

My most important discovery in those years was Gordon Tomkins himself. Whenever two facts tickled his fancy, Gordon generated an idea. As a result, his ideas accumulated at an alarming rate, and it was our task to pick and choose among them. He freely admitted that 90% of his ideas were wrong. Still, the remaining 10% was plenty enough, providing we chose the right 10% to tackle. To my astonishment, Gordon took being wrong with perfect equanimity. The demise of a cherished notion elicited a characteristic response: "Good. Now I'll think about something else."

Gordon's curiosity and imagination triggered discoveries everywhere he went. At the NIH, his colleague Julius Axelrod told how Gordon advised him to set about studying the biochemistry of drug metabolism: "Julie," Gordon said, "For biochemistry you need only two tools: a liver . . . and a knife." In liver slices, Axelrod discovered the first drug-metabolizing enzymes, described in chapter 3.

In San Francisco, Gordon was a Pied Piper—endlessly enthusiastic, always encouraging, brimming with ideas. We talked about science all the time. To get away from his telephone, Gordon would lead sneak expeditions to obscure conference rooms in other buildings, where his secretary couldn't find him and we could plan experiments undisturbed. Sometimes we speculated wildly. In one free-wheeling session, we convinced ourselves that cells might perform their complete regulatory repertoire with only two signals. One of them, we imagined, was cyclic AMP. This idea, like many we dreamed up, was wrong—but I was learning that death of an idea was not an occasion for mourning. Gordon made me feel the supply of new ideas would never end.

I learned a new vocabulary and a new way of thinking. Normal S49 cells were *wild-type*, by analogy to the "wild" bacteria in our gut or fruit flies in the orchard. We think of ourselves as tame, but most of us—and most of our genes—are truly wild-type. We talked constantly about *phenotype*—the traits of a cell (or organism) that are dictated by a gene. "Mutation" and "mutants" became staples of conversation. An inherited mutation causes all cells in a clone to share a particular *genotype* and phenotype. We *selected* the mutant clones out of a population of mostly wild-type cells by treating the culture with agents that killed every clone of wild-type cells. A cell *expresses* a mutant protein from the corresponding mutated gene, just as another cell may express a wild-type protein from the corresponding wild-type gene. In either case, the cell makes a protein whose building blocks (amino acids) are arranged in an order specified by the order of a set of chemical links, called bases, in the corresponding gene. (The mutant gene, of course, carries a sequence of bases that differs subtly from that of the wild-type gene. The difference is the mutation itself. With the DNA revolution yet to come, however, we couldn't document mutations as changes in the sequence of bases in DNA.)

Mutant phenotypes allowed us to make strong inferences about normal regulation. One example was the negative feedback cyclic AMP exerts on its own accumulation. Further experiments strengthened and refined the central notion that PKA is responsible for cyclic AMP's actions in S49 cells. For instance, Paul Insel selected cyclic AMP-resistant clones with different phenotypes. One set of clones was completely resistant to cyclic AMP and totally devoid of PKA, while other clones were sensitive to killing, but only by very high concentrations of the cyclic AMP analog.[3] In the latter cells, PKA associated less tightly with cyclic AMP, compared to PKA in wild-type cells.

These "relatively" resistant cells allowed Jacob Hochman, an Israeli postdoc in the lab, to do some nifty biochemistry to take the story a step further.[3] Biochemists already knew that PKA is composed of two kinds of "subunits," encoded by different genes. One kind binds and detects cyclic AMP, while the other contains the enzymatic activity that stimulates downstream responses. Jacob found that a mutation in the gene for PKA's binding subunit caused PKA to require very high cyclic AMP concentrations for activation, further reinforcing our inference that cyclic AMP acts via PKA to kill cells.

———

Attending Gordon Conferences during the early 1970s, I learned that two questions fascinated most researchers in the cyclic AMP field. The first question—how does cyclic AMP act in cells?—had already begun to yield to hard-core biochemical techniques. First identifying, and then purifying, PKA and its target enzymes in the liver and other tissues established PKA's crucial role in cellular responses to elevated cyclic AMP. Genetic evidence from our PKA mutants strengthened the evidence by extending it to another cell type and additional responses.

The second question, which was to guide my own research for the next 25 years, was already proving much harder to answer. How does the hormone's message penetrate the cell membrane to be translated into cyclic AMP as a second messenger inside the cell? This was really a series of nested questions. Most generally, how does the message-transmitting machinery perform two quite distinct functions—detecting the hormone outside the cell and making cyclic AMP inside? Are these functions performed by separate subunits, analogous to the binding and enzymatic subunits of PKA? In other words, is the hormone's stimulus transformed into cyclic AMP by one protein, or two? Already, the fact that many hormones stimulate adenylyl cyclase activities in different tissues made it easier to imagine the latter scenario—that a single cyclase would be triggered by a host of distinct detector elements, or "receptors," for different hormones.

Everyone agreed that it would be a tall order to tackle these nested questions with classic biochemistry. First we would have to separate and purify all the proteins (receptor, cyclase, and whatever else was important), and then we'd have to determine whether one or both of these components traverses the membrane itself. And in the fullness of time (a long time hence, I thought), we would eventually be in a position to figure out how this machinery transmits the biochemical message from outside the cell to the enzymatic activity that makes cyclic AMP inside.

Working with Gordon, Phil Coffino and I thought we might dance around the biochemical difficulties by using genetics to determine whether receptors and cyclase were products of separate genes. We first imagined a mutation that would make cells resistant to killing by ISO but leave them sensitive to killing by the cyclic AMP analog. Such a mutation, we predicted, would destroy the receptor for ISO, but leave the cyclase intact. The experiment was surprisingly easy—selection with ISO produced lots of ISO-resistant clones, and most of these turned out to be still susceptible to killing by a cyclic AMP analog. This result set Phil and me to performing a quick dance, like clumsy dervishes, in the tissue culture room.

We calmed down a bit, however, when it turned out that our specific prediction was dead wrong. If the ISO-resistant, cyclic AMP-sensitive clones lacked the ISO receptor, prostaglandin or cholera toxin should elevate their cyclic AMP quite nicely. To our surprise, none of these agents did so, nor did they stimulate adenylyl cyclase in membranes from the same cells. OK, if the receptor isn't mutated, we thought, the cells must lack adenylyl cyclase. Accordingly, we termed these cells adenylyl cyclase-deficient, and gave them a genetic acronym, cyc^-. The acronym made us feel good at the time, but turned out to be a serious mistake, as the next chapter will show.

The paper describing our findings began by asking whether adenylyl cyclase might comprise multiple different proteins. Our results did not resolve the question, although they showed that at least one gene (and presumably one protein) was necessary for many different stimuli to increase cyclic AMP production. So we hedged our bets, concluding that the question "cannot be answered rigorously without extensive purification and separation of adenylate cyclase . . . and other components of membranes, followed by their functional recombination in vitro—a daunting task." (Note: years later, biochemists changed "adenylate" to "adenylyl," which is more correct, for arcane reasons much too involved to go into here.)

Although the mutant did not cleanly establish whether receptor and cyclase were distinct, Paul Insel had a bright idea. If they are separate, he reasoned, then cyclase-deficient membranes from cyc⁻ cells should contain normal amounts of receptor. Paul talked with Al Gilman, a bright young scientist whose lab was located in Charlottesville, Virginia. Al's lab was measuring receptors for ISO (called β-adrenergic receptors) by assessing binding of a radioactive compound to these receptors in membrane extracts. Paul brought our cyc⁻ cells to Charlottesville. Sure enough, the ISO receptor was present in cyc⁻ membranes. Paul's paper gave a "yes" answer to the question in its title—"β-adrenergic receptors and adenylate cyclase: Products of separate genes?"

———

As we prepared to submit our paper on the cyc⁻ mutant, in mid-1975, Gordon began to experience mild vertigo, and a neurological workup revealed a benign acoustic neuroma in his brain. He traveled to New York, to be operated on by a celebrated brain surgeon.

I was at a weekend "retreat" of Ken's clinical pharmacology program when a friend called to tell me that Gordon had been in a coma for 24 hours after the surgery, and probably would not survive. Barely aware where I was, I somehow made my way back to the meeting and sat down. There I found myself sobbing desperately, among colleagues who had no idea what had happened, and barely knew who Gordon was.

A week or so later, Gordon was gone. He was only 50 years old. The endless flow of new ideas ceased, and life lost its fun and excitement. Everyone who worked with him was devastated. Perhaps experiments would eventually become exciting again, but for now I was emotionally paralyzed.

I felt doubly bereft, for losing Gordon as a person and for a different reason, scary and selfish. My three short years with Gordon had changed my whole approach to science, at a time when biology itself was entering a new era. He had taught me the explanatory power of genetics, the delight of surprise, the lack of shame in being wrong, and the value of imagining multiple possible connections between facts before testing any of them. Now I was afraid I might never learn anything again.

The last lesson Gordon taught me is one I formulated on my own, years later. It is simply that young scientists must learn how to deal with two very different, but equally necessary, motivations for doing science. For me, Gordon epitomized one of these motivations, Ken Melmon the other. I call them delight and ambition.

Ken valued science—questions, ideas, experiments, published papers, and pretty much everything else scientists do—almost exclusively as a set of opportunities to satisfy ambition. He persuaded me to tackle cyclic AMP, a sexy molecule, in human white blood cells because that would attract the attention of our biomedical peers. He taught me that ambition can convert results in the lab into publications, credit from peers, and academic tenure. In his world, Ken was right—that is precisely "how the game is played."

In Gordon's very different world, science was a playground for ideas and a source of unending delight in testing them. His emphasis on imagination and refusal to fret about being wrong opened my eyes to thinking about experiments in new ways. Those same attitudes led some of Gordon's peers to judge him brilliant but not altogether sound. Wrong more often than his seniors thought proper, Gordon was not elected a member of the National Academy of Sciences. This failure distressed him, because he lived at least part of the time in the world of ambition, and needed recognition like the rest of us.

Looking back at my youth, I see myself as stuck almost exclusively in ambition mode, because I depended for satisfaction primarily on getting praise from others. It worked fine for a while, but the flow of praise stopped at Harvard and didn't resume at the Richmond News Leader. When I was 20, fortunately, Nancy and a great deal of good luck led me to medicine. At Hopkins and Columbia I was driven by ambition, to be sure, but I discovered the delight of asking and answering questions. After all the switchbacks and dead ends that led to me experimental biology, meeting Gordon finally made it clear that delight was both possible and necessary. For that I shall always be grateful to him.

The motivations of most scientists, like mine, oscillate constantly between poles of ambition and delight. Perhaps a few geniuses sustain themselves on delight alone. At the other extreme, a few may derive sufficient satisfaction from their carefully burnished reputations. The rest of us strive to balance and reconcile the two.

CHAPTER 6

Dancers and Bulldozers

ANATOMY OF A DISCOVERY

We were climbing the second flight of stairs when the lights went out. Nancy waited with the luggage, while I set off to find a flashlight. Groping down the stairs, I reflected that five dollars a day wasn't enough to light hotel corridors in Paris, even if the rest of Europe had discovered how to keep the lights on.

Unaccountably, lights in the lobby shone bright. Ignoring my heroic effort to borrow a flashlight in French, the manager flicked a switch on the wall, pointed to the re-illuminated stairway, and mumbled something I didn't understand.

The second plunge into darkness came as I fumbled with the key to our room. Experimentally, I sought a switch I had glimpsed on a corridor wall, and flicked it. Magically, the lights came on. Nancy and I laughed at our innocence. In our experience, light switches turned on and stayed on—until you turned them off. Other switches, like doorbells, stayed on only while you pushed and turned off when you stopped pushing. Here, to save a few centimes, the hotelkeeper had put these lights on a timer, like a parking meter. *Vive la belle France*!

That hotel corridor went suddenly dark in 1964. I vividly remember it, because it helps me to understand the working of a biological switch, discovered a dozen years later. This discovery transformed the way biologists think about how cells detect and respond to external signals. It was the greatest discovery I had anything to do with.

I'll tell the story of that discovery as a two-act play, combining a detective story and a comedy of errors. My role—more than a walk-on, but not the star turn I coveted—gives me close-up views of the principal actors, as they puzzle over the mystery, stumble into pratfalls, and mistake one another's meaning. Their performances tell us a lot about how experimental biology works or, sometimes, fails to work. The play does have a happy ending—before the curtain falls, the mystery is solved.

The mystery was straightforward: how do cells transmit hormonal signals outside the cell to the machinery inside? Hormones, it was clear, do not need to penetrate cells. Instead, cells somehow convert the hormonal message into biochemical events that result in an appropriate response. Sutherland's discovery of cyclic AMP had provided a glimpse at one mechanism for getting the message across, first in the case of adrenaline and then for several other hormones. By 1975, when Gordon Tomkins died, more than a half dozen labs were focusing their curiosity on how hormones trigger production of cyclic AMP inside cells. It was becoming clear that membranes at the cell's periphery contain two separate components. One of these, the hormone receptor (R), acts as a sort of catcher's mitt, with its pocket oriented to the outside. When it detects entry of hormone (H) into the pocket, the mitt somehow switches on the second component, adenylyl cyclase (AC), an enzyme oriented to the inside of the cell, where it can associate with a small chemical precursor and convert it into cyclic AMP. More succinctly stated,

$$H \rightarrow R \rightarrow ? \rightarrow AC \rightarrow cyclic\ AMP.$$

The question mark represents the unknown switch mechanism that links receptor to cyclase. Thoughtful people realized it wasn't possible to rule out the possibility that the membrane-traversing mechanism might involve yet a third component. (Unlike those thoughtful worthies, I had assumed that receptor and cyclase were the only key players, and even named our mutant *cyc⁻*, to indicate that it had lost adenylyl cyclase.)

Before introducing the detectives who solved the mystery, I shall have to give the mystery's solution away—because if I don't, audiences will have real trouble following the story. At the time many of the detectives were themselves thoroughly bamboozled, even after the mystery was solved. The solution was not just dauntingly intricate and counter-intuitive—it was downright peculiar. Nonetheless, it is worth understanding in its own right, because it represents a mechanism evolution has adapted to control thousands of biological functions, not limited to actions of a few hundred hormones and neurotransmitters.

The solution involved a third component, in addition to R and AC. This extra component was a new kind of biochemical switch, a protein I'll call the "Genie," or plain G. That is,

$$H \rightarrow R \rightarrow G \rightarrow AC \rightarrow \text{cyclic AMP}$$

Letters and arrows don't do the Genie justice. Figure 6-1 shows some of the mechanism's intricacies. In this Figure, the receptor is represented as a box and the cyclase as a light bulb (dark or lighted). The Genie is depicted as a hand, which can assume three shapes—a fist closed around a small object, an open hand, and a partial fist, grasping a different small object while extending an index finger. (When they became available later, the 3D structures of the Genie protein didn't look remotely like a hand, of course. But the inactive form did tightly grasp a molecule I'm representing with one small object, and the active form similarly grasped the other kind of small object. Instead of pointing a finger, however, activation changed the shape of a region on the Genie's surface so it could nuzzle up to exactly the right spot on adenylyl cyclase and stimulate production of cyclic AMP. Thus the signal relay device works pretty much the way our metaphor says. We'll see one of these 3D structures in a later chapter.)

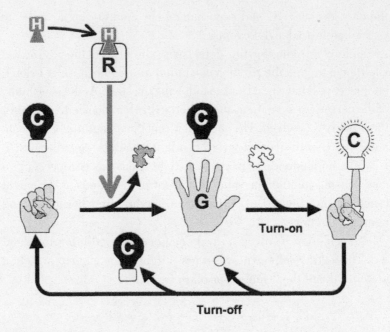

Figure 6-1. Metaphorical representation of how the Genie switch (formally named Gs) carries the stimulatory message from an activated hormone receptor to adenylyl cyclase. Hormone (H) binds to its receptor (R, the box at the top left). The activated hormone-receptor complex then stimulates (gray arrow) a change in the shape of the Genie switch (G, the hand) from a closed fist to an open shape. The Genie's shape change causes it to release a dummy totem (dark gray irregular object). Then the "empty" Genie (open hand in the middle) grasps the magic totem (white irregular object), which causes it to take on a new "active" shape—a fist with the index finger extended. In this active state the Genie activates adenylyl cyclase (C), represented by the illuminated light bulb. After a short while in the active shape (and a brief illumination of the light bulb, C), the Genie inactivates itself by converting the magic totem into a dummy totem. The magic leaves (small white circle) and the hand no longer stimulates adenylyl cyclase, as indicated by the light bulb returning to its inactive dark state. Now the inactive Genie (fist holding dummy totem) must be reactivated again by the hormone-stimulated receptor.

As a switch, the Genie's "on" position is the hand whose finger extends to turn the light on (in the diagram) or, in the cell, to induce adenylyl cyclase to make cyclic AMP. The Genie switch itself turns "on" when it grasps a magic amulet or totem, represented by the funny-shaped white object that enters the open hand (center), causing it to form the "active" shape (right). Totems are hokey, I know, but for now I'll defer details of how the magic totem is "really" a small chemical found in all cells, which . . . blah, blah, blah . . . .

The magic totem is the core of the Genie's timer mechanism, which is broadly analogous to the timer we met in the Paris hotel corridor. This timer works because the Genie removes the totem's magic after it sits in the fist for about 10 seconds. As a result, the Genie and the light bulb (adenylyl cyclase) remain "on" only for that brief 10 seconds. Afterward, the Genie's fist is left tightly clasping a modified totem, exorcised of its magic. (In Figure 6-1, the lost magic is the circular fragment that comes off the totem, and the closed fist clutches an irregular spotted object, the de-magicked "dummy" totem.)

If grabbing a magic totem to turn on a light seems bizarre, just wait! Once the magic is turned off, the Genie hand won't let go of its relic, the dummy. As a result, the Genie switch remains fixed in the "off" position for several minutes, until the hormone-activated receptor tickles it. This tickle causes the Genie's hand to open and release the dummy totem. Because cells contain lots of free-floating magic totem molecules, one of them is always readily available to fall into the Genie's open hand, causing it to form a fist and extend its index finger once again. In this way, the receptor re-activates the Genie switch simply by causing it to release the dummy totem left over from the last round of activation. As a result, the light bulb (adenylyl cyclase, that is) turns on for another 10 seconds, until the new totem loses its magic.

Ready availability of magic totems in cells allows the hormone-activated receptor to keep the Genie active (and the light on) nearly all the time, interrupted only by flickers to the "off" position during brief intervals required to release the dummy—that is, receptor-induced regeneration of an "active" Genie requires only milliseconds, while the Genie remains active for much longer, 10 seconds. In the absence of hormone-activated receptor, by contrast, the Genie switch spends most of its time in the "off" position (fist with dummy totem, at left in Figure 6-1), with a rare 10-second burst of activity, once every five minutes or so, when the Genie fist spontaneously opens and drops the dummy.

As the curtain rises on our mystery drama, let's admit a glaring esthetic problem. The timing mechanism I've described seems a wildly improbable solution for resolving any mystery, novel, fairy story, or cell. An ordinary tourist (like me) had trouble imagining a light switch hooked to a timer. What about this positively rococo switch, with all its flourishes of Genie and totems? Doorbells and ordinary light switches are straightforward. How could nature put up with such folderol?

Real cells do abound in biochemical switches that act like doorbells or light switches, but timed switches like this Genie have also captured significant market share in the regulation business. In a later chapter, we'll come back to how evolution may have taken advantage of the totem strategy to build a timer. For now, we can be sure it was not a trick to save centimes.

———

In our play's first act, detectives stumble on the magic totem and try to figure out what it does.

The story began in the lab of Marty Rodbell, at the NIH. Marty and his colleagues were trying to understand how a hormone, called glucagon, stimulates adenylyl cyclase in liver membranes. Glucagon, a short chain of amino acids, elevates blood sugar by releasing sugar from stores in the liver. It does so, like adrenaline, by stimulating cyclic AMP production in liver membranes. Marty's lab worked with the peripheral membranes of liver cells. Broken into tiny pieces, these membranes expose both their inside and outside surfaces to the water and chemicals in a test tube. Researchers in Marty's lab measured adenylyl cyclase, with or without glucagon (the hormone), using an assay like the one I learned from Gopal Krishna years earlier. They assessed receptors with a binding assay that involved adding radioactively tagged glucagon to membrane fragments floating in a test tube, followed by separating receptor-bound and free (unbound) radioactivity from one another. They separated the two by pouring the membrane-fluid mixture over a filter, which let free glucagon molecules through but retained membranes, including the receptor-bound hormone.

One group in Marty's lab measured effects of glucagon on the cyclase, while another measured binding of radioactive glucagon to its receptor. In 1971, a sharp postdoc in the lab, Lutz Birnbaumer, suggested a nitpicking control experiment. (A control experiment applies a condition or manipulation designed to rule out spurious influences that might influence an observed result.) This control experiment led to a momentous discovery.

A tall, thin biochemist, Lutz hails from Argentina. His sleepy eyes mask a sharp mind and a penchant for noticing key details others consider trivial. At the time of his suggestion, the lab had been pleased to find that the concentration of glucagon required for efficient binding to the receptor was virtually identical to the concentration that stimulates cyclic AMP production by the cyclase, measured in a separate assay.

"I just pointed out a possible problem," says Lutz. "The cyclase had to be measured in a solution containing the chemical precursor of cyclic AMP, but this precursor was left out of the receptor assay. I said you have to do both assays under the same conditions, and that means adding the precursor to the receptor binding assay. I didn't think it would really make any difference, and neither did anybody else."

To everyone's surprise, adding the precursor *inhibited* binding of radioactive glucagon to receptors. With the precursor around, receptors would bind glucagon only when the total free glucagon concentration was significantly higher than that required for equivalent binding in the absence of precursor. This was a real puzzle. It wasn't only that hormone concentrations for binding and activation were so different. More worrying, nobody could imagine why the biochemical precursor of cyclic AMP should affect hormone binding.

Fortunately, Marty's colleagues didn't just stand around clutching their pipets. Instead, they asked whether chemical relatives of the precursor molecule might also inhibit receptor binding of glucagon.

They found one relative that acted at much lower concentrations than the precursor itself. They didn't know it yet, but this compound—which is abundant in every cell—was the magic totem itself. (Later, they discovered that the totem compound was a 1% contaminant of the purportedly "pure" chemical they had been adding as a precursor for production of cyclic AMP. Without the contaminant, the system would not have efficiently converted the real precursor model into cyclic AMP.)

Soon thereafter, in 1974, Marty's lab found a remarkable synthetic molecule, chemically similar to the magic totem but not present in any cell. This new totem's super-magic stimulated adenylyl cyclase more strongly than the normal totem, and did so in membranes from tissues of rats, cows, fish, and frogs. Incidentally, this super-magic molecule resisted biochemical degradation and inactivation by enzymes in cells that normally destroy the "ordinary" magic totem.

(This parenthetical note is reserved for those not averse to acronyms. The precursor of cyclic AMP is ATP, or adenosine-5'-triphosphate, the principal energy currency of cells. Commercially available ATP at the time was contaminated by the totem, which is GTP, or guanosine-5'-triphosphate. GTP gives its first initial to the G-protein family, described later in this chapter and exemplified by the Genie molecule. The super-magic totem, Gpp(NH)p, resists degradation by enzymes called GTPases, which remove a phosphate group from GTP to convert it into GDP, or guanosine-5'-diphosphate. To avoid sprinkling the story with acronyms, I shall almost always refer to GTP as the "magic totem", Gpp(NH)p as the "super-magic" or indestructible totem, and GDP as the "dummy totem".)

It wasn't easy to put all these new findings together. Always a visionary, Marty loved to make complicated models to explain everything. His models suggested that hormone binding to receptor increased the likelihood that the magic totem would associate with some site on receptor or cyclase. He and his lab remained agnostic about the number and nature of the proteins involved, and made no serious attempt to separate and purify the possible components. Paraphrasing one of his critics, Marty later confessed to having "applied clean thoughts to dirty enzymes," essentially because thinking was easier and more fun than mucking around with difficult biochemistry. Thus he uncovered an exciting problem, but danced around it rather than plunging in.

That said, I should emphasize the extraordinary importance of the control experiment Lutz suggested, which led to discovery of a molecule whose association with the Genie led to unraveling the mystery. Control experiments can be boring, because ruling out a spurious explanation is not very exciting. But controls sometimes bring to light unanticipated facts that open avenues to new knowledge. Lutz's control experiment did exactly that.

At this point an Israeli lab took the story a crucial step further. The lab's chief was Zvi Selinger, a serious, thoughtful man who brought passionate intensity to every problem he tackled. Zvi and his postdoc, Danny Cassel, were intrigued by the report from Marty's lab that the super-magic totem resisted degradation by cellular enzymes. Could it be that hormones not only stimulate adenylyl cyclase, but also regulate the magic totem's degradation? To find out, they measured biochemical degradation of the magic totem in membranes prepared from turkey red cells. (Turkeys were a meat staple in Israel, so turkey blood was easy to obtain from slaughterhouses; and turkey red cells had lots of adenylyl cyclase.)

Their first finding was surprising but unequivocal. In turkey red cell membranes, the adrenaline analog, ISO, stimulated *both* adenylyl cyclase *and* degradation of the magic totem molecule. These results generated a paradox, because ISO seemed simultaneously to stimulate adenylyl cyclase and stimulate breakdown of the magic totem that was required for adenylyl cyclase activity. Zvi and Danny imagined a resolution for the paradox. It began with the idea—similar to Marty's—that the hormone promotes binding of the magic totem to a specific site on the cyclase enzyme, which it stimulates. To this they added a clever but counter-intuitive codicil—that the same totem-binding site also converts the magic totem into a dummy, inactivating the cyclase. ISO then re-activates the cyclase by somehow inserting into its binding site another molecule of magic totem, which is subsequently degraded. In other words, Cassel and Selinger imagined a cycle similar to that I drew earlier for the Genie, except that the Genie was part of the cyclase itself, rather than a separate protein.

The Israelis' idea seemed nearly as fanciful as Marty's, but the proposed cycle had the advantage of being testable—and was proved substantially correct. I learned of the clincher experiments from Zvi when he visited San Francisco on a trip, sometime in 1976. In these experiments the super-magic totem blocked ISO from stimulating degradation of the real totem, presumably by competing for binding to the same site. Even more convincing, treating red cell membranes for a few minutes with ISO plus the super-magic totem *irreversibly* activated adenylyl cyclase—that is, membranes merrily persisted in making more cyclic AMP even after ISO and unbound totems, super-magic or otherwise, had been removed. The light stayed on, because ISO had inserted into the switch a totem molecule whose magic could not be dispelled. In contrast, if the light had been turned on with ISO plus the "ordinary" magic totem, removing ISO turned it off immediately.

Influential scientists greeted the turkey red cell results with a conspicuous lack of enthusiasm, possibly because they didn't understand (or want to understand) Zvi's interpretation. The *Journal of Biological Chemistry* turned down his first paper, Zvi told me, based on Marty Rodbell's review of the manuscript. In his review, Marty had written that the paper represented "prejudice, not science," because "if anything, the hormone should inhibit" degradation of the magic totem. (Scientific papers are usually reviewed anonymously, leaving the authors to guess the reviewers' names. In this case, the journal mistakenly sent Zvi the *signed* version of Marty's review.) Marty's mistake was a common one: working hard to come up with our own explanation of how something works, we tend to reject opposing views—a "sin" I have committed several times. Thank goodness experiments can prove us wrong!

———

If the first act discovered how the crime was committed, the second act identified its perpetrator. Knowing how the magic totem works did not specify where it works, or how many proteins might be required for a hormone to stimulate adenylyl cyclase. Al Gilman's lab understood this better than anyone. He had spent several years valiantly trying to purify adenylyl cyclase, summarizing the results in a 1975 paper entitled "Frustration and adenylate cyclase."

Al Gilman felt strongly—and correctly—that Gordon's genetic approach wasn't enough. Instead, understanding hormone-stimulated adenylyl cyclase would require separating its components biochemically. But his frustration with adenylyl cyclase reflected serious biochemical difficulties. First, the enzyme is located in cell membranes, and thus could not be separated from other components of the system without dissolving it in water. Enzymes that normally reside in the water inside cells (the "cytosol") are readily water-soluble, but membrane-bound proteins are not. This is because membranes are made of greasy, fatty molecules called lipids, which do not mix easily with water. To reside in the membrane's grease, a protein has to make itself comfortable both with grease in the plane of the membrane and with water on either side. It does so by exposing greasy surfaces to the membrane and non-greasy, "water-loving" surfaces to the water on either side. As a result, such a protein cannot dissolve in water alone or in grease alone.

The obvious compromise, in washing dishes or dissolving and purifying proteins, is to use a detergent. Greasy on one side, water-loving on the other, detergent molecules dissolve a membrane-bound protein by orienting their greasy sides to the greasy surface of the protein and exposing their water-loving sides to water, thereby lending a water-loving character to the entire surface of the protein-detergent complex. That, at least, is the theory. But reducing the idea to practice requires handling delicate proteins delicately, using the right detergent and the right conditions to avoid destroying the protein or leaving it attached to membrane lipids.

A second difficulty compounded the first. The cyclase system might comprise two proteins, receptor and cyclase, or even more. Each separate component could require a different detergent. Even if each individual component were dissolved and purified, to understand how they work would require putting them back together, "reconstituting" hormone-dependent function in the proper environment, a lipid membrane. In the event, every one of these difficulties had to be resolved. In reviewing our *cyc⁻* manuscript before it was accepted for publication, Al had twitted me for complaining that separating adenylyl cyclase components would prove a "daunting task." In reality, Al knew the daunting complexities much better than I.

Having given almost no thought to detergents or membrane proteins, I was very excited by a letter Gordon Tomkins received in the spring of 1975. Elliott Ross, a graduate student at Cornell, was asking for a postdoctoral position in Gordon's lab. Elliott made an exciting proposal: apply detergents to normal cell membranes to dissolve the component missing in *cyc⁻*; then dilute the detergent and insert the component into *cyc⁻* membranes. Successful reconstitution of hormone-dependent adenylyl cyclase activity in *cyc⁻* membranes would serve as an assay for the missing component. Such an assay would be invaluable for the next task—purifying the missing component from some abundant source of plasma membranes. Gordon and I were delighted. Elliott, a real biochemist, should know a lot about detergents because he came from a department engaged in purifying membrane-bound proteins from bacteria.

Gordon promptly invited Elliott to join his lab. But it was not to be, because Gordon died a few months later. Suddenly left without a postdoctoral position, Elliott decided to join Al's laboratory in Charlottesville. There he would also be able to work with *cyc⁻* cells, because Paul Insel's collaboration with the Gilman lab (described in chapter 5) had brought *cyc⁻* cells to Charlottesville.

After Elliott joined Al's lab, Paul and I had a long talk—one I shall never forget.

"Look," Paul said, "Elliott's letter described the very best way to understand how hormones stimulate cyclic AMP production. Shouldn't we try to do it ourselves?"

"You're right," I agreed. "But how? Elliott knows detergents and biochemistry, which is more than you and I do. It would take more than a year even to get going here in San Francisco."

In the end, I chickened out. For many years thereafter, I was to feel deeply troubled for not having tackled the challenge. Decades later, the mists of embarrassment and chagrin have cleared, and my timid choice looks as much like prudence as like cowardice. Lacking previous experience with protein purification, detergents, and functional reconstitution, I would have had to learn every scrap of the strategy from scratch. In my hands the effort would have progressed at glacial speed, and I would have given up well before another lab succeeded. Elliott and Al were bolder, undaunted, and—most important—better prepared.

Elliott and Al were quite different characters. A fresh-faced ingénu, Elliott was not sure of himself but full of ideas, as well as detailed reservations and concerns about the meaning of every experiment. Brow furrowed with effort, he worried endlessly over detergent concentrations, biochemical details, and how to devise clever controls. He was tightly wound, especially when experiments did not go well. Sometimes it showed in his gait: muscles taut, he would seem to walk on the balls of his feet. Still, Elliott never lost sight of the big picture. And he was damned if he was going to accept easy explanations without questioning them first. I've never known anyone more adept at imagining the myriad nasty artifacts and mistakes that might account for an exciting result—his own, or anyone else's. Consequently, Elliott's experiments meant what he said they meant.

Al was an altogether different animal. In 1971, when I met him, at my very first Gordon Conference, he was already famous for devising a new way to measure cyclic AMP. This method was faster and vastly more convenient than the cumbersome procedure others had struggled with for more than a decade. He accomplished this feat during two draft-dodger years at the NIH, which began very soon after I left. There he worked in the lab of Marshall Nirenberg, who had just received the Nobel Prize for solving the genetic code. Al didn't like the project Nirenberg assigned him, and came up with a plausible alternative. He proposed to use PKA, described in the previous chapter, to construct a cyclic AMP assay.

Immediately Nirenberg pronounced this a terrible idea. For hours the boss tried to persuade his postdoc that neurons were more important than a cyclic AMP assay. "This will be a disaster for your career," he told Al.

Al opted to try the cyclic AMP assay anyway, and soon got it to work. Investigators all over the world, including me, latched onto the method as soon as it was published, in 1970. Convenient, accurate, and reproducible, the "Gilman assay" accelerated the pace of cyclic AMP research. Contrary to Nirenberg's prediction, developing the new cyclic AMP assay was a superb career move for Al—the first step in an illustrious career. It did not escape my attention that Al's NIH experience differed sharply from my own.

Al retained the same intensity, drive, and determination he showed at the NIH. Scientifically, he is quick to understand a problem, imaginative in tackling it, and always aware of its larger significance. He is unnervingly perceptive about people—taking everyone's measure, he manages expertly to direct and orchestrate others' efforts, whether in the laboratory, editing a major textbook, or running an academic department. These efforts succeed because Al's own goal soon belongs to his colleagues, as well. He is a controlling figure, but his colleagues benefit.

Even for Elliott and Al, separating adenylyl cyclase components was a task that teemed with obstacles. Elliott spent more than a year just trying to dissolve functional "adenylate" cyclase from normal, wild-type membranes. Almost ready to give up, he finally found the right gentle detergent, plus an effective way of applying the detergent extract to cyc^- membranes. Both ISO and the super-magic totem molecule stimulated the "reconstituted" membranes.

Al told me this result during a long drive from Boston to a Gordon Conference in New Hampshire, in 1976. It seemed clear to me that he and Elliott were reconstituting cyc^- membranes with a receptor-cyclase coupling protein distinct from both receptor and cyclase, and that a site on this coupling protein must bind and degrade the magic totem. Al and Elliott considered such a separate "Genie" protein as one possibility, but only one of several.

The decisive experiments came in Elliott's 1978 paper,[1] a year later. The new results confirmed my excited take on the earlier results, but also showed that separating components was the way to go. First, the term cyc^- was a woeful misnomer. Despite the name, detergent extracts of cyc^- membranes did contain adenylyl cyclase activity.

In addition to the cyclase, wild-type detergent extracts contained a second activity, less sensitive than the cyclase to mild heating. This activity belonged to the Genie (that is, the hand in Figure 6-1). Hereafter I shall call it the Genie or Gs (think of it as the *G*enie that *s*timulates adenylyl cyclase), more or less interchangeably. Adding the heat-resistant Genie to *cyc*⁻ membranes reconstituted cyclase sensitivity to the super-magic totem as well as to ISO. The *cyc*⁻ mutation abolished the Genie's activity. Now it was clear that hormone-sensitive adenylyl cyclase contained at least three separable components—receptor, Genie/Gs, and cyclase. The Cassel-Selinger model of GTP binding and degradation is still correct, providing we revise it to specify that the Genie and the cyclase (hand and light bulb in Figure 6-1) are separate components.

Al quickly recruited a cadre of smart, hard-working postdocs to complete the story. Within three years they had purified Gs, the "stimulatory regulator of adenylyl cyclase," identified its protein subunits, and shown that it reconstituted hormone—and magic totem-dependent adenylyl cyclase in *cyc*⁻ membranes. Soon thereafter they separated and purified all three components—the receptor for ISO, adenylyl cyclase itself, as well as Gs—and put them back together to reconstitute hormone-dependent production of cyclic AMP. Over the next 20 years the Gilman lab led research on Gs and related signaling proteins, including other G-proteins, adenylyl cyclase itself, and additional regulators. They purified each of these proteins, obtained DNA sequences of the corresponding genes, and finally solved the three-dimensional (3D) structures of the proteins, revealing the specific arrangements of atoms that allow them to do their job.

Introducing Al before he delivered a prestigious lecture, I once described him as a scientific bulldozer, relentlessly crushing or pushing aside any obstacle between him and his goal. The comparison was apt, but I was afraid Al might be slightly offended. Instead, he was delighted. He knew his bulldozing style had made Gs and adenylyl cyclase two of the best understood hormone-dependent regulators in nature.

———

A quarter-century later, Gs has spawned a large family of G-proteins. New chapters of the G-protein story still appear every week, in every nook and cranny of animal and plant biology. We have "big" G-proteins, siblings of the same Genie Al and Elliott resolved from receptors and adenylyl cyclase. In addition, myriad cousins of the big G-proteins take responsibility for controlling how cells grow, divide, migrate, stick to one another, secrete and localize membrane proteins, change their shape, and find their proper place in the embryo. In nearly every case, G-proteins switch between active forms and inactive forms, which bind, respectively, the same magic or dummy totems Rodbell's lab identified back in the 1970s. The grasping, pointing hand of Figure 6-1 metaphorically depicts the way all these proteins act, although many of the Genie's relatives receive input signals from sources that are not necessarily receptors, and can transmit their signals to output proteins quite different from adenylyl cyclase.

In 1994, Al Gilman and Marty Rodbell were awarded the Nobel Prize in Physiology or Medicine, "for their discovery of G-proteins and the role of these proteins in signal transduction in cells." This well-deserved honor recognized a discovery comparable to Sutherland's Nobel-winning discovery of cyclic AMP.

I learned about Al's getting the prize during a long-distance conversation with Elliott, who was sitting in his office in Texas. Someone popped his head in Elliott's door and told him "Come quick, Al's celebrating the Nobel!" Elliott never said anything about it, but ever since I've wondered whether he feels he deserved a share of the prize himself. I think he did deserve it, as one of the primary discoverers of Gs. His idea led to the protein's discovery and his hands performed many of the key experiments. Some thoughtful scientists argue differently, partly because Al's later contributions to understanding G-proteins were much more outstanding than Elliott's. In addition, at the time of the first discovery Elliott was a postdoc, and postdocs rarely share Nobel Prizes—no just as Lutz didn't share Marty's.

Aside from its significance in biology, the G-protein story offers lessons about the process of scientific discovery. It thoroughly debunks the popular notion that great discoveries originate in flashes of inspiration during creative frenzies of lucky scientists. Instead, real discoveries unfold in fits and starts, over months or even years, in the experiments and minds of many different individual scientists. Like artists, participants begin by covering the canvas with crudely penciled lines, often before anyone knows what they represent. With time some lines are erased, others emphasized. Inked figures in the final drawing rarely look much like anything in the early sketches.

A second lesson relates to the very different roles of biochemistry and genetics. In the form of cyc^-, a dollop of genetics was useful, but hard-core biochemistry carried most of the burden. This was hardly surprising before the DNA revolution, of course. Now genetics more often occupies stage center, but still generates surprises better than it explains them—which is why we need biochemistry, cell biology, and organ physiology.

Another lesson is a matter of different scientific styles, dancing vs. bulldozing. Marty's lab danced around the problem, and so did I. Danny Cassel and Zvi Selinger performed the exquisite *pas de deux* that explained the central mystery of how the Genie worked, but didn't specify what the Genie actually was. The bulldozer crunched and pushed aside every obstacle to clear the highway for the rest of us. Al, even more than Elliott, kept his eye on the road ahead, constantly moving forward rather than dancing in and out of the problem.

Finally, the discovery had enormous consequences for me. I was profoundly disappointed at my failure to rise to the Genie's challenge. Later I found long-lasting delight in the exciting questions it raised. The first installment of that story comes next.

CHAPTER 7

Out of the Woods

A LAB OF MY OWN, AND TWO DISEASES

In early 1975, I turned 35. The collaboration with Larry Lichtenstein on white blood cells was winding down, but our big review article was in press in a prestigious journal, and I felt ready to turn to the ideas Gordon kept generating, by the dozen. We seemed poised to discover how cells transmit hormonal signals across their membranes. New S49 mutants, Gordon's enthusiasm, and publishing papers in good journals filled me with delight, encouraged my ambition, and bolstered my confidence. In July, I would travel to England for a year, to study in a lab focused on regulation of cell growth. I had Ken's blessing, Gordon had suggested the lab I should go to, and a foundation would fund my salary for the year. Ken and I had patched up our tiff about his not being listed as an author of a review. His grants amply supported the lab, and his clever maneuvering was about to engineer my advancement to tenure. In the middle of my life, I felt sure I would be able to make a life in science.

The preceding three chapters focused on Ken, Gordon, and discovery of the Genie, Gs. I told each story separately, like movies simultaneously showing in different theaters of a modern movie house—not just for clarity and convenience, but also because my memory seems to have stored the three films on separate reels. Ken didn't intrude on my relation to Gordon, and *vice versa*. When the Gilman lab discovered the Genie, Gordon was gone and Ken was not interested.

While my cognitive self was working hard to keep the reels separate, my emotional self did not, especially as each story approached its end. Gordon died in 1975. In 1976 and 1977, Al Gilman and Elliott Ross used *cyc⁻* cells to discover Gs. And in 1978, Ken Melmon decamped for Stanford. Three successive losses. Like the pilgrim in Dante's *Inferno*, I found myself "midway on our life's journey, . . . in dark woods, the right road lost."[1]

Finding a path out of the woods would not be easy.

The first and hardest blow, which I described in chapter 5, was losing Gordon. His operation took place a few days before we were scheduled to fly to London, and he died a few days after we arrived. Suddenly I had lost Gordon and found myself thousands of miles from all the people, questions, and experiments I cared about.

In other ways, the London year turned out splendidly. Our children loved their new school and we hugely enjoyed our life as a family in a strange new world. Vacations in England and the continent were marvelous fun. But I continued to miss Gordon terribly, as a person and as a mentor. My sabbatical research seemed to move too slowly, although the new lab was a good one. Discouraged, I stubbornly pretended that all was well, just as I had as a medical intern and in Brodie's lab.

I managed not to confess my troubles to Nancy until Spring, when our time in London was nearly over. I vividly recall walking down a green lane in Devonshire, under a bright sun and blue sky.

"Nancy, I have a problem," I began, and then blurted it out. "I'm disappointed, and feeling sad. Right now I'm not getting much done in the lab, but I'm even more worried about going home. Without Gordon and all his ideas, what the hell will I do? I've been riding on Larry's coat-tails, and then on Gordon's. I'm afraid I may not be cut out for research after all."

Nancy already knew I wasn't happy, of course, but was surprised by how intensely I felt. "Is that everything?" she asked.

"Well, one thing, but it's less important," I replied. The week before, I'd had a disturbing conversation with the chief of the London lab, a man I liked and respected, and who felt the same about me. I told Nancy what he said—"Who is this guy, Ken Melmon? You say he's got the grants and is always on your papers? Henry, is that a good idea?"

As butterflies fluttered around us, Nancy and I kept on talking. She said I had to learn to say what was bothering me, at least to her—and she was right. We should just take this year for what it was—right again. "And then let's see what life in San Francisco is like. It'll be a lot better than you think."

Returning to San Francisco worked very well, at least at first. The lab was exciting, and intriguing questions had not disappeared. Some reflected Gordon's old ideas, some required thorough revision, and others were brand-new.

Then Elliott and Al began to unfold their great discovery. We had never really competed with them, of course, because I had not dared to attempt Elliott's proposed strategy for identifying the protein missing in cyc^-. To put it simply: in the search for Gs, the Charlottesville team left us in the dust. This discovery struck serious blows to my ambition and self-esteem. Less able to rely on the profound lack of self-awareness I enjoyed in youth, I now saw myself as a chump with no one to blame but myself. Of course I also worked, as always, at pretending not to care, and sometimes almost convinced myself. But it would take years to realize that the temperament and skills of a bulldozer were not absolutely necessary for a satisfying career.

Slowly it began to look as if Ken and I would be able to disentangle ourselves from one another. I began to apply for grants on my own, and Holly Smith, chair of the Department of Medicine, leaned on the Pharmacology Department to give me lab space. Ken also supported my move to Pharmacology, perhaps in response to Holly's urging, perhaps because he saw my new Pharmacology space as an addition to his own domain. Of course I saw it as the beginning of my real scientific independence, and looked forward to organizing a lab quite separate from Ken.

In 1978, just as our relationship seemed to be healing itself, Ken made his decision to take the new job at Stanford, leaving the trail of deception I described earlier. He was about to move his family and lab equipment to Stanford when I got a call asking me to come talk to Dick Havel, who was head of a research institute at UCSF and PI of a program project grant (separate from the one Ken had headed). Havel's grant included part of my research, focused on isolating S49 mutants.

"Ken came by here a couple of weeks ago," Havel said, "and asked me to let him take your part of our program project grant with him to Stanford." I was about to protest that Ken had said nothing to me, but Havel went on. "I heard him out, but then I told him 'No, let's see what Henry can do with it.'"

So Ken's parting shot was an attempt to purloin the grant that supported most of my research. I expressed heartfelt gratitude to Havel, a man I had always thought barely aware that I even existed. Ken Melmon's betrayal not only deprived me of a hero and laid bare my abject gullibility, but also came close to stopping my research in its tracks. I remained furious with Ken for more than two decades.

Soon Ken's departure confronted me with rather more practical challenges. One of these was welcome. Now I would direct my own lab, truly independent of Ken or anybody else. I would have to obtain NIH funding to replace grants Ken did take with him to Stanford. This was not the dire emergency it would represent now. The lab had done good work, I was good at writing intriguing research proposals, and the timing was fortunate. Relative to the number of scientists competing for support, the NIH then was much richer than it is now, so it was easier for a young scientist to find support for a lab.

The other challenges revealed how much Ken had really done for me. Now I had to take on his clinical and administrative responsibilities as well—that is, serve more frequently as "attending physician" on the medical wards, and inherit Ken's position as head of the "Division" of clinical pharmacology. Once a gung-ho clinician, I could probably do the clinical work. But I was more doubtful about the clinical pharmacology empire, a disparate gaggle of labs held together more by Ken's magnetic personality than by common needs and interests.

Over the next several years, it gradually became clear—first to me, and then to the Department—that I would not meet these two challenges as well as I dealt with the lab. My clinical performance began well, but deteriorated as I focused more and more on the research effort, which afforded much greater real satisfaction. Teaching clinical medicine requires enormous knowledge, intelligence, and dedication. I felt bad about shirking this task, and tried to tell myself I wasn't. The epiphany came one day in the early 1980s, when I returned to a conference room to retrieve my attending physician's white coat.

The coat was there, but my stethoscope was stolen. The theft filled me with guilty joy! After that I stopped attending on the wards.

The clinical pharmacology empire was easier to deal with, because it withered away on its own, pretty much unlamented. Its best researchers had already chafed under Ken's leadership and were as glad as I to gain their independence. I lacked the necessary vision, chutzpah, personal magnetism, and determination to hold them together. In addition, under Ken the division had earned little in the way of clinical income, and earned even less now. From my point of view, it seemed a mercy to let the poor beast fade away.

In medical academia, such problems usually resolve themselves at a glacial pace. In this case, final resolution came five years after Ken's departure—in 1983, that is, when I was asked to take the chair of a pre-clinical Department, an adventure I'll relate in a later chapter.

I was of course not the first scientist to harbor doubts in mid-life or to smart from defeat at the hands of more successful competitors. For many in that predicament, the most effective therapy is to tackle new questions in the lab. In my case, the discovery of Gs served up a platter loaded with treasure, in the form of fascinating questions to pursue. In the five years after the last of my three losses, my lab sought to answer a number of questions. Let me tell two stories from this time, both of which involve the role of Gs in human diseases.

———

The first story begins with Zvi Farfel, an Israeli MD who came to the lab because Ken Melmon's reputation attracted him to take a fellowship in the clinical pharmacology program in San Francisco. Zvi may have harbored a vague idea that working in a lab like mine would make him more valuable as a faculty member in his clinical department in Israel. As for me, I felt I was doing Ken a favor to take him into the lab. He would add little, I guessed, because he knew almost nothing about genetics, biochemistry, cell biology, or even cyclic AMP.

So, I assigned Zvi to work with a postdoc in the lab and to focus on a somewhat pedestrian question about Gs activity in red blood cells.

He was as clumsy and inept in the lab as I was when I started at the NIH, but gradually learned how to use a pipet and do reproducible experiments. And his results did eventually confirm our predictions, as we meant them to.

I had not reckoned, however, with another of Zvi's qualities. Although he was gentle, kind, and easy-going, the inner Zvi was a true Israeli—determined, stubborn, persistent. Refusing to take no for an answer, sometime in 1978 he began to pester me with his idea about Gs and his favorite hormone-resistance disease, which was a rare endocrine disorder with a jawbreaker name, pseudohypoparathyroidism.

I had never seen a patient with the disorder, but re-read what I was supposed to have learned in medical school. Patients inherit the disorder from their parents, and suffer from low blood calcium and mild mental retardation. They are short in stature, with round faces and stubby fingers. Most of their clinical problems reflect inability of a single hormone, parathyroid hormone, to stimulate normal cyclic AMP accumulation in bone, kidney, and gut cells. This hormone is secreted from "parathyroid" glands in the neck, just behind the thyroid gland. The disorder is "pseudo" because it resembles a different condition, in which those glands make too little parathyroid hormone, while patients with the "pseudo" disorder make the hormone in perfectly normal amounts. Instead, their tissues respond so weakly to parathyroid hormone that it cannot do its job. To avoid a jawbreaker on the one hand, and a distracting acronym on the other, I shall refer to the disease as a "disorder of hormone resistance".

An endocrinologist, Zvi raised the possibility that resistance to this hormone might be the human counterpart of the cyc^- mutation we had described in S49 cells—that is, he proposed that the patients, like cyc^- cells, inherit a mutation affecting Gs. I pooh-poohed his idea, pointing out that patients without Gs would not be able to survive. It was much more likely, I argued, that the patients inherit a genetic defect of the receptor for parathyroid hormone.

One day Zvi asked to talk with me about his idea, for the third time. Not for nothing, I reflected, did the Lord call the children of Israel "a stiff-necked people." This time he walked in and announced, without further preamble: "Here's something new. This will change your mind."

In a textbook, Zvi had found a fact that made the single-receptor idea very unlikely. Some patients with the disorder, he read, show resistance to a second hormone, thyroid stimulating hormone, which also promotes production of thyroid hormone in the thyroid gland by stimulating adenylyl cyclase. In addition to low blood calcium and retardation, patients resistant to this second hormone suffer from hypothyroidism—low concentrations of thyroid hormone in the blood make them lethargic and coarse-skinned, thin their hair, cause them to gain weight, and increase their mental dullness.

With this new information, I had to agree that the patients might have a defect in Gs, which we could probably measure in their blood cells. The pesky, stiff-necked postdoc had turned the tables and acted as my mentor. His idea would lead us to identify the molecular basis of an inherited human disease, a discovery that gave both of us immense satisfaction. Zvi's persistence kept me from persisting in a serious mistake—that of letting my ego make my ideas look better than they were. Ideally, scientists avoid this recurring danger by wanting the right answer intensely enough to doubt their own notions as vigorously as they deserve. That does happen, of course, but in practice we (perhaps I should say I) rely more often on our colleagues. As Zvi showed me, and as I have learned many times since, the great value of the mentor-student relation for research is that it requires two minds to concentrate on a problem at once.

I found an endocrinologist in Los Angeles, Arnold Brickman, who treated a number of patients with this disorder, who were rare in San Francisco. Zvi set up a quantitative assay for Gs activity in human red blood cells. We had already found Gs (but not adenylyl cyclase) in red blood cells, by virtue of its ability to reconstitute normal regulation of adenylyl cyclase in cyc^- membranes (that is, the Ross and Gilman procedure). Zvi's assay was reproducible in red cells of "normal" individuals, including Zvi and me. Then Arnie sent us blood samples from his patients. To my delight, accompanied by exultant crowing from Zvi, the patients' red cells proved to contain only 50% of the Gs activity we measured in red cells from normal subjects.

We proposed that the 50% deficit in Gs activity reflected loss or inactivation of one of the two Gs genes in the genomes of normal humans.[2] (Most human genes come in two copies, one on each of a pair of chromosomes, present in almost every cell. The exceptions are genes on the unpaired X or Y chromosomes in males.) When the DNA revolution finally made it possible to identify Gs genes on chromosomes, our idea was confirmed. The idea seemed to explain why the patients did not die. Presumably, we imagined, half of the normal amount of Gs protein suffices for survival, but not for normal responses to parathyroid hormone and thyroid stimulating hormone. The reduced amount of Gs apparently allows most hormones, however, to stimulate adenylyl cyclase activity strongly enough to maintain normal responses.

Gordon Tomkins would have been delighted to learn that cyc⁻ helped to identify the molecular defect of a human disease. (He would have been even more pleased by a bizarre version of the same disease, which I'll describe in a later chapter.) People who study human diseases often like to brag that "medicine is the tutor of biology." If so, the reverse is also true—with this disease, experimental biology served as a tutor of medicine. The discovery of Gs by Ross and Gilman, combined with the behavioral defect of cyc⁻ cells, told Zvi and me to look for a hormone-resistance disorder with the same defect. And we found it.

We knew more than a dozen hormones whose receptors activate Gs to stimulate cyclic AMP production. Why, then, did the patients resist the actions of a mere handful of hormones, such as parathyroid hormone and thyroid stimulating hormone, but respond normally to the rest? Once we found the 50% reduction in Gs activity in red blood cells, I made up a semi-plausible explanation. Presumably only a few hormones, I suggested, need nearly 100% of the available Gs activity in their target cells to trigger increases in cyclic AMP sufficient for normal endocrine function. This notion would be hard to test, of course. (Later work in other labs added a wrinkle to the story, which begins to tell us why one hormone response would need so much more Gs than another. For an account of that wrinkle see my brief note.[3])

Finally, I should note that discovering the molecular basis of this disease produced a sudden, almost magical effect—my lab became "important." The discovery itself was fun, but made no change in the medical outcome for patients with the disease, and failed to change thinking about causes or treatment of other diseases. Still, it carried a certain cachet—just as Ken Melmon had intimated, a decade earlier, when he told me I should study adenylyl cyclase in human white blood cells. Zvi and I knew perfectly well, objectively speaking, that this cachet was balderdash. But it's worth noting that neither of us balked at claiming bragging rights for our accomplishment. Ambition and delight, our twin cravings, were equally served.

———

The second disease we studied during this period is more lethal and more common than the rare endocrine disease caused by loss of a Gs gene. This second disease was the scourge of tropical countries, cholera. Growing in the small intestine, the cholera bacterium produces a toxin that causes death-dealing diarrhea. The toxin does so by stimulating the cells lining the gut to make too much cyclic AMP. The cells respond to excess cyclic AMP by secreting salt and water into the intestine, and the secreted fluid becomes copious watery diarrhea.

The molecular mechanism triggered by cholera toxin was a great boon to our research, although in fact the actual mechanism is not very relevant for treatment of cholera. The treatment, which is effective and embarrassingly straightforward, depends on the fact that the lining of the human gut normally replaces its cells every few days. Consequently, it is enough to insert an intravenous tube and replace the lost fluid and salts for the few days required for new cells to take the place of cells exposed to the toxin. When the bacteria are gone, the patient recovers and intravenous fluids are no longer necessary.

How, we wondered, did cholera toxin stimulate adenylyl cyclase? Before Gs was discovered, as described in the previous chapter, Cassel and Selinger had proposed that adenylyl cyclase turns itself off by inactivating the magic totem that turns it on. Soon they went on to find that cholera toxin not only stimulates adenylyl cyclase, but also prevents de-activation of the magic totem. Thus cholera toxin sustains cyclic AMP production not by repeatedly turning the switch on (which would mimic the receptor), but rather by forbidding the timer to turn the switch off. Once Gs was discovered, it appeared likely that this new protein contained both the switch and the timer. Consequently, we and others immediately imagined, cholera toxin must act directly on Gs, more or less as shown in the metaphorical scheme of Figure 7-1.

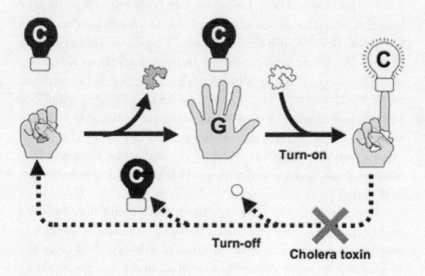

Figure 7-1. Cholera toxin prevents de-activation of Gs. As in Figure 6-1, the hand represents Gs as the hand of a Genie, and adenylyl cyclase as a light bulb, illuminated when activated, dark when not. The magic totem is the white irregular object held by the active form of Gs (fist with extended index finger, activating adenylyl cyclase, right), and the dummy totem is the dark irregular object grasped by the inactive Gs (fist form, left). Cholera toxin prevents the timer from turning off the switch (indicated by the X and the dotted arrows). As a result, the magic totem stays in the binding pocket of Gs (the closed fist) and keeps Gs active, so that the light glows. Activation by hormone receptor is not necessary because the inactive form of Gs relaxes now and then, even in the absence of activated receptor, and thus releases the dummy totem. Because the toxin prevents inactivation of Gs, with time all the Gs molecules become active.

To me the Gs switch was little more than a blob of protein, but I hoped cholera toxin could help us to find the timer that controlled the switch. The first step would be to determine whether the toxin acts directly on Gs. The toxin was already known to enter cells, where it acts as an enzyme, transferring a part of a small chemical compound (NAD^+) to a membrane protein, which had not yet been identified. Perhaps an unusually astute postdoc could identify that protein, by showing whether it was Gs itself.

The postdoc was Gary Johnson, a tall, burly fellow Ken Melmon had interviewed for the job while Nancy and I were in London. When I returned, Gary became the first postdoc I supervised after Gordon's death, while I was working out my independence from Ken. Gary was the perfect person to help me at that time, not just because he was a superb scientist, but also because he so perfectly exemplified independence himself. For instance, about six weeks after we began working together, I apologized to Gary for only talking with him about experiments once a week. "Henry," he said, "I've already talked more with you than I talked with my PhD adviser during four years in the lab."

Working efficiently and very hard, Gary found that the toxin could transfer radioactivity from a radioactive version of NAD^+ to a protein that was present in membranes of wild-type S49 cells, but lacking in cyc^- membranes. Because Ross and Gilman had shown that cyc^- lacked Gs, the toxin's target must be Gs. Thus we could publish a paper saying that the toxin almost certainly did act directly on the Gs switch.

(Gary may have been referring to that paper when he reminded me, only a year or so ago, that I once returned to him a manuscript criss-crossed with red ink. Next to a key paragraph I had written a single word, in capital letters—"LAUGHABLE!" His story made me cringe. There I was, a young man just beginning to run my own lab, and unable to imagine that anyone shared the self-doubt and anxiety I felt every day. Although it may have hurt, Gary's calm self-trust protected him from my quite unnecessary arrogance. I hate to think what I may have said to less hardy souls than Gary, and hope that with age I've learned better behavior. In any case, I suspect that Gary, now chair of a department and enjoying a distinguished scientific career, treats his own postdocs with more dignity and constraint than I showed with him.)

Once we knew the switch protein is the toxin's target, the next step was to identify the specific site in Gs to which the toxin attaches a portion of the NAD^+ molecule. We weren't good enough biochemists to dream of doing that experiment. Indeed, at that point in time, the experiment was beyond the skills of Gilman's lab also, because it was too difficult to obtain large enough quantities of pure Gs. A year later, after Gary left the lab to take an academic job, we got very lucky. The lucky break was simple—I attended a seminar by Lubert Stryer, a Stanford biochemist.

Lubert's lab had discovered that the eye detects light with protein machinery similar to hormone receptors and Gs. The eye's receptor-like protein, rhodopsin, responds to photons by activating a protein he called transducin. ("Trans" means "across," and "ducin" refers to the Latin word for "leader," so that the name "transducin" signifies the protein's ability to *lead* a signal from the retina's light detector molecule *across* to other machinery in the cell.) The protein is also called Gt, because it acts like Gs. It converts the same magic totem into the same dummy, and then rests in an inactive state until the photon receptor knocks the dummy out of the protein to allow re-entry of another magic totem. Gs and transducin were to become founding members of a large family of receptor-activated G-protein switches.[4]

We were especially lucky that the retina's sensitivity to light depends on huge amounts of transducin, amounting to 10% of the total protein in the eye's photoreceptor cells. (Compare this with less than 0.1% for Gs in liver cells!) For our purposes, transducin's abundance made it an ideal biochemical target. Lubert's lab had already shown that light causes rhodopsin to promote association of the magic totem with transducin, which (like Gs) inactivates itself by converting the magic totem into a dummy. Working with them, we found that treating transducin with toxin plus NAD^+ profoundly inhibited its ability to convert magic into dummy totem molecules. The toxin's ability to inhibit the self-inactivation of both transducin and Gs meant that the two proteins must use very similar turnoff mechanisms.

By this time (1983, approximately), Neil Van Dop, a first-rate biochemist, had joined my lab. Neil decided to search for cholera toxin's target site in transducin. To tag the site, he treated large amounts of transducin with toxin plus radioactive NAD^+, and then used an enzyme to cut the transducin into many pieces. One of these pieces was radioactive. J. Ramachandran, a protein chemist then at UCSF, found that this fragment contained four amino acids—serine, arginine, valine, and lysine, arrayed in that order. The radioactive portion of NAD^+ was attached to the arginine. Now we knew that cholera toxin does its job by chemically modifying a specific arginine in transducin. By analogy, it was likely to do so in Gs as well.

Why was this new information useful? Sure, it was nice to know that cholera toxin modifies a specific arginine in transducin, and that this modification prevents transducin from inactivating itself. And it was satisfying to infer that cholera toxin acts on a corresponding arginine located in Gs, which is the toxin target responsible for cholera in real patients. More fundamentally, the arginine was exciting because it was the first specific biochemical clue to the molecular nature and location of the timing device that turns off G-protein switches. We knew that Gs and transducin are chains of amino acids that fold into specific shapes, which create a switch and a timer. Consequently, we felt sure that the arginine we found would ultimately point to how these devices work.

"The game's afoot," Sherlock Holmes would have declared. Hunting the timer took several years, but in the end we would run our quarry to ground.

———

Guided by the poet Virgil, Dante's pilgrim found the right path and eventually ascended to Paradise. In my case Virgil was busy elsewhere, and Purgatory and Paradise were not on the itinerary. But with time I recovered personally from each of my three episodes of loss and defeat. Healing came in various ways. I would like to claim that insight brought me out of the wilderness, but for the most part I relied on my standby strategies, steadfast denial and skillful dissimulation.

Once I stopped actively mourning Gordon's death, I realized that for me it was more appropriate to mimic Gordon's style than to despair at inability to imitate a bulldozer. I would never match Gordon as a dancer, but with effort I could learn the steps. Not a very profound insight, but it worked.

Rather than lament another lab's discovery of Gs, I pretended the kind of delight Gordon would have felt. With time, astonishingly, the delight became real. I was least successful at quenching my anger at Ken, but gradually came to appreciate Ken's contributions to the early stage of my academic career, and learned to remember his example whenever my own ambition needed tempering.

Friends, family, sheer good luck, and interesting experiments ushered me out of the forest. Support from others made healing faster. Nancy, who knew me best, played the biggest role. Administrators like Dick Havel and colleagues like Phil Coffino helped me also. Like me, Phil had to recover from Gordon's death and direct his own lab. For several years we kibitzed on each other's work and brought our groups together for joint lab meetings, to our mutual profit. Finally, the people in my lab furnished valuable support—more so than they probably knew—if only by accepting at face value my pretense that I knew what to do and how to do it.

Then the great DNA revolution brought me as close to Paradise as I think I'll ever get—as I shall show in the next chapter.

CHAPTER 8

Bliss in the Afternoon

RIDING THE DOUBLE HELIX

One morning, early in the 1980s, I stopped to listen to a vigorous discussion at the blackboard in my lab. Holding forth was Vince Groppi, a bright, gregarious postdoc from Phil Coffino's lab, next door. This time he wasn't joking about his family's connections to the Mafia back home in New Jersey. (Connections that were in any case, I think, non-existent.) Instead, he was talking about experiments in one birthplace of the DNA revolution, a UCSF lab four floors below ours.

"So they slap this DNA into PBR322," said Vince, first drawing a red line (the plasmid with its special DNA sequence). "And then they put the plasmid into another bacterium," he added, surrounding the red line with a white ellipse, representing a bacterium. "Lo and behold, the bug makes the protein! For them this is routine."

Vince had learned of about recombinant DNA experiments through the postdoc grapevine. Despite our constant palaver about genes and mutants, neither Phil's lab nor my own had learned how to experiment with DNA, and the two postdocs listening to Vince knew almost nothing of plasmids or bacteria.

Equally ignorant, I had been offended and cowed by the arrogant self-assurance of DNA jocks at UCSF, who kept claiming their experiments were easy, while at the same time exuding an aura that told us old farts (I had turned 40 in 1980) we could never learn their tricks. My own lab was progressing nicely, I thought, by using cells and biochemistry to mop up details of the hormone resistance disease and the action of cholera toxin, as described in the last chapter.

Vince's charm and postdoctoral status made him less intimidating, so I ventured to ask questions. He assured me the arrogant molecular biologists were right—DNA is easier to work with than proteins or animal cells, because its chemical stability makes it less temperamental than either. "A couple of months, and you're skating fast, doing experiments and getting real results. Putting the genes into cells and seeing what happens."

Or so Vince claimed. The pioneers had already developed procedures for cutting DNA into manageable fragments, splicing the fragments together, and reading long stretches of its sequence. They were beginning to introduce the DNA into animal cells as well as bacteria. He and others directed me to key publications, manuals, and people I should talk to.

Conceptually, the DNA revolution was almost complete in the early 1960s: Avery had identified DNA as the material that transmits heredity, Watson and Crick had described a DNA structure that implied its own replication, and Nirenberg had deciphered the DNA code that specifies sequences of amino acids, the links in protein chains. For most biologists, however, practical discoveries in the 1970s ushered in the real revolution. In 1974, Stan Cohen, at Stanford, and Herb Boyer, at UCSF, introduced "recombinant" DNA from a frog into a bacterium. In the same year, Paul Berg, also at Stanford, spliced together DNA from two organisms. Later Boyer co-founded the San Francisco company, Genentech, which expressed the insulin gene into a bacterium in 1978. By the early 1980s, scientists were already reveling in a treasure house of new genes, new proteins, and newly created organisms. In principle, we could tailor DNA molecules to our own specifications, recombine them into the DNA of a bacterium or cultured cell, and produce cells or creatures with novel biological properties. The revolution made recombinant DNA an essential element of our working lives, giving us tools to tap a bottomless reservoir of nature's secrets.

About a very different revolution, Wordsworth wrote, "Bliss was it in that dawn to be alive/But to be young was very heaven." My entry into the DNA revolution was less enthusiastic, at least at first. By 1983, biochemistry and luck had taken us as far as they could.

We badly needed help from DNA, but I was leery of a mysterious new technology and had put off the transition for far too long. I had no inkling of the real "bliss" the DNA revolution would bring, even though it began in my own backyard. As a result, I was a latecomer to the revolution, joining in early afternoon rather than the dawn Wordsworth praised.

———

A late start did give us the real advantage of piggybacking on the pioneers' clever new strategies for handling sequences of DNA. At every step, we could copy or adapt ideas and procedures from our predecessors, snapping up insights from handbooks of experimental methods, textbook accounts of protein structures, obscure and main-line journals, and—more and more—word-of-mouth ideas, guesses, and plain gossip of faculty and postdocs around us at UCSF. Although we praise and envy other scientists' creativity, we praise most sincerely when we borrow products of their creativity to answer our own questions. Scientists have never copied one another with greater élan or more spectacular results than during the DNA revolution. We tackled the G-protein switch by applying new tools and ideas, and then following our noses.

The behavior and personalities of individual scientists determined whether, when, and where the revolution's miracles took place. My lab profited immensely from the generosity of others—scientists at UCSF, elsewhere in academia, and in burgeoning biotech companies. They gave us strategic advice, provided valuable reagents, and taught us the fine points of manipulating DNA. By revealing each technical secret or new discovery, the original discoverer enjoyed an opportunity to taste the fun again. Part of their generosity reflected revolutionary fervor, but generous scientists outnumber cut-throat competitors even in non-revolutionary times.

(Undoubtedly, other motivations also played a part. For instance, a year after we joined the DNA revolution, I became chair of an academic department at UCSF, a story told in the next chapter. This made it easier to ask for and get advice, cooperation, and reagents, because "one hand washes the other," as one of my Israeli friends used to say. Now I was recruiting for faculty positions at UCSF—positions that might be filled by candidates from labs that helped my own.)

In my lab, the most critical contributors to the DNA revolution were the people who did the work. The adventures I recount here involve aspiring DNA revolutionaries who joined the lab from 1983 to 1986. I tried hard to attract postdocs who had worked with DNA, but most were headed to labs already versed in the new technology. One recruit was a clinically trained MD with little previous lab experience, while the others were PhDs with research training. Among these, only Kathleen Sullivan knew how to cut and splice DNA, and how to detect specific DNA fragments by binding them to other DNA molecules. Most important, she was not afraid of DNA—a quality that made her a virtual genius in comparison to the rest of us, as well as an invaluable teacher of basic skills new to everyone in the lab.

These young people were remarkable for their courage. Excited to learn, they remained undaunted by their ignorance or by mine. They read scientific papers, pored over how-to manuals, unabashedly sought advice from colleagues in other labs, and learned by doing. Despite many mistakes, their projects usually succeeded. A confession: I myself never learned to do DNA experiments. Before the revolution, I could have performed any procedure in the lab. After it, my practical expertise became almost irrelevant to our progress. As with many scientists, this transition came at a time when the lab was expanding (and when I was becoming a department chair). I am not proud of the transition, but did little to prevent it.

In addition to their courage, these young people were remarkable for their ability to work together, support one another, and have fun. I can remember no group of lab people enjoying themselves more than this one. The atmosphere reflected excitement of biologists all around us, but this group was unusual in a special way. With a single exception, noted below, they laughed together constantly—at practical jokes, at one another's foibles, and at their own. Laughter was possible because they liked and trusted one another.

Except for me, everyone in the lab was between 25 and 33 years old. Many were starting families. Babies burgeoned, it seemed, every month or two. A huge sign in the lab warned "Beware: Acute Pregnancy Zone." Amid all this fecundity, one pregnancy was alarming. Pale and shaken, an unmarried woman returned to the lab from her first visit to a gynecologist, who began their interview on a terrifying note: "I see in your chart that you have a positive pregnancy test." The patient, our lab-mate, said that could not be true. No one in the lab could imagine a less likely candidate for unwanted pregnancy. Raised in a more reticent era, I was amazed by her frankness, and also by the trust she placed in her co-workers. But she trusted the right people. Everyone supported her. Physicians in the group suggested that the test result could be an artifact, and should be repeated. In the end, the scare resulted from a mixup: the test was positive, but performed on blood from a different patient with a similar name. Acute Pregnancy Zone, indeed!

The kind of trust this woman placed in her lab-mates helped to make each young person in the lab more successful than he or she could have been alone. Here's an example. One day an unusually outspoken postdoc, Susan Masters, pointedly quizzed a visiting Nobel Prize winner. "Is that really true?" she asked. "What's the evidence?" At the next day's lab meeting, a postdoc had an announcement. From under a chair he pulled two shark hats, decorated with wicked-looking cardboard fins. To general merriment, he awarded one shark hat to Susan, one to me, for daring to ask hard questions. Within a few weeks, everyone in the lab had earned a shark hat. For years I had preached to everyone in the lab that questions help both questioner and speaker to learn, but young people often fear revealing their ignorance by confronting a speaker directly—especially, perhaps, if the questioner is scheduled to present data at next week's lab meeting. During the 1980s my lab learned to behave differently—a lesson I know has stood them in good stead.

A postdoc I shall call Julian—he's the exception I mentioned above—figured prominently in a second example. A first-rate scientist, he proved difficult as a person. He repeatedly caused trouble by surreptitiously appropriating reagents from others, and also by accusing them later of sabotaging experiments that didn't work. One night, needing to incubate bacterial cultures at 41°, Julian turned up the incubator temperature from its usual 37°. The higher temperature ruined cultures Kathleen Sullivan had put into the incubator earlier.

When she discovered what had happened, Kathleen yelled at Julian, and he yelled back. People in labs down the hall heard the din, and other lab members had to intervene to calm the antagonists. (I was out of town, and heard the tale two days later.)

At other periods in my lab's history, a Julian could have irretrievably poisoned the lab's delicate ecosystem. Instead, everyone else supported Kathleen and made it clear to Julian that he needed to clean up his act. After a short sulk, he did. In this case the group's generosity and social skills allowed them to stick together and support one another. As a result, everyone was able to succeed, even Julian. I don't think scientists' ability to cooperate differs much from the rest of the population. My lab in the 1980s showed that ability in abundance, however, at just the right time to allow us to enjoy the DNA revolution. How lucky we were!

Looking back, I suspect that one reason the lab worked so well in this period is that many of the new generation of postdocs and students were bright, capable women. Brodie's lab, Ken's, and mine—at least in the 1970s—had been mostly male, with a few female technicians. Now, by bringing more women into graduate training and scientific research, the feminist revolution complemented the DNA revolution. My lab, like many others, became a much more interesting place to work.

At the time I didn't even notice the correlation with the presence of women, but I should have, because the entry of women into the workplace had made a big difference in my own family. As the children grew, Nancy had worked part-time as a teacher, and then started a pottery studio, selling pots and teaching students. Eventually she went to law school, and in 1983 became a lawyer. I'm ashamed to admit that at first I told her that the law was a bad idea, but fortunately it didn't take long for me to realize how wrong I was.

For our first major foray into DNA, Dan Medynski, a postdoc
in the lab, chose a formidable task: he would "clone" the fragment
of DNA whose sequence encodes transducin. Cloning such a DNA
fragment means identifying and modifying it for propagation in the
lab, usually by incorporating it into a rapidly growing "clone" of
bacteria.[1] No one in the lab, including Dan, had ever cloned a DNA,
and we needed all the help we could get. An invaluable gift gave
Dan a welcome initial boost. This was a DNA "library" containing
fragments that encoded proteins expressed in photoreceptor cells of
the retina, where transducin is one of the most abundant proteins.
The gift-giver was Jeremy Nathans, then at Stanford, who had recently
obtained DNA encoding the photon receptor, rhodopsin, from the
same library. Each DNA fragment in the library was carried by an
individual bacterium growing in culture broth along with bacteria
carrying other DNA fragments.

We hoped that transducin's abundance as a protein in the
retina would mean that the library contained many transducin
DNAs. Even if that was so, how could Dan identify which of many
thousands of bacterial colonies contained the transducin DNA?
He read extensively and consulted with experts about alternative
approaches. In the end he chose to tweak the DNA library so that
each bacterium contained a DNA fragment that would cause the
bacterium to make the corresponding protein. He would identify
which bacterial colonies make transducin by using a rabbit antibody
to detect transducin protein. The approach was technically difficult,
a real long shot. Bravely, Dan performed the preliminary procedures,
then did the experiment. Much to our delight, the anti-transducin
antibody identified a single bacterial colony, among thousands Dan
tested. Knowing that lonely colony would tell the tale, Dan and I
were equally anxious.

To determine for sure whether that colony's DNA encoded
transducin would require isolating the DNA and determining its
sequence, in order to compare with that of the actual transducin
protein. We could do this because both DNA and protein are long
strings of chemical compounds, each of which can be thought of

as a "letter" in a coded message. The DNA sequence of a gene
is a string composed of only four different letters, which are
compounds called bases, while a protein is a string of different
letters, 20 of them, called amino acids.[2] Any three successive
letters (a so-called "triplet") in the DNA encode a single letter,
or amino acid, in the corresponding protein. We shall return to
the coding business again in this and later chapters.

We could look up the DNA code in a textbook, but none of us knew
how to isolate the actual DNA we needed and determine its sequence.
Fortunately, our lucky streak continued. Dan collaborated with
Peter Seeburg, a DNA pioneer then at Genentech. Peter did know
how to make DNAs and determine their sequences, and found that
Dan's lone DNA was the right one. The sequence of 1,050 bases in
the DNA predicted the amino acid sequence of the corresponding
protein,[2] which should comprise 350 amino acids. We were sure
the protein was transducin, because parts of the amino acid
sequence predicted by the DNA sequence perfectly matched
the amino acid sequences of transducin fragments produced by
cutting it with a digestive enzyme, trypsin. (Enzymes like trypsin
cleave bonds between particular amino acids in a protein, allowing
biochemists to separate the fragments and determine their amino
acid sequences.) Indeed, one of the trypsin fragments was the short
string of four amino acids at the site targeted by cholera toxin, a
site Neil Van Dop identified a year earlier, as I described in the
previous chapter.

Soon after celebrating victory, we found we were not the only
lab with a G-protein DNA sequence. Others had climbed onto the
same bandwagon. In 1985, the year Dan's paper was published,
a G-protein "cloning frenzy" produced reports of the DNA and
predicted amino acid sequence of transducin from two other labs,
plus the closely related sequence of Gs, from the Gilman lab. The
frenzy continued. In 1986, Kathleen Sullivan determined the DNA
sequence and the predicted amino acid sequence of yet a third
G-protein, Gi, which had been discovered earlier by the Gilman
lab and dubbed G*i* because it *i*nhibits adenylyl cyclase (unlike
G*s*, which *s*timulates adenylyl cyclase). Over the following decade

researchers identified a total of 16 G-protein genes similar to those that encoded Gs, transducin, and Gi. Each of these G-proteins links a subset of receptors—stimulated by hormones, neurotransmitters, photons, or chemicals we smell or taste—to regulation of a specific cell function.

Meanwhile, G-protein sequences didn't yield their secrets easily. Each DNA sequence predicted an unappetizing word salad of amino acids, apparently thrown together in random order. The order seemed random to me, of course, because I was ignorant. Until now I had managed to think of proteins as amorphous blobs that float inside cells. They could be purified and shown to perform specific biochemical functions, but I didn't bother to worry exactly how the blob did its job, or how it might be shaped.

Now I had to learn, instead, that each gene encodes a protein with a unique 3D shape. In fact, biochemists and crystallographers had discovered, years earlier, that the order of amino acids in a protein chain determines precisely how the chain folds itself in three dimensions, and that this fold allows it to perform a specific molecular function. Now the DNA revolution would force me to take account of these 3D shapes, and how they generate specific functions. A decade earlier, Gordon Tomkins had shown me how genetics could reveal the cell's machinery for responding to hormones. Again, I had a lot to learn—this time from textbooks, manuals, and even Judson's superb account of the origins of molecular biology, *The Eighth Day of Creation*.[1] I got invaluable help from a host of teachers, including structural biologists at UCSF like Bob Stroud, Bob Fletterick, and Fred Cohen.

My very first intimation that sequences of proteins related to Gs might not be random came from a 1983 paper by Karen Halliday.[3] She examined the published amino acid sequences of two families of proteins known to bind and inactivate the same magic totem that regulates Gs. One family comprised "Elongation Factors", first discovered in bacteria, which are essential for making proteins. These factors help cells to "elongate" proteins by adding, one at a time, the amino acids designated by the sequence of a "messenger" nucleic acid.[2] The second was the Ras protein family, whose members normally control cell growth and proliferation. Ras mutations were known to cause cancer and to prevent Ras from converting the magic totem to a dummy totem, a finding I'll return to in a later chapter. Sequences of Elongation Factors and those of Ras proteins appeared unrelated, with intriguing exceptions: in four short stretches, each 10-15 amino acids long, Halliday found remarkably similar sequences in both. These four stretches—which she dubbed A, C, E, and G—appeared in the same order in both sets of proteins (see Figure 8-1)

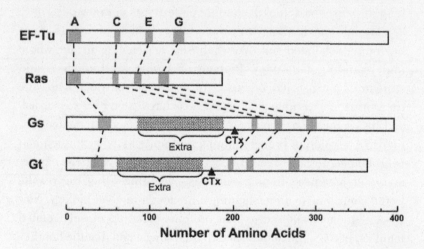

Figure 8-1. Regions of similar sequence (A, C, E, and G) in four G-proteins. In Gs and transducin (Gt) an "extra" region, absent in Elongation Factor-Tu (EF-Tu) and Ras, intervenes between A and C. Ctx indicates the site targeted by cholera toxin in Gs and transducin.

We were delighted to discover that transducin and Gs contain similar "Halliday sequences," arranged in the same order as in Ras and Elongation Factors (Figure 8-1). Protein structure gurus told us that such conserved stretches of sequence indicate that the proteins to which they belong are *homologous*—meaning that, like a man's hand and a raccoon's paw, they share a common precursor in evolution and are likely to perform similar functions. Although evolution assigned different tasks to Elongation Factors, Ras, transducin, and Gs, these proteins all share the ability to grasp the same magic totem and convert it to the same dummy totem. Consequently it seemed likely that the four homologous regions lined a similarly shaped totem-binding pocket located in each of these proteins, while amino acid sequences of the rest of each protein had diverged in order to perform functions unique to each. Protein structure gurus told us that the entire protein chain of each of these proteins must fold in similar ways, however, in order to orient the Halliday sequences correctly toward the pocket. For the moment we had to take the whole idea on faith, because the actual 3D folding pattern was unknown.

My lab and I, along with thousands of other biologists, were beginning a belated but overwhelming sea-change in our whole understanding of biology. Pioneering molecular biologists and structural biologists had preceded us by a decade or two, but now the transformation was unavoidable, because it revealed new ways to ask and answer questions about how life works. Even more fundamentally, the DNA revolution brought intellectual unity to every branch and twig of biology. Earlier, each biologist worked on an isolated enzyme, organ, or organism, hoping—but also doubting—that the results would contribute to understanding a broader swatch of biology. Now DNA sequences showed us that proteins make up closely related families, like Gs, transducin, and their siblings, and that the families themselves make up super-families (e.g., like the enormous and still growing family that includes not only Gs and its close relatives, but also Ras, Elongation Factors, and many others).

Suddenly biologists found themselves almost required to begin at the "big picture" level, using inferences drawn from multiple species and genes to form testable conjectures about how nature works. And our experiments on almost any function of almost any organism would help us to understand the workings of multiple genes, proteins, organs, and organisms. A whole generation of biologists felt the same thrill. Stated another way, by revealing the unity of biology, the DNA revolution converted a whole generation of experimental biologists from Darwinian fellow travelers into true believers in evolution.

Gordon Tompkins had always loved pushing the logic of any set of facts as far as they would go—farther than they could go, some of his colleagues claimed. The new unity of biology would have brought him ecstasies of delight, because the DNA revolution unleashed both intellectual creativity and the practical know-how needed to convert ideas into new molecules, cells, and organisms. Now we could entertain abstract ideas and plan risky experiments our predecessors would have laughed out of the laboratory. When each gene, protein, or organism appeared unique, argument by analogy seemed at best a risky business. Now analogies became transformed into a powerful strategy for designing experiments. And knowing the amino acid sequences of a progressively growing number of proteins, we could cut, splice, mutate, and recombine their DNAs to order—and, by extension, the proteins themselves.

———

At this point, yet another thrill emphatically confirmed for me both the unity of biology and the predictive power of analogy. Frances Jurnak reported the 3D structure of a specific bacterial elongation factor:[3] lo and behold, its homology regions *did* line its totem-binding pocket! Old hat to the gurus, the 1D-to-3D principle came to me as practical revelation rather than abstract pronouncement. One-dimensional (1D) facts—that is, shared sequences of amino acids in different protein chains—had suggested a shared 3D structure, the totem binding pocket. The Jurnak structure told us that the elongation factor DNA (a 1D sequence) really did magically transform itself into three dimensions, shaped in a predictable way. The gurus had known this already, from comparing the amino acid sequences and 3D structures of hemoglobins and their relatives. Now, much closer to home, we could see for ourselves that they had got it right—the sequence of amino acids in one dimension specifies precisely how the chain folds together. The gurus told us also that the 1D-to-3D transformation depends on the different "side chains" of the 20 amino acids, each with its own unique shape and chemical characteristics. Greasy side chains stick to one another; small or large ones fit snugly into interstices of corresponding size, gluing the protein together; electrical charges seek out opposite charges or situate themselves at the protein's surface, etc. As a result, the protein chain folds into a unique, stable 3D structure, rather than an amorphous blob.

Transformation of 1D sequence into 3D structure is a perfect example of an abstract idea that begets adventurous experiments. No one knows exactly how a protein folds into its unique 3D shape, and no one will ever watch it happen. But knowing that similar 1D sequences of amino acids dictate similar 3D structures gave my lab (and many other labs) the license to ask structural questions and an effective strategy for answering them. We had only to take the leap of faith that 1D sequences would transform themselves predictably into 3D structures, despite the fact that we had never seen the actual structures, and might never do so.

This bold leap, combined with new DNA technology, allowed us to ask new questions. What part of Gs contacts the receptor? What part contacts adenylyl cyclase? How does the totem binding pocket convert magic into dummy? We had remarkably few qualms about risking valuable time and effort to exploit our faith in the relation of 1D and 3D structure. To make the task easier, we adapted an effective experimental strategy already pioneered by others. The strategy begins with making mutations at specific sites in the DNA for the "recombinant" protein—whose DNA sequence is "recombined" into a larger sequence that allows it to be manipulated. Experimenters then devise a cell system lacking that protein, insert the mutant proteins into it, and ask what mutations do to function.

As a first step in that direction, Susan Masters constructed a crude 3D model of a generic G-protein, based on the Jurnak structure of the elongation factor. Exciting then, the model now is humbling. Working with Bob Stroud, Susan proposed that the magic and dummy totems fit into a binding pocket in Gs that is pretty much identical to that of the elongation factor Jurnak studied. Years later, when other labs managed to shine X-rays at crystals of transducin and Gs, this prediction proved correct. The rest of our model, however, was mostly wrong. Most egregiously, we failed to predict that the totem-binding pocket must include the target site for cholera toxin, which Neil Van Dop had identified in transducin.

Kathleen Sullivan and Tyler Miller, another postdoc in the lab, realized that a published S49 mutant might have already pre-empted our chosen strategy for assigning functions to different parts of Gs. The Gilman lab had isolated a mutant S49 cell line, called *unc*, in which adenylyl cyclase was "uncoupled" from the receptor for isoproterenol (ISO), a hormone analog that stimulates cyclic AMP accumulation in normal S49 cells—that is, Gs was present in *unc* cells, where it allowed cholera toxin, but not ISO, to activate adenylyl cyclase. For a variety of reasons, we were sure that the *unc* genetic defect resided in Gs itself. Kathleen and Tyler cloned and sequenced the Gs DNA from S49 wild type and *unc* cells. Compared to wild-type, the *unc* DNA showed one difference—a single substitution, which would lead to substitution of a different amino acid (proline) for the amino acid (arginine) that is normally located six positions from the distal end of Gs. By inference, we proposed—correctly, as we and others later found—that receptors interact with the distal end of Gs.

To prove the point, Kathleen and Tyler put the *unc* mutation in a different Gs DNA and tried to incorporate it into a Gs-deficient *cyc*⁻ cell. Unfortunately, *cyc*⁻ cells were not hardy enough to stand the rough procedures then used to insert DNA into cells. Again, a colleague's generosity came to the rescue. Harold Varmus, then a UCSF faculty member, suggested a gentler strategy. Following his advice, Kathleen and Tyler put a DNA carrying the *unc* mutation into a retrovirus and used the virus to infect *cyc*⁻ cells: the infected cells stably incorporated *unc* DNA, and made *unc* Gs. Just like the original *unc* mutants, adenylyl cyclase in recombinant *unc* mutants was stimulated by cholera toxin, but not by ISO. This result formally demonstrated that the arginine-to-proline substitution prevents Gs from being stimulated by the ISO receptor.

Susan's G-protein model, plus the idea that similar sequences indicate similar structures, gave her an idea for a strategy more daring than just substituting a single amino acid—she would create a "chimeric" G-protein. In Greek myth, the world's first chimera was a creature with the head of a lion, the body of a she-goat, and the tail of a dragon. Susan's chimera would contain parts from only two DNA "creatures": she would splice the front end of the DNA for Gi, the G-protein *inhibitor* of adenylyl cyclase, to the back end of the DNA for Gs, the G-protein *stimulator* of adenylyl cyclase (Figure 8-2).

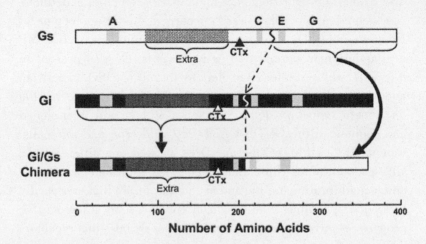

Figure 8-2. Susan's Gi/Gs chimera was constructed by splicing the front end of Gi (the end on the left in the diagram) to the back end of Gs (on the right in the diagram). The ISO receptor could activate the chimera to stimulate adenylyl cyclase, indicating that sequences within the back end of Gs include contact sites with both the receptor and the cyclase.

"The back end will make the chimera respond to stimulation with ISO, as we know from the *unc* mutation Kathleen and Tyler found," Susan suggested. "And we think the part of Gs that triggers cyclic AMP production is in the front end. So the part of Gi that inhibits adenylyl cyclase will probably be in the front end, too. That means ISO will *reduce* cyclic AMP production in a *cyc⁻* cell that expresses the Gi/Gs chimera! Neat, huh?"

I thought this was a risky experiment, because we knew almost nothing about the 3D structures of the back or front ends of either protein, so the front end of one might not fit very well with the back end of the other. If so, the chimera could prove unstable. Furthermore, our notion that the front end of each protein "talked to" adenylyl cyclase was based on weak evidence and even looser analogies—that is, on suggestions from other labs that the regions of Elongation Factors and Ras (located between Halliday regions A and C), exert the effects of these regulators on other proteins. But the experiment would not be extraordinarily difficult, now that we knew how to cut and splice DNA and express DNA sequences in cyc^- cells.

Riding on Pegasus's back, the Greek hero Bellerophon vanquished the lion-goat-dragon chimera with a single spear-thrust. Susan's chimera confirmed one prediction, and definitively destroyed the other. Expressed in cyc^-, her chimera acted like wild type Gs, allowing ISO to stimulate cyclic AMP accumulation. Thus the 40% of Gs sequence at its back end (see Fig. 8-2) conferred not only the ability to respond to the ISO receptor, as we had proposed, but also the ability to *stimulate* adenylyl cyclase—not at all what we had imagined. Eight years later, the labs of Steve Sprang and Al Gilman solved the 3D structures of adenylyl cyclase bound to Gs or to Gi, showing that each G-protein used amino acids in its back half to interact with adenylyl cyclase, and nicely confirming Susan's findings. Susan's chimera made us wonder what those extra 100-plus amino acids between the A and C regions really do. The answer is that they fine-tune the G-protein switch—a story I'll tell in another chapter.

———

For my generation, the DNA revolution divided science into two epochs. By discovering new tools for asking questions, the revolution dramatically changed the way biologists think about nature. Now younger researchers cannot imagine even asking questions, much less answering them, without reaching into the DNA toolbox. For my part, I pity them for having missed the bliss of the revolution itself. Unlike most revolutions, this scientific revolution was fun, from first to last. We had the time of our lives.

At the simplest level, DNA provided the tools we needed to unravel the question that fascinated us most: how does the

Genie protein work? But the revolution in fact changed our whole perspective on biology, in two directions. Now we had to think about genes, proteins, and biochemical reactions in the unifying frame of evolution, from bacteria to humans. And the sequences of DNA and proteins opened windows into a set of revelations quite new to me, based on using 3D structures of proteins to understand how cells and bodies work. In the late 1980s and the 1990s, these revelations were to drive almost every project in my lab.

Another transformation was similarly crucial, although many of us didn't fully realize it: biologists were poised on the verge of an Age of Miracles. In that new age, life in the lab would move faster—new ideas would generate thrills every few months, rather than every few years, and experiments would confirm or negate those thrills within weeks, not months.

At very nearly the same time, I found myself beginning a quite different and completely unexpected adventure. The next chapter tells that tale.

CHAPTER 9

A Gamble Pays Off

DEPARTMENT CHAIR

One afternoon in 1983, the telephone's ring interrupted me as I pored over a manual on cutting and splicing DNA. Would I meet Holly Smith, chair of the Department of Medicine, tomorrow at 11 a.m.? One didn't say no to Holly, but I couldn't think why he suddenly wanted to see me. I returned to the manual.

The next morning Holly opened his door, revealing two other senior faculty seated at a table. Both were shining stars in the firmament of basic research at UCSF—Bill Rutter, an outstanding molecular biologist and chair of the Biochemistry Department, and Mike Bishop, who would later win a Nobel Prize for discovering oncogenes. To me Holly was an august presence, benevolent but distant. I had never had a conversation with Bill or Mike. What might this formidable triumvirate want with me?

Mike indicated a chair. Puzzled and uneasy, I gratefully sat down.

"Henry, we'll get right to the point," Bill said. "We want you to become chairman of the Department of Pharmacology."

Dumbstruck, I stammered that I wasn't a real pharmacologist. "But you're a good cell biologist," Mike replied, "and the department needs a leader."

They told me Pharmacology had been without a permanent chair for several years, and had not hired a new faculty member for even longer—so the department had six unfilled faculty positions. The Chancellor was about to appoint a new Dean for the School of

Medicine, and developing the department would be one of the new Dean's highest priorities.

I told them I wasn't ready to make a decision, but wanted to think about it. Explore it further, they advised, by talking with the Dean-to-be. I said I would, and escaped as quickly as possible.

The person I really needed to talk with was Nancy. That night we talked about problems and opportunities. First, running a department would steal time and energy from my research, which I loved. Second, Pharmacology was in serious disarray, and in ways that might prove impossible to fix. So the risk of failure was real. Third, I had no training or expertise for this new task. And it didn't help that I had not proved a conspicuous success as head of Clinical Pharmacology, a smaller academic entity with fewer problems.

To my surprise, I found myself countering these negatives with arguments for taking the job. It would be a new challenge, a real adventure, and it ought to be fun to attract and hire new faculty. And if I could keep the lab going, I would have an escape route if chairmanship proved a total disaster. Finally, I knew that the new chairperson of a department often comes to the job without training, with little in the way of experience, and at an age comparable to mine. I was 43. Nancy felt I should do it. "If you don't, you'll always wonder whether you should have. Take a hard look at the problems, sure. But if you think there are ways to deal with them, take the job."

I knew something about the department, mainly because Holly Smith had engineered a transfer of my lab into space he commandeered from Pharmacology after Ken Melmon's departure for Stanford. In addition, for seven years I had delivered a few lectures in Pharmacology courses. It was a small department. One professor, Roger Nicoll, was a leading researcher on synapses in the brain. He talked mostly to other neuroscientists, and interacted minimally with department faculty. Two other senior faculty, Bert Katzung and Tony Trevor, had previously conducted active research programs but now were shifting their primary responsibility to teaching.

For years the department had suffered from weak leadership. Years earlier, I had learned this first-hand, while teaching a Pharmacology course. At a meeting of teachers, held in the course's sixth week, I sat down at a round table with six older men and one young woman. The chair at that time was Bob Featherstone, a bald, taciturn older Professor. On my right sat a small man with gray hair, a white shirt, and a bow tie. I had met the woman, an Assistant Professor I'll call Dr. Earnest, who had taught two weeks of lectures. She seemed unusually serious, but smart and capable. The chair offered routine announcements, and asked for comments on the course.

"I have a comment," announced the Bow Tie. "Dr. Earnest's lectures were atrocious, from beginning to end." For 15 minutes, he anatomized a long list of defects in organization and presentation, made more egregious by ignorance of key facts. I had never heard a diatribe like this one, and wondered who would take him on. Dr. Earnest's face took on a tight, controlled expression, but she kept silent. So, to my amazement, did everyone else. Featherstone, the chair, spoke not a single word. Bow Tie finally subsided, and the meeting proceeded as if nothing had happened. I kept my mouth shut, but resolved not to attend this meeting ever again. (Bow Tie's attacks, I later learned, were usually unprovoked, and by no means confined to women. Featherstone's passivity was characteristic. Earnest soon transferred to another institution, where she had a successful career.)

By the time I was asked to take the chair, Bow Tie had retired and Featherstone had died. Under his leadership, the department had gradually accumulated a small "Old Guard" of problematic faculty, who occupied most of its lab space and ran old-fashioned research programs. They bickered among themselves, but were united in opposition to change. The department's resources—lab space, departmental funds, research grants, and number of permanent positions—had dwindled steadily for two decades. As a result, Pharmacology was the weakest basic science department in the school. This was why Holly had been able to engineer my earlier move to Pharmacology space.

At the other end of the spectrum, Bill Rutter's Biochemistry Department was by far the strongest, with a cadre of excellent scientists, well supported by research grants from the NIH. For years their superior scientific prowess had made it easy for Biochemistry to garner the lion's share of new resources, so that it had twice as many faculty positions as Pharmacology, twice as much lab space per researcher, and many fewer courses to teach in professional schools. Biochemistry was a magnet for excellent graduate students, who were much better than those who applied to the Pharmacology graduate program.

The other basic science departments—Physiology, Microbiology, and Anatomy—were better off than Pharmacology but less prosperous and respected than Biochemistry. Invincibly parochial and isolated, each department feared the others might at any moment steal one of its labs or faculty positions. Each also had its own graduate program, whose faculty and students rarely crossed borders to talk with people in other departments. Pharmacology faculty railed about "those selfish snobs in Biochemistry." Soon after Roger Nicoll joined Pharmacology, one Biochemistry professor asked him, "How did you end up with those idiots?"

The School of Medicine had made repeated efforts to refurbish Pharmacology, trying for almost a decade to recruit eminent scientists to take the chair. Al Gilman, whose lab discovered Gs, was one candidate. Another was Jared Diamond, an outstanding physiologist and ornithologist (now known as the author of *Guns, Germs, and Steel*, as well as *Collapse*). These and other luminaries turned the job down, partly because they didn't relish the prospect of battling the department's truculent and well-entrenched Old Guard, but also because they wanted more faculty positions and lab space than UCSF had to offer. In the interim, the Dean's office prevented Pharmacology from hiring new faculty members. This had one salutary effect—over time, attrition produced six unfilled positions.

I had long talks with the incoming Dean, Rudi Schmid, a blunt, charming Swiss biochemist and liver specialist who bristled with readiness for combat. Rudi said he would give me all the support I might need to turn the department around—that is, to re-distribute and renovate lab space and to recruit new faculty. The Old Guard, he claimed, were nothing but paper tigers.

Holly Smith, dry-witted, droll, and silver-haired, surveyed the academic landscape with a keen, discerning eye. He urged me to realize that real change in academia comes slowly. I should make deliberate, unhurried decisions. Change, he said, often requires replacing older faculty with new. "Remember, Henry, where there's death, there's hope!" (Death was not strictly necessary—retirement or moving to positions elsewhere would do the job nicely.)

With help from Bert Katzung, the department's acting chair, Rudi and I carefully reviewed the department's existing resources and problems. One of the latter was a faculty member I'll call Jack Jones. Jones's irascible behavior and inability to get along with departmental neighbors had led to exile in a lab off campus. Rudi, Bert, and I decided to look at this off-campus space to see whether something useful might be done with it. On the way, I told Bert and Rudi about the visit Neil Van Dop, a postdoc in my lab, had paid to the Jones lab the day before.

Jones had circulated a notice inviting prospective buyers in the department to look at an old scintillation counter he wanted to get rid of. The Professor was away when Neil arrived, so one of his lab people took Neil to the scintillation counter. To reach it they walked through a battered door, hanging crazily on its hinges. Neil was told that Jones had come to the lab the previous weekend and discovered he didn't have a key to open this door. Whereupon, his postdoc said, Jones opened a red firebox on the wall, removed a huge ax, and beat the door down. I couldn't wait to meet this Grendel in a lab coat.

The Professor himself greeted us at the lab, all smiles and charm. He asked us to call him Jack. Touring the lab, we came to the famous door.

"My God, Jack, what happened here?" I asked.

"Oh, we often have these vandals," Jones replied. "They sneaked in this weekend, took an ax and beat the door down. Didn't steal anything, though."

The three of us managed not to laugh out loud, but giggled all the way back to campus.

In the end, ambition trumped self-doubt. Somehow I persuaded myself that this would be an exciting challenge. I was too ignorant to realize how hard a task I was about to tackle, how ill-prepared for it I was, or how much I had to learn about medical academia, and about myself.

and—my own special interest—responding to external signals, or "signaling."

I might be ignorant, but I was also an adept hand at grabbing an idea and running with it. A Cell Biology Graduate Program, it seemed to me, would go a long way toward solving Pharmacology's big problem. The new program would attract first-rate graduate students and excellent faculty for our department. We would draw its core faculty from new recruits in Pharmacology, who would join the growing group of outstanding cell biologists in other departments. For the moment, I decided to ignore the lack of any obvious close connection between cell biology and Pharmacology's official function, which was to teach medical students about drugs. We'll deal with that later, I thought.

For me the immediate difficulty was that I didn't really know the prominent cell biologists at UCSF. Most were Biochemistry faculty, who notoriously disdained anyone outside their exclusive club. I recognized the unease I had felt many years before, when I decided to sit next to Gordon Tomkins on a commuter bus. Perhaps, I hoped, this venture will turn out just as well.

So I screwed up my courage and called a meeting, sometime in 1984. A dozen faculty were invited, including the best cell biologists at UCSF. Trying not to look intimidated, I stood before the blackboard and outlined a plan for organizing a new interdepartmental graduate program. I pointed out the benefits of such a plan to all the basic science departments, emphasizing the opportunity to attract outstanding young cell biologists to unfilled faculty positions in Pharmacology. (I knew, but didn't say, that Biochemistry and the other departments had filled all their positions.) I watched the audience for reactions, but couldn't read them. Were they disdainful? Hostile? Or just bored? When I asked for questions and nobody said a word, I thought the game was lost.

Finally I heard a question. "Who should head the program?" asked Marc Kirschner, a brilliant member of the Biochemistry Department. I replied that we would probably recruit a senior person from outside, using one of the Pharmacology positions. I was to learn that Marc was a genial, relentless locomotive, chugging inexorably ahead and insisting that you climb aboard or get out of the way. In this case, Marc's locomotive chugged in the right direction. He soon had the group discussing possible senior figures we might bring to UCSF, and visibly warming to the idea of a Cell Biology Program. As they talked, I was struck by how little I myself knew about the rapidly expanding field. Outside of cell signaling, every candidate they named was unknown to me. I had a lot to learn.

Before the meeting was over, we had decided to set up a Cell Biology Program. Its faculty would include cell biologists in many departments, but would be located administratively in Pharmacology. We would seek a senior person to head the program. The rest would be assistant professors. By 1985, we were setting up a prototype program, with a core faculty and a flagship course in cell biology. Marc wrote a grant application to the NIH, asking for money to support graduate stipends, and I prepared a formal proposal for a new graduate program and shepherded it through endless administrative channels on the campus and at the level of the University.

Our most important move, by far, was to organize and teach a core Cell Biology course. The faculty included Marc (cell shape and movement), plus Mike Bishop from Microbiology (cell division and cancer), as well as Reg Kelly and Peter Walter from Biochemistry (secretion and vesicle traffic in cells), and me (cell signaling). Graduate students from many departments flocked to the course, and so did the faculty. All the lecturers were excited enough about the course to attend every lecture, where they asked one another probing questions that pushed each subject as far as it would go. Excitement about the course kindled our enthusiasm and gave us a chance to learn more about one another, making it much easier to organize a cohesive Cell Biology Program.

We also learned more about the subject, most of which was completely new to me. After Gordon died, I had narrowly focused my attention on hormone action and G-proteins. As a result, I probably learned more from the cell biology course than anyone else. I had expected that chairing Pharmacology would interfere with my lab's research, but the result was just the opposite. At first, as I mentioned in the previous chapter, the cell biologists and their departments saw me mainly as a convenient conduit for new faculty positions. Working together to organize the course and the Program, however, triggered exciting conversations about biology, so that I gradually gained access to advice, criticism, and new ways of thinking. People already aboard the DNA bandwagon grabbed our hands and hoisted us up to join them. Their help and the opportunity to buttonhole a host of experts with questions were magnificent rewards for jump-starting a graduate program.

As I had foreseen, we were not able to pretend forever that cell biology and pharmacology are identical disciplines. We dealt with the very real discrepancies in two ways. First, new knowledge produced by the DNA revolution rapidly rendered much of old-fashioned pharmacology pretty much irrelevant to medical students. Now they need to learn mechanisms of disease and of drug action, rather than memorize endless minutiae about myriad diseases and hundreds of individual drugs. Our new faculty—cell biologists, chemical biologists, structural biologists—had already acquired basic knowledge and expertise highly relevant to the new curriculum. As the new biology began to explain mechanisms of human disease and drugs, learning and teaching about them could become an exciting challenge, rather than a dreaded duty.

The second strategy was to hire additional faculty who specialize in teaching basic sciences to medical and other professional students. The first such person we hired was Susan Masters, a PhD in pharmacology. As an extremely bright postdoc in my lab, Susan spearheaded many exciting projects, some described in the previous chapter, others in the next. Shortly before the end of my stint as chairman, Pharmacology hired Susan to direct several professional courses. As Bert Katzung and Tony Trevor neared retirement, Susan took over their roles and skillfully supervised the teaching of all our faculty. More recently, she played a guiding role in a comprehensive revision of UCSF's entire basic science curriculum, and now supervises courses that combine biochemistry, organ physiology, and pharmacology. A few years ago she was joined by another Pharmacology faculty member, Marieke Kruidering. Together they have assumed direct responsibility for much of the acclaimed new curriculum. Some of these changes took place after I retired from the chair, but I am especially proud of having lured Susan into teaching Pharmacology.

———

For ten years, Pharmacology kept me very busy. I had to move faculty from poorly utilized labs into smaller offices, renovate vacated space for new labs, and recruit candidates for faculty positions. Now I marvel at how I found the chutzpah to tackle so many tasks I knew nothing about. Without strong support from the Dean's office, Bert, Trev, and Roger in Pharmacology, and faculty in other departments, it could not have happened.

Dealing with Old Guard faculty was sometimes hard. Jack Jones, fortunately, reached age 70 before federal law abolished a university's ability to ask faculty to retire at that age. I had never thought I'd need to know the actual birth date of a faculty member, but Jack's birthday and the number of days before his retirement were red-inked on my calendar. The rest of the Old Guard saw that the department was moving in a new direction, and they didn't much like it. Several eventually took positions elsewhere, but in the meantime I faced a certain amount of petty opposition and latent hostility.

Riding my bike home one summer evening, I suffered a scary moment of black comedy. Climbing a steep, slow hill, I glanced over my shoulder and saw the angriest member of the Old Guard driving the car behind me. Paranoia suggested he was planning to push me over the guard rail, but to my intense relief the car passed by, and disappeared. In retrospect, I'm sure its driver had no notion that the cyclist slowing his progress up the hill was his bête noire of a chairman.

With Old Guard faculty I could assume a confident, decisive manner and learn as I went along. In the critical business of finding and attracting new faculty, such a policy felt risky. I had never participated in any hiring decision, and didn't even have a clear notion of how I myself was hired. Ken Melmon seemed to have brought me onto the faculty by sleight of hand, without interview or competing candidates. My guess is that he had to persuade Holly, and that was enough in 1971. The formal procedure for hiring assistant professors was new to me, and I had no idea how to judge young scientists.

Although we did make a few mistakes, most of the people we chose were excellent. This was because I followed good advice in the very first step of the "search" for each position. That is, I found highly qualified faculty to serve on each search committee, individuals who did know how to judge young scientists and would work hard to do it right. The committee began by advertising the position and contacting colleagues elsewhere to recommend likely candidates. Then, after perusing dossiers of more than a hundred candidates, they would invite the top five or six to UCSF for interviews and a formal seminar. Finally, we would offer one of them a Pharmacology position.

The first step was crucial. Indeed, in four of the seven searches we conducted, the candidate we eventually chose was "discovered" by a cell biologist at UCSF. One was a postdoc in a UCSF lab, and two came from labs well known to our own faculty but located at other institutions. I brought the fourth—a young man I had met at a signaling Gordon Conference—to the committee's attention. The other successful candidates applied in response to advertisements.

I chaired most of our committee meetings, which meant I could elicit others' opinions and run less risk of revealing my ignorance. I learned a lot by listening. At one meeting, a colleague exclaimed, "This guy is amazing. He thinks he can purify a nuclear membrane protein just like that—without knowing any biochemistry!" I nodded sagely, reflecting that I was nearly as naïve as the candidate in question. Other committee members frequently pointed out logical flaws or unfeasible experiments, dashing my unspoken enthusiasm about the "big picture" a candidate painted in his seminar. I came to know which colleagues were expert at assessing a candidate's accomplishments and potential success or failure in competition with other labs. The criteria for selecting a young person were obvious. She or he had to be smart, capable, and accomplished. We awarded extra points for success in two different fields, as a graduate student and then as a postdoc, because this suggested the person could adapt to new questions and unforeseen results. The proposed research had to be feasible, interesting, and likely to attract NIH funding.

Obvious criteria, perhaps, but applying them in practice required experience in hiring faculty, which I lacked. I thank my lucky stars for my colleagues' well-honed judgment.

An additional criterion occasionally proved decisive. For instance, we interviewed a brilliant, highly recommended young man, whom I'll call Albert. He had authored outstanding papers and delivered an outstanding seminar. Interviewing him, I was bothered by hints of arrogance in Albert's demeanor. The eventual committee vote split evenly on whether to offer Albert a position. (I kept silent.) Five committee members argued eloquently for the high quality of the candidate's research and his extraordinary promise as a scientist. The other five agreed about his unusual scientific ability, but adamantly opposed hiring him. Their arguments boiled down to one—"I don't want Albert as a colleague." (In a separate search, we judged one candidate more succinctly—"Being an asshole is not enough.")

For me, the divided vote was decisive. When I told Albert we couldn't offer him a position, he abruptly hung up the phone. Decades later, both our committee's judgments were proved correct. Albert's research is original, well known, and highly productive. But he is also a notorious thorn in the side of his department and his host institution, a loner whose interactions with fellow faculty are often tinged with acrimony.

I think we made the right decision. Some departments and institutions, to the contrary, claim to choose colleagues solely on the basis of scientific ability. I think they are wrong, because a close-knit, cooperative community that chooses to put up with a jerk incurs a huge cost. The community not only loses an opportunity to work with a more generous and communicative person, but also pays for overt damage the jerk wreaks among its faculty and students. Perhaps my debt to colleagues' generosity tempts me to exaggerate, but my own experience suggests that many basic science faculty at UCSF perform at a level well above their own intrinsic ability, because their colleagues help them to be smarter than they really are.

Years of observation have also shown me that scientific ability and personal character are not linked to one another in any way, genetically or otherwise. In my experience, personalities of excellent scientists vary pretty much like those of the general population, whether we talk about generosity *vs.* selfishness, cooperation *vs.* exploitation, or drive *vs.* laziness. Consequently, the cost of refusing to hire a jerk is likely to be small, because with the same amount of effort we can find an excellent scientist who is also a good person.

In his best oracular style, my friend Zach Hall extends this idea further: "Any scientific enterprise is at the mercy of the unlinked genetic traits of its alpha-scientists." Scientists tend to follow the leadership of "alpha-scientists," so we should pay close attention to every candidate's unlinked character traits. If the candidate we choose becomes an alpha-scientist, as we hope, her or his unlinked character traits may very well shape the future of the department, or of the institution itself. It is easy, unfortunately, to cite alpha-scientists whose unlinked personality traits promote misery and conflict in departments, institutions, and even entire fields of research.

One of our searches was aimed at identifying a person to direct the Cell Biology Graduate Program. The leading candidate, Professor Eminent, provoked a wrenching controversy. He was a vigorous elder statesman of cell biology, an alpha-scientist world-renowned for his ground breaking discoveries. After falling out with his colleagues at another institution, he let it be known that he could be attracted to a job elsewhere. Professor Eminent met with the Dean, Rudi Schmid, and with many cell biologists at UCSF. The latter were sharply divided. They didn't question the candidate's scientific quality or his capacity to judge research and researchers, but many judged him dogmatic, autocratic, and out of tune with the goals and new research directions of the program. Because I agreed with the latter opinion, and worried that Professor Eminent would prove a difficult colleague in Pharmacology, I asked the Dean for help.

"I worry about this guy for just the same reasons. We shouldn't take him," said Rudi.

"But," he added with a sly grin, "You're the one who has to tell him no."

This was more than I had bargained for. Who was I to say no to a scientific giant whose ability and research accomplishments dwarfed my own? The prospect of confronting this imperious fellow terrified me, but I couldn't get out of it. Someone from the Dean's office brought Dr. Eminent to my tiny office. There he stood, towering in the doorway. I invited him in, we shook hands, and sat down.

"Professor Eminent," I said, "After a lot of thought, we've decided that our program and you would not be a good fit for one another."

"Thank you for telling me," Dr. Eminent replied, and abruptly left the room. I collapsed with relief. Ultimately we chose to commit our positions to young scientists, and to appoint a member of our current faculty to direct the Cell Biology Program. It turned out we didn't need a giant, after all.

Overall, the combination of my inexperience and energy, plus stalwart help from many colleagues, brought five excellent young scientists to UCSF. Most of them are now national and international leaders in cell biology, and three are chairs of departments—two at UCSF, one elsewhere. We made mistakes, as well.

One serious mistake was hiring a brilliant young man I'll call Frank. As a postdoc, he had been first author of two ground breaking papers from an outstanding laboratory. His job talk at UCSF was superb, his technical skills and gift of gab outstanding. As an assistant professor, however, Frank's work never got off the ground. Despite help from me and from several senior colleagues, he had no success in attracting grant funds. I found an internal contradiction in the main argument of one of Frank's grant applications, and pointed it out to him. He argued a bit, but eventually agreed that it was a contradiction. In the end, however, he failed to correct the contradiction, which the NIH's reviewers used as grounds to turn the application down. He seemed unwilling or unable to profit from advice.

Although Frank couldn't tell me why he ignored my advice, I did learn more about his postdoctoral work, before he came to UCSF. There he had been very closely supervised. His PI carefully reviewed the planning, execution, results, and analysis of every individual experiment—so closely that Frank never felt a need, or perceived an opportunity, to think on his own. The PI, a scientist of immense intellect and overwhelming personality, never gave him a chance to be wrong. Perhaps as a result, he performed experiments superbly, but couldn't think effectively about what experiments he needed to do.

Frank was in fact a textbook example of an experimenter who failed to incorporate thinking into the fabric of his life. As a result, we asked him to leave UCSF. He took a position working for a biotech company, where he had similar difficulties. I'm not sure where Frank is now.

In a separate case, the search attracted a group of mediocre candidates, but I felt pressed to hire someone, took a gamble, and lost. The person we chose proved worse than mediocre. I had not taken seriously enough the lesson a hard-nosed academic tried to teach me, just after I took the chair. "Henry, think of all the money and effort we put into a new faculty member. Hiring a marginal candidate is always a disaster. Remember: hiring no one may be the best choice, because you can search again next year."

————

Recruiting new faculty and watching Cell Biology develop were satisfying, but were soon overshadowed by a more comprehensive revolution, which involved UCSF's entire biomedical science community. Fueled by the world-wide DNA revolution in experimental biology, the local revolution gave me and my colleagues a second wave of exhilarating bliss in the afternoon of that revolution, with lasting effects that extended beyond UCSF.

I would like to think it began with the Cell Biology Program, with its successful flagship course and magnetic attraction for first-rate new faculty and graduate students. In fact, UCSF furnished other examples of ecumenical graduate programs. Zach Hall, in the Physiology Department, had founded an excellent interdepartmental Neuroscience Graduate Program in the 1970s. Soon, Ira Herskowitz and other geneticists were organizing a Genetics Graduate Program.

The tinderbox of new ideas needed only a spark. In 1988, the Markey Charitable Trust struck that spark by awarding UCSF $13 million to improve basic biomedical research and graduate training. Leaders at UCSF envisioned an extraordinary opportunity. Holly Smith persuaded the Markey Trust, as he put it, "to invest a substantial amount where it will make a difference, rather than waste their funds in scattered dribs and drabs."

Rudi Schmid, Dean of the School of Medicine, also played a key role. I can still see Rudi announcing the Markey Award to a group of department chairs and leaders of graduate programs. Laced with boring rhetoric, his speech lasted almost 30 minutes, but its core was unprecedented. Rudi promised that the Dean's office would not dole out the funds itself, nor would it levy the customary "Dean's tax" on awards. Instead, he would trust the basic sciences to spend the money for the common good. To connoisseurs of Deanly behavior in any academic setting, this was a rare gesture indeed. Even rarer, the Dean's Office did precisely what Rudi said it would do.

Mike Bishop and Bruce Alberts, who had recently replaced Bill Rutter as chair of Biochemistry, took up the challenge of transforming vision into reality. They envisioned forming an umbrella graduate program, with the goal of uniting research efforts and faculty recruiting by all the basic science departments. The umbrella would comprise interdepartmental programs, which would replace the programs sponsored by departments. The intellectual rationale was obvious—the DNA revolution was already uniting disparate research fields in ways that crossed old departmental boundaries.

Called the Program in Biological Sciences (aka PIBS), the umbrella initially comprised four interdepartmental graduate programs—Cell Biology, Genetics, Neuroscience, and Biochemistry/ Molecular Biology. Each program chose its own faculty, admitted students according to its own criteria, and organized courses of its own or in collaboration with other programs. Students in each program were permitted to do their thesis work with a faculty member in a different PIBS program.

Such umbrella programs are the rule nowadays, rather than the exception. In 1988 they were rare, owing to departmental chauvinism and fears that interdepartmental research and teaching would reduce the power of departments and their chairs.

UCSF became the birthplace of one of the first umbrella programs for two reasons. The first was the vision and personalities of Bruce Alberts and Mike Bishop, combined with strong support from others, including Ira Herskowitz and chairs of other departments—such as Zach Hall, who became chair of Physiology in 1988, and me.

The second reason is that we devised a remarkably effective way to distribute and monitor expenditure of funds from the $13 million Markey Award. The key was to vest the crucial power of the purse in PIBS's Steering Committee. This Committee was composed of representatives of the individual programs and chairs of five basic science departments (Biochemistry, Physiology, Pharmacology, Anatomy, and Microbiology). It controlled access to the Markey money, which could be used for supporting graduate students, purchasing lab equipment, and paying travel expenses of seminar speakers.

The most critical expenditures would be start-up funds for recruiting new faculty members—that is, money required to buy essential equipment and pay salaries and research costs until grant funds became available. Here the rules were strict. Every faculty candidate proposed for such funds must be identified by a search committee that included faculty already in PIBS graduate programs, and nominated for PIBS membership by one of the programs. In every case, the new person's membership, as well as her or his start-up funds, were subject to approval by the Steering Committee. Thus a department could hire any candidate it chose, but PIBS would control that person's access to PIBS graduate students and PIBS-derived start-up funds. Departments could preserve their own graduate programs as long they were willing to pay for them. As a result, within a few years departmental programs withered away. More important, under this new arrangement the resources needed by new faculty members depended directly on cooperation among multiple programs and departments. As a result, PIBS's success was very much in the interest of everyone.

And it worked. Now, 20 years later, PIBS has turned out to be a huge success. Faculty and students routinely collaborate across departmental lines. PIBS has incorporated new graduate programs (Development Biology and Chemical Biology, for instance) and continues to promote effective cooperation between departments in recruiting new faculty.

Dissolving rigid boundaries between departments also enhanced our ability to retain faculty members courted by "raiding parties" from other institutions. This happened with Ron Vale, an outstanding young cell biologist I recruited to Pharmacology. Ron chafed at UCSF's tight space constraints, which crammed his lab into tiny facilities on two separate floors. In contrast, the raiding party from another school offered luxurious new lab space, higher salary, and generous start-up money. By itself, Pharmacology could not compete. Then PIBS jumped into the fray, mobilizing money for renovation and equipment, and Zach Hall and his Department of Physiology allowed us to borrow lab space for Ron, at the cost of delaying a faculty appointment in Physiology. Fortunately, Ron decided to stay at UCSF, where he is currently chair of Cellular and Molecular Pharmacology (the department's new name). This was the first of several such rescues engineered by PIBS-promoted cooperation between departments.

Since 1988, many schools have followed our example and organized umbrella graduate programs of their own. Still, I have the impression that the basic science community at UCSF remains more cooperative and cohesive than such communities at most other institutions. If so, PIBS is partly responsible.

PIBS's success seemed almost miraculous, but resulted from a combination of three elements required for transforming any academic enterprise. The first was a perceived need that could not be accommodated by existing arrangements. Created by the DNA revolution, this need made traditional departments and graduate programs quite irrelevant to the new questions biologists cared about.

The second element was money. Without it, no department chair would have dreamed of merging "his" graduate program with others, and many faculty, especially in weaker departments, would have refused to risk the possibility that researchers in another department could lure graduate students away from their departmental program.

The third and most essential element was the leaders who made PIBS happen, and in particular two qualities they shared—imagination, combined with unselfish generosity. Holly and Rudi had the imagination to see that the Markey money was a rare opportunity, and that Mike, Bruce, and their colleagues could be trusted to spend it well. Bruce and Mike, widely respected for their scientific prowess, worked long and hard to transform their environment, more to the benefit of their present and future colleagues than to their own. Without their moral certainty that cooperation would improve everyone's lot, and the generosity of their example, the transformation would not have worked. PIBS would never have existed if it were not for the salutary unlinked traits of these alpha-scientists.

———

In June of 1989, I noticed dark blood in my stools. Unwilling to believe this could be serious, I protested that colonoscopy wasn't necessary. Finally the gastroenterologist persuaded me to undergo the procedure.

Lying on my side, I watched the colonoscope's view on a video monitor. The scope slowly snaked its way up a pink tunnel. Suddenly a big bulge loomed, purple and shiny, on one side of the tunnel ahead. "My God, what's that?" I cried. A voice said, "Give him some more," and an extra dose of sedative put me under.

Afterward, the gastroenterologist wanted badly to say, "I told you so," but suspected it wouldn't sound right. Instead, he held my hand, told me the cancer was in the sigmoid colon, and asked me to choose a surgeon. Surgery was scheduled for the next morning, and I returned home, pretty much on autopilot. I drank a few glasses of malt whiskey, and Nancy and I polished off a delicious bottle of white wine. I was instructed to drink "clear liquids only," and these were the clearest liquids I could find. In the morning my hangover headache made me welcome anesthesia.

The recovery process laid bare my characteristic response to adversity. I tend to glide through difficult situations by pretending they don't exist, as I had in college and immediately afterward. This time I gave the tried-and-true policy a new twist. In the hospital, my doctor told Nancy and me what the pathologists had found. The cancer's appearance, plus small pockets of metastatic cancer in two lymph nodes, predicted a 50% likelihood of surviving five years after surgery. In my mind, I magically transformed this into an 80% survival rate, which I sincerely believed and blithely relayed to friends. Nancy had heard the 50% figure clearly, however, and a year later my oncologist confirmed that 50% was correct. So, I met the threat with psychological denial, unconscious but powerful.

Remarkably, denial worked. Within a couple of months I stopped worrying that every belly pain signaled a metastasis. Soon I more or less forgot to worry about the future, despite a year of weekly chemotherapy, when an oncologist would remind me of the cancer by giving me an intravenous dose of 5-fluorouracil. Better still, I happened to fall in the fortunate 50% of the population, and have survived 20 years post-surgery—another example of my life's extraordinary streak of good luck.

Colon cancer did have one major effect on my life, by helping me to realize it was time to retire from the chair of Pharmacology. A month or two after the surgery, I asked the new Dean of the School of Medicine—Joe Martin, an eminent Harvard neurologist—to replace me as chair as soon as he could. The cancer, I said, showed me I would really prefer focusing my passion on research rather than administration, but I would be willing to stay on for a year or two while the school found a replacement. Joe said he understood, and I think he did. Still, it was five years before a new chair took over.

What I told Joe about preferring research was correct, but only part of the story. The more decisive reason for giving up the chair was that I had stopped enjoying the job. I knew I lacked the clear scientific vision of my administrative heroes, Holly, Bruce, and Mike. This didn't bother me much, because I was good at recognizing and applying the visions of others—as I did with the idea of a Cell Biology Program, and in my research as well. More critically, my temperament wasn't right for the task—that is, I couldn't muster the kind of equanimity and patience I would need over the long haul. A first-rate leader manages not to take mistakes to heart, but I certainly did. My peers might occasionally hire an Assistant Professor who was not superb, but seemed not to let it worry them, while such a misstep bothered me for years.

My tendency to righteous anger posed a greater problem. As a young man I had rarely shown anger, even when it was justified—for instance, against Gopal Krishna at the NIH or Ken Melmon in my early years at UCSF. In contrast, between 1988 and 1994 I gave way to expressions of anger several times. I don't know what had happened in the interim. Perhaps I unconsciously felt that anger could bring damaging retribution to an Assistant Professor, but not to a Chairman. (Although it's hard to imagine that even my unconscious was that crazy!) In any case, these episodes occurred during the last half of my chairmanship, often in conflicts with Biochemistry, which (I felt) violated PIBS's ecumenical principles by unfairly monopolizing money and space that should be shared with other departments.

On one of these occasions, another university was vigorously trying to steal an outstanding researcher in Biochemistry, and I strenuously opposed the Dean's plan for retaining this person at UCSF. The plan, I argued, would endanger everything PIBS had created, by setting up a privileged research enclave within UCSF's research community. My first act in opposing the plan was to confront the man who was its object. I told him that if he accepted the Dean's offer he would breathe up all the oxygen PIBS was supplying to bright, capable investigators, and destroy a healthy, growing research community. As far as I could tell, our conversation had no useful effect.

Then I wrote all these arguments in an accusatory, burn-my-bridges letter to power brokers at UCSF, including Dean Joe Martin, Holly Smith, and Ira Herskowitz, the new chair of Biochemistry. My arguments were correct, and the letter gave me a brief but delicious rush of self-righteous pleasure, but I have repented sending it ever since. A wiser man would have opposed the plan by mobilizing consensus among like-minded colleagues. Instead, my irate letter alienated a friend (Ira), and Holly and the Dean quietly ignored it. Thus anger failed to achieve its object. In the end, fortunately, the outstanding researcher succumbed to the other university's blandishments, so the plan became moot. I would like to think that my confronting him helped sway his decision, but it is likely that he simply responded to a better offer.

Angry episodes did not even accelerate my retirement from the chair. Two years after my surgery, and repeated requests from me, the Dean had made no effort to identify a new chair. Pharmacology was stable, its new faculty prospered, and the Dean's office had more pressing issues to deal with. Clearly I would have to find the new chair myself.

The choice was obvious: Keith Yamamoto, Professor of Biochemistry at UCSF. An internationally renowned investigator whose research focused on the action of steroid hormones, Keith had come to UCSF as a postdoc in Gordon Tomkins's lab in the 1970s. During my years in Pharmacology, Keith had taken on important roles in PIBS. He had every quality a leader needs. Without a word to anyone else, I approached Keith to propose that he take the Pharmacology chair. His response was a characteristic mix of charm, mild interest, and no hint of commitment either way. As always, Keith knew how to keep his own counsel, but I guessed that the possibility of leading a young department intrigued him. I reminded him repeatedly, for almost a year. Finally he gave his permission to raise the issue with the Dean.

Keith's qualities had certainly not gone un-noticed. In fact, the Dean leapt at the opportunity, and worked hard to gather resources to attract Keith to the position. In 1994, Keith became chair of the Department of Pharmacology, where he did a magnificent job. He recruited a stellar group of young scientists, all five of whom have become leaders in their fields. In addition, he presided over the founding of a Chemical Biology Graduate Program, a collaboration between the Schools of Medicine and of Pharmacy, which has attracted a growing team of brilliant young chemists and outstanding graduate students. His vision, patience, and ability to build consensus played decisive roles in moving most of UCSF's basic science community to a new campus at Mission Bay, in 2003. That same year, he handed the Pharmacology chair to Ron Vale and moved to the Dean's office. Now, as Executive Vice Dean of the School, Keith has taken on broader responsibility. And he still runs a superb lab, engaged in ground breaking research.

The day Keith became chair of Pharmacology was one of the happiest days of my professional life. Persuading him to consider the chair may have been my most substantial achievement.

———

Years later, I look back fondly on the conference room where that august triumvirate offered me a splendid but daunting opportunity. The triumvirate and I took a considerable risk, but in the right place and at the right time. Our mutual gamble paid off, in the sense that I was able to make a significant contribution to an institution that has done so much for me.

More personally, as a scientist, I profited from the huge boon of getting to know many colleagues willing to share their knowledge and advice. It was thrilling to work with so many gifted academic leaders—Holly, Bruce, Rudi, Joe, Zach, Marc, Ira, Keith, Ron, and many more—and, by watching them, to learn what it takes to become an effective leader. I also learned a bit about how academic institutions work, and much more about myself.

CHAPTER 10

All in the Timing

SWITCHES, TIMERS, AND PITUITARY GIANTS

After the DNA revolution, we could no longer bury our heads in the little sandboxes that surrounded our own narrow questions and experiments. A few years earlier, cancer would have seemed medically important but irrelevant to my lab's focus on Gs and cyclic AMP. But in the 1980s we suddenly found that a mutant cancer gene called Ras was also a G-protein switch—a switch locked in the "on" position.

Oncogenic (cancer-causing) Ras mutations, found in more than 80% of human pancreatic cancers, were all located in Ras's "homology regions" of amino acid sequence (Figure 10-1).

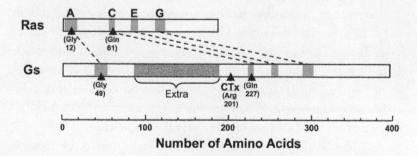

Figure 10-1. Sites of key mutations in Ras (top) and Gs (bottom). Three-letter abbreviations and numbers in parentheses indicate the names and locations of the normal amino acids that are targets of mutation in the two proteins. Gly = glycine; Gln = glutamine, Arg = arginine.

From Halliday and from Jurnak's structure of an Elongation Factor,[1] we had learned that these regions almost certainly lined the pockets that embrace the totem molecules in Ras, Gs, and transducin—totems that regulate their activities.

Because normal Ras promotes cell growth, mutations that maintain Ras in the "on" position cause rapid cell growth and cell division—and therefore cancer. This reminded us of the persistent activity of Gs in the gut cells of patients with cholera. In both cases, the magic totem molecule fails to lose its magic, and the affected protein persists in stimulating its customary cell response.

Oncogenic Ras mutations cause a "wrong" amino acid to substitute for the right one at either of two sites, which are located in homology regions A or C (Figure 10-1). (Both amino acids are close to the magic totem molecule in Ras's 3D structure, reported later in the 1980s.)

Gazing at Ras and Gs sequences, Susan Masters, a postdoc in my lab, was intrigued to find that the normal amino acids at positions that are mutated in oncogenic Ras corresponded to identical amino acids in Gs (Figure 10-1). She predicted that substitution at either position in Gs should increase Gs activity and cyclic AMP production. Retroviral transfection, the procedure Harold Varmus had taught us earlier, allowed her to put Gs with Ras-like mutations into Gs-deficient cyc^- cells, and then to measure adenylyl cyclase in membranes of those cells.

Susan still remembers her intense excitement as results rolled out of the scintillation counter, which counted radioactive cyclic AMP made from ATP. As compared to wild-type membranes, membranes from Gs with a mutation at a site corresponding to the Ras mutation in region C made 10 times more radioactive cyclic AMP. For that short, magical moment, Susan was the only person in the world who knew that Gs and Ras turn off in nearly the same way.

She also adapted an indirect method, originally devised by another lab, for measuring the turnoff rate of Gs and adenylyl cyclase in membranes. Half the population of GTP-bound wild type Gs molecules turned themselves off in less than 10 seconds. We express this in scientific shorthand, saying that the "half-life" of active Gs is less than 10 seconds (just as a physicist might say that the half-life of radioactive

^{14}C is 5,730 years, meaning that half of this isotope decays in that time). By contrast, the half-life of activity in mutant Gs carrying one of Susan's mutations was greater than 30 minutes. Thus the similar 1D amino acid sequences of Ras and Gs furnished the clues, and Susan's experiment told us that their 3D structures are also similar, and almost certainly evolved from a common precursor, millions of years ago.

In contrast, Susan's second Gs mutation, located at the other site often mutated in region A of oncogenic Ras, did not fit her prediction. Compared to wild-type Gs, cells expressing the second-site Gs mutant accumulated less cyclic AMP, even after activating receptors with ISO. Adenylyl cyclase in membranes was similarly reduced with this mutant, compared to wild type. The half-life of activity in this mutant was longer than in wild type (2 minutes vs. 10 seconds) but much shorter than in first mutant she tested (more than 30 minutes).

(Michael Graziano, working in Al Gilman's lab, confirmed Susan's results with experiments on the same Gs mutants and wild-type Gs, purified from bacteria expressing mutant or wild-type DNAs.[2] His paper, immediately following Susan's in the *Journal of Biological Chemistry*, showed that the biochemical turnoff activities of the pure proteins, measured directly, were almost identical to the Gs turnoff rates Susan measured indirectly in cell membranes.[2] Thus the different timer functions were intrinsic properties of the mutant and wild type Gs molecules.)

We rationalized the fact that one of the mutations failed to mimic its Ras counterpart by arguing that Gs and Ras are not identical proteins, so their totem-binding pockets need not be absolutely identical either. More important, we also began to toy with an intriguing idea—perhaps the G-protein switch was functionally distinct from the timing device that controls it. One mutant Gs could barely elevate cyclic AMP, but could nonetheless turn itself off, albeit more slowly than wild-type. Thus it seemed to be a wimpy switch with a slow timer, in contrast with the other Gs mutant's ability to switch on quite strongly, but turn itself off even more slowly, like a perfect switch with a very slow or absent timer.

The normal switch responds to a magic totem by inducing Gs to undergo what biochemists call a "conformational change"—that is, the magic totem molecule induces Gs's shape to change from an inactive to an active form, able to deliver a stimulatory tickle to adenylyl cyclase. In terms of our Genie-hand metaphor, this conformational change causes the hand's "index finger" to extend so that it can flick on the light switch (aka adenylyl cyclase). According to our new, more subtle metaphor, transplanting one of the Ras mutations into Gs permitted the hand to flick the switch on quite normally, but not to inactivate the totem's magic, so the light shines and keeps on shining. The second mutation somehow weakens the extended finger but slows exorcism of the totem's magic only slightly—thereby producing a dim light.

This idea fitted perfectly with just-published papers showing that the intrinsic ability of biochemically pure *normal* Ras to turn itself off is vanishingly low—that is, the half-life of a magic totem molecule bound to pure (unmutated) Ras protein is greater than half an hour, which is similar to the half-life of a magic totem molecule bound to Gs carrying the first of the Ras mutations. Normal Ras can dispel the totem's magic as fast as normal Gs, however, but only if it is accompanied by a second protein, which acts as an *extrinsic* timer. (The extrinsic timer was called GAP, for **G**TPase-**A**ctivating **P**rotein.) Oncogenic Ras mutations leave the Ras switch intact, but impair its susceptibility to regulation by the extrinsic timer.

The distinction between switch and timer raised an interesting question. Why is the intrinsic turnoff rate of normal Gs (half-life of 10 seconds) more than 100 times faster than the intrinsic turnoff of normal Ras (half-life greater than 30 min, or 1,800 seconds)? Perhaps, we were beginning to think, Gs might contain an *intrinsic*, built-in timer, while Ras could turn itself off only with help from a separate extrinsic timer.

———

One day in 1987, about the time Susan was putting Ras mutations into Gs, a journal called *Nature* asked me to review a manuscript on an unexpected subject—pituitary giantism, also called acromegaly. As a medical resident, I had seen sad cases of this rare endocrine disease. The patients had big, flabby muscles; thick bones, lips, and noses; enlarged hearts, livers, and kidneys; and immense hands and fingers (acromegaly means "big digits"). The tongue of one patient, too big for her mouth, protruded onto the pillow when she slept.

The disease is caused by excessive secretion of growth hormone, which is made in tumors of the pituitary gland, located in the middle of the head, just below the brain. The normal pituitary makes several hormones, of which growth hormone is critical for growth in childhood and adolescence. If the tumor appears early in life, the patient becomes a "pituitary giant," because too much of this hormone stimulates long bones to grow excessively, until puberty stops them from getting longer. Growth hormone is normally secreted by pituitary cells that are responding to stimulation of cyclic AMP accumulation by another hormone, called growth hormone releasing hormone. The releasing hormone's receptor, like the receptor for ISO, stimulates Gs and adenylyl cyclase. Tumors of patients with pituitary giantism and acromegaly make growth hormone on their own, without input from the releasing hormone.The manuscript I reviewed contained a surprise and a puzzle. Pituitary tumors from acromegalic patients showed elevated cyclic AMP and adenylyl cyclase activity. These increases appeared to result from increased Gs activity, because adding extracts from the tumors to Gs-deficient *cyc⁻* membranes restored the ability to make cyclic AMP in response to ISO and GTP. Just as we busied ourselves putting Ras mutations into Gs, it seemed that nature might have done the experiment for us. A lovely surprise!Curled up inside the surprise, however, lurked an intriguing puzzle. The authors reported[2] that cholera toxin could enzymatically modify a Gs-sized protein in normal pituitaries, but not in tumors with increased cyclic AMP and Gs activity. Fascinated, I wrote a commentary[2] to accompany the paper, suggesting possible solutions to the puzzle. In one solution, the tumors make a cholera toxin-like enzyme, which elevates cyclic AMP and adenylyl cyclase activity. Because this hypothetical toxin-like enzyme would have already modified the amino acid of Gs normally targeted by cholera toxin, the real toxin would be unable to modify the same site.

The second solution, which I thought more likely, was simply that Gs mutations in the tumors might have substituted a different amino acid for the arginine that Neil Van Dop had identified as modified by the toxin. The toxin would be unable to modify the mutated site because it specifically acts on the arginine Neil had found there. This second solution also would indicate that this arginine is a necessary part of the Gs timer, so that altering it (whether with a mutation or with a toxin modification) would prevent Gs from turning off and increase adenylyl cyclase and cyclic AMP.

On the day the pituitary paper was published, I wrote to its first author, Lucia Vallar, a scientist in Milan, Italy. Would she like to look for Gs mutations in pituitary tumors? Could she bring a few tumors to my lab? When? In the meantime, I recruited a young nephrologist, Claudia Landis, to join the project. Tyler Miller (another postdoc, also a nephrologist) had persuaded Claudia to join the lab, arguing that G proteins could furnish scientific opportunities for her future career in academic medicine. Claudia was bright, eager, and profoundly innocent, especially with respect to lab procedures. But she was also logical, earnest, and determined—ideal qualifications for the task ahead. Claudia's job would be to learn a powerful DNA technology called the "polymerase chain reaction", which was new to my lab. This reaction would be an ideal way to obtain DNA sequences from tiny tumor fragments, because it "amplifies" DNA—that is, it creates billions of identical DNA sequences from a single designated sequence in cellular DNA. Showing the bulldog-style tenacity for which she would become known in the lab, Claudia overcame multiple obstacles and made the new assay work.Then Lucia landed at the San Francisco airport, carrying a plastic bucket filled with dry ice and frozen pituitary tumors. Blonde, sophisticated, and European, Lucia had a deep voice and a direct, no-nonsense tone, burnished by cigarettes. (I had just stopped smoking myself, and was consumed by envy.) At first I worried that she and Claudia were too different to work together productively, but fortunately I was wrong. Lucia made extracts from the precious tumors and measured their adenylyl cyclase activities. From the same extracts, Claudia amplified Gs DNAs with the polymerase chain reaction and determined their sequences. Analyzing the results was not easy, because in the process of amplifying DNA the chain reaction makes occasional "mistakes"—that is, random substitutions of one base for another—mistakes we might misinterpret as tumor-associated mutations. Fortunately, however, the reaction rarely makes precisely the same mistake in separate experiments. As a result, identifying the same mutation in repeated amplifications from a single tumor would mean that the mutation occurred before the chain reactions and is therefore "real." Because the tumor fragments were smaller than the tip of a child's little finger, Lucia had to husband the extracts carefully for Claudia to perform multiple chain reactions. Brusque sophistication and bulldog tenacity complemented one another. (And not only in the lab. Later, I learned that Lucia introduced Claudia to a French perfume, Mitsouko, which she still uses.) Finally, Claudia put all her sequences together. She painstakingly reviewed the data, searching for consistencies and inconsistencies before finally "diagnosing" genuine mutations. She found mutations at either of two sites in Gs, but was so proud of having made the polymerase chain reaction work that she had not thought much about roles of specific amino acids in Gs. Shyly, she told Susan and me that she had some results. Would we like to see them? Susan and I exploded with delight when Claudia showed us what she found. The Gs mutation in one tumor was a lovely example of life imitating art. This mutation replaced an amino acid at the very same site where Susan's "art" had already shown that a Gs mutation would lead to increased cyclic AMP and adenylyl cyclase. This was a site that is also mutated in oncogenic Ras. In other tumors, however, the Gs mutations were located in the cholera toxin target site—the arginine Neil had identified was replaced by an amino acid called cysteine in two tumors, and by a histidine in another. Apparently, substituting any other amino acid for this arginine mimicked the toxin's effect. This told us that the side chain of this amino acid does indeed play a specific role in Gs's timer, just as I had predicted after reading Lucia's paper.

To confirm these results, Susan put each of the mutations Claudia found into recombinant DNA encoding Gs, and then put the mutant DNAs into cyc⁻ cells. As predicted, mutations at the cholera toxin target site increased cyclic AMP accumulation, dramatically slowed turnoff of Gs, and—mimicking Lucia's results with the actual tumors—prevented enzymatic modification by cholera toxin.

Damaging the timer at either position caused Gs to maintain the totem's magic, so that the light bulb remained bright (Figure 10-2).

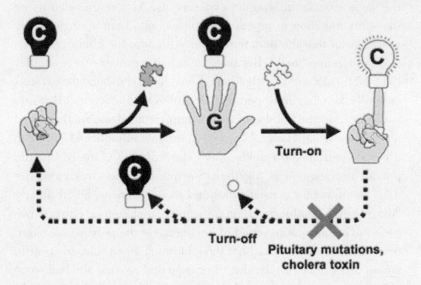

Figure 10-2. Like enzymatic modification by cholera toxin, the mutations in pituitary tumors of acromegalic patients prevent Gs from turning itself off.

Cholera and acromegaly, different diseases in different tissues, shared almost identical molecular defects.

[At this point, alert readers may wonder how acromegalic patients inherit a Gs mutation that is specifically located only in pituitary cells. The answer is that they don't. This disease is not inherited in families. Instead, it results from a mistake in copying the DNA sequence that probably occurs early in embryonic development, in a precursor cell that will divide to produce progeny cells that contribute to the pituitary. As one of the Gs genes in this precursor cell is copied, the copying machinery mistakenly replaces one correct base in the DNA sequence with a "wrong" base. The mistake is then reliably inherited by all of that cell's progeny, producing cells in which the Gs protein cannot turn itself off. The elevated cyclic AMP in those cells increases the rate of cell doubling, as well as their production of growth hormone, so that years later the patient has a small tumor in the pituitary and all the consequences of making too much growth hormone. Indeed, the vast majority of human cancers originate in much the same way—as mistakes in copying the DNA of a precursor cell, which result in expression of mutant Ras (or of another mutant protein) in the progeny cells, which form a tumor.]

Once we had quaffed champagne to celebrate Claudia's sequencing results, we sat down to prepare our story for publication.[2] Now we felt ready to propose an explicit model for the Gs turnoff mechanism. Unlike Ras, we imagined, normal Gs can turn itself off in 10 seconds because it possesses its own built-in (intrinsic) timer. (Ras, remember, turns itself off *very* slowly unless it is acted on by an extrinsic timer protein, called a GAP.) As shown in the metaphorical diagram at the left of Figure 10-3, the built-in timer inserts a finger, the side-chain of a specific arginine, into the totem-binding pocket, where the finger accelerates the magic totem's conversion into an inert dummy.

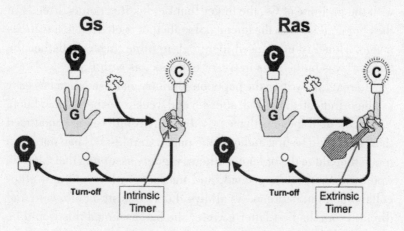

Figure 10-3. Intrinsic vs. extrinsic timers. The left and right panels of the cartoon depict the turnoff reactions in Gs and Ras, respectively. In Gs, a cross-hatched finger of the Genie's hand serves as in intrinsic timer. Located in the right spot to dispel the totem's magic, it causes the hand to release the white circle and consequently return the light bulb to the dark state. In the case of Ras, a separate protein serves as an *extrinsic* timer, but works in a similar way. Biochemically, both the intrinsic mechanism and the extrinsic mechanism use the same amino acid, arginine, to promote the enzymatic reaction that exorcise the G-proteins magic.

We could even propose a function for the mysterious "extra" 120 amino acids immediately preceding this arginine in the sequences of Gs and transducin (see Fig. 9-1): serving as a rigid scaffold, it nuzzles up to the totem-binding pocket, where it orients the arginine into the right position to terminate the totem's magic—that is, together the arginine and the "extra" region act as an *intrinsic* GAP.

Years later, we showed biochemically that the intrinsic timer really does work this way, and that the extra region does present the arginine to Gs's totem-binding pocket.[3] That conclusion was confirmed by the 3D structure of transducin, solved at almost the same time in Paul Sigler's laboratory[3]. Soon after, the wheel came full circle, with 3D structures of Ras and other Ras-like proteins, each crystallized in the embrace of its extrinsic timer (GAP) protein. In every case, the extrinsic timer pointed its own "arginine finger" into the totem-binding pocket of its partner (Figure 10-3, right). Just as with the arginine of Gs, the finger that tickles Ras points directly at the chemical bond in the totem molecule that is cleaved to negate its magic. Thus evolution used identical arginine fingers, whether the "finger" was built-in, as in Gs, or extrinsic, as with Ras.

In real life, writing the paper on pituitary giantism wasn't as easy as I have indicated. Instead, after several weeks of experiments, Lucia Vallar asked to speak with me privately. In my office, she announced that she should be first author of the paper. Carelessly, I had not given much thought to the order of authors, vaguely assuming that Claudia would be first, Lucia second, and me last, with Susan and other collaborators in between. As always, Lucia was straightforward and direct. From the first letter I wrote, she had assumed this would be her paper. Moreover, she counted on first authorship to give her the kind of high-profile, first-author publication necessary for academic advancement in Italy. I could see how she came to that assumption, and also that a woman lacking Lucia's strength and determination would find it hard to make her way in the male-dominated world of Italian biology. But I also feared an authorship dispute, especially since I had contributed to it myself by failing to deal with the issue earlier. Claudia, the least senior contributor to the paper, would find first authorship just as useful as Lucia would. Far too experienced to make such a stupid mistake, I had nonetheless failed to foresee Lucia's legitimate claim to first authorship. To Lucia I proposed a possible solution: Claudia would be first author, Lucia last author, and I next-to-last. Lucia readily agreed to this compromise because, according to prevailing convention, first authors and last authors together share almost all the prestige of authorship. The first author is usually considered to have made the major experimental contribution to the paper, while the last author is usually chief of the lab in which the research was done and/or the project's primary instigator. The proposed compromise would give Claudia credit for her first-rate work, and Lucia's peers would see her as the person who spearheaded the project—a true characterization, because without her discovery of excess Gs activity in the tumors there would have been no project. If the compromise cost me anything, I deserved it for not having paid attention to the order of authors.

Readers unversed in the arcana of scientific authorship may find this story puzzling or even ridiculous. How could grownups care so much about authorship order, or contrive a resolution based on such artificial conventions? The answer is simple. The principal currency of reward in our world is authorship, valued according to the order of authors' names in each published report. (In my own career, Ken Melmon's inclusion as an author of my papers had proved a major bone of contention.) The authorship order we devised for the Landis-Masters-Bourne-Vallar paper was the most intricate resolution of such issues I can remember in my lab, but I have witnessed far more disruptive and bitter disputes in other labs, and resolutions much more convoluted than ours.

The DNA revolution gave scientists the vast pleasure of answering fascinating questions and licensed us to talk grandly about learning to understand "nature." But it did not alter our need for artificial conventions to help manage our selfishness.

———

When Claudia deciphered the Gs mutations in pituitary tumors, I was 17 years older than that young man who met Gordon Tomkins on a commuter bus in 1972. In the meantime I had learned that genetics really does generate surprises, and that mutations can point unerringly to critical steps in signaling pathways that regulate cells and organisms. We saw earlier how inherited mutations in a human disease of hormone resistance revealed the essential role of one regulator, Gs, in the action of several hormones. Tools forged in the DNA revolution revealed sporadic mutations in the Gs genes of pituitary cells because they cause a second disease, acromegaly. These mutations show how important it is for Gs to turn itself off.

Now let us return for a moment to a knotty question about the G-protein switch. When I first introduced the switch, I apologized for using such an elaborate and esthetically clumsy metaphor. Reprised in Figure 10-2, that metaphor involves a Genie's hand, a magic totem molecule, a magical transformation that enables the hand to turn on a light bulb, delayed exorcism of the totem's magic, and (although omitted from this version of the Figure) re-activation by another *deus ex machina*, the activated hormone receptor. However rococo it may appear, the metaphor accurately reflects the way Gs works in real cells. Its improbable absurdity would not amount to one jot less if I related it in "scientific" language, replete with acronyms, chemical reactions, and a larger cast of molecular players than the metaphor can accommodate.

So here's the question—what kind of artist would cobble together all this rococo folderol? Proponents of "Intelligent Design" argue the opposite way—that organs like the eye are so beautiful and complex that chance could never have concocted anything like them. The principal answer to my esthetic joke or to their purported evidence for divine intervention is straightforward. Biology's immense variety—especially when brightly lit by the DNA revolution—makes it clear that *only* chance could account for the unimaginable complexity of organs like the eye or improbably rococo molecular machines like G-proteins. Indeed, once presented with a useful kernel of novelty, chance and evolution invariably weave many different variations on the basic theme. Richard Dawkins pointed out,[4] for instance, that visual organs like the eye evolved independently in many widely separated lineages—not once, that is, but at least 40 times! And, it turns out, many of these eyes use a photon detector very similar to the rhodopsin in our own eyes. Given a good photon detector, evolution exploits it by forming dozens of different kinds of eyes to present the detector to the world.

The baroque complexity of Gs and its relatives reflects a parallel tendency of evolution to elaborate variations on the molecular machine itself. The magic totem molecule itself is a chemical precursor of one of the nucleotides in the genetic material of every organism. As a result, virtually every organism contains enzymes that convert the magic totem into other molecules, including the one we called a dummy totem. Biochemically, every G-protein is really just an enzyme, and not a very efficient enzyme at that. Most enzymes convert their target molecules into a product molecule in milliseconds, rather than the near-eternity of 10 whole seconds required for Gs, or the many minutes required for Ras! And most self-respecting enzymes, unlike G-proteins, release their molecular product quickly after making it, so as to pick up another target molecule right away.

It looks as if their relative ineptitude as enzymes accounts for the large market share of G-proteins in biological regulation of animals, plants, bacteria, fungi, and other microorganisms. This is because that enzymatic ineptitude offers opportunities to superimpose many additional layers of regulation. The leisurely rates at which G-proteins convert magic totem molecules to dummies, and then release the dummies, invites regulating them with proteins that speed up inactivation (by accelerating removal of the totem's magic, as with the extrinsic timer proteins that turn Ras off) or accelerate release of the dummy (as with the several hundred hormone receptors that tickle Gs and its close relatives, plus a host of proteins that similarly turn on Ras and other G-proteins).

In addition to their versatility as targets for regulation, G-proteins are crucial for so many cell functions because almost everything in life requires correctly set timers. Consequently, G-proteins play key roles in constructing proteins from separate amino acids; exert force to change a cell's shape; move and direct the location of vesicles that carry critical cargo to and from every structure in the cell; control trafficking of small and large molecules into and out of the nucleus; determine the location, migration, and division of cells in embryogenesis; augment or calm the electrical neurons in the brain; and, as emphasized in this book, mediate cell responses to many hormones and neurotransmitters.

If G-protein timers didn't exist, cells would have had to invent a similarly useful timing device.[5]

CHAPTER 11

The 0.7-Angstrom Click

RESOLVING A PARADOX

To avoid the question, Taroh banters with the sushi chef. I ask again: "Did the experiment work? What does it tell us?"

Taroh Iiri is a postdoc in my lab. He is a marvelous scientist, but—as I have learned over the past year—he is often reluctant to tell unpleasant truths. I hoped dinner would loosen him up, but now wonder whether I want to hear his answer. Eventually, sake and maguro work their magic.

"We got it! It's beautiful," he answers, with a delighted smile.

Taroh's smile marked the turning point of a long effort to solve the tantalizing puzzle of a bizarre genetic disease. The disease, new to medical science and very rare, was caused by a mutation in my lab's favorite protein, Gs. But the mutation was subtle, adding only a single tiny oxygen atom to a protein 3,000 times its size. In April we had thought a few experiments would do the trick. Now, in San Francisco's rainy December, we floundered still. The answer lurked in plain view, but we saw only part of it—and even that part was blurred. Finally, Taroh's experiment gave us a new fact: with a nearly audible click, every piece of the puzzle locked into place.

I tell click stories whenever I can, to share the fun. It's almost as much fun to hear a colleague's click story as to tell my own. Now, rather than sharing click stories with scientists in neighboring labs, I shall share this one with you.

What do I mean by "click"? Most people are used to the mundane but satisfying clicks they get from puzzles—the little rush of satisfaction when a jigsaw piece falls into place or the name of a rare bird suddenly links vertical and horizontal rows of a crossword puzzle. Clicks can be part of almost every human activity, but they give more pleasure when the task is harder. Will you ever forget the first time you rode your bike without falling? For adults, a really good click brings the same visceral thrill. Concentrating hard on a problem, you mull it over in the shower, seek advice, and wake up in the middle of the night to think about it some more. The click itself can come out of the blue or develop incrementally, at first without your knowing it. Finally, you discover how to manage a conflict at work, add just the right flourish to an abstract design, come up with a decisive legal argument, or make sense of a haunting but difficult poem. After the click, you want to tell someone about it, to share the pleasure and to feel it again.

———

This story began in 1993, four years after Claudia Landis and Lucia Vallar found the Gs mutations that cause pituitary giantism. First I sensed a premonitory mini-click, a tentative tug of the fish on a line. Searching for something new and different, I was trolling through short abstracts of talks that were to be delivered at a meeting. A little tug in the title of an abstract interrupted the tedium. The tug was a jawbreaker name (pseudohypoparathyroidism) that I knew very well—the name of an inherited endocrine disease caused by a mutation that inactivates Gs, and thus makes patients resistant to effects of hormones that act by stimulating Gs. As I described in chapter 7, the disease results from a mutation that disrupts one of two Gs genes, causing patients' cells to contain only about 50 percent of the normal amount of Gs protein. (This is because cells rapidly destroy the 50 percent encoded by the mutated gene.) The patients suffer from mental retardation, subtle bone defects, and low blood calcium.

The abstract described two boys with identical mutations in one of their two Gs genes. In addition to the hormone-resistance disorder, each suffered from a second, even rarer endocrine disease, called precocious puberty. As two-year-old toddlers, the boys had abundant pubic hair, hair under their arms, fully developed genitalia, and high blood testosterone. To find both rare disorders in the same patient was a real surprise. Indeed, adult males with the hormone resistance disorder often have almost the opposite problem—they can't be fathers, because they make abnormally low numbers of sperm.

I was sure this tug on the line would turn out to be a real fish, and the gene mutation described in the abstract said the fish would be big enough to keep. The mutation was very specific: at position 366 in Gs, it substituted serine for another amino acid, alanine. Involving only one of the 394 building blocks composing Gs, this change would add one oxygen atom to a protein 3,000 times bigger than oxygen.

How could one extra oxygen atom inflict so much woe on these boys and their families? How did it cause not one but *two* rare diseases, resistance to hormones and precocious puberty? The two disorders represented diametrically opposite defects of signal transmission. The hormone-resistant patients have plenty of hormone, but respond to it weakly. Precocious puberty precisely reverses this picture. The testes pour out testosterone, as if in response to hormones, but the hormones that should be elevating testosterone aren't even present. (In normal puberty, the pituitary starts releasing hormones called gonadotropins, which stimulate testosterone secretion by cells in the testes. Gonadotropins in these boys were undetectable.)

The paradox went deeper still. The other elements in the Gs signaling pathway include the hormone receptor (R), adenylyl cyclase (AC), and cyclic AMP, acting in the following order:

$$\text{Hormone} \rightarrow R \rightarrow Gs \rightarrow AC \rightarrow \text{cyclic AMP} \rightarrow \text{Response}$$

Gs, adenylyl cyclase, and cyclic AMP are essential for normal responses to both parathyroid hormone and gonadotropins. In these boys' paradoxical endocrine disorder, we knew that *loss of Gs* causes hormone resistance. This didn't fit with what we knew about the normal testis at puberty, when increased testosterone secretion reflects *increased Gs activity*, which is a change in exactly the

opposite direction. How could the same defective Gs switch relay
the message triggered by one hormone much too weakly in the body,
and simultaneously work overtime to relay spurious signals from
undetectable hormones in the testes?

These questions were on my mind when Taroh arrived in the lab,
fresh from MD and PhD training in Japan. Our first task was to pick
a juicy lab project for him to tackle, one that suited his skills and
piqued our mutual interest. Taroh's PhD research had focused on G
protein biochemistry, and his medical training was in endocrinology,
so it didn't take long for the double-dipper endocrine paradox to rise
to top priority.

I quickly telephoned the abstract's senior author, Neil Van
Dop. As a postdoc in my lab eight years earlier, Neil had identified
the amino acid that is targeted by cholera toxin in transducin, a
molecular relative of Gs. Now on the pediatrics faculty at UCLA, Neil
had initiated a comprehensive survey of mutations in patients with
the hormone resistance disorder. His lab determined the Gs coding
sequence in DNA from blood samples sent by pediatricians from
all over the country. The samples included blood from the unlucky
boys described in the abstract. This was a remarkable coincidence,
because the boys and their families lived in states more than 1,000
miles apart and were unaware of each other's existence. Neither Neil
nor I could guess how the same Gs mutation in these boys caused two
diseases. I suggested we collaborate to figure it out. His lab would
provide the mutant DNA and the clinical story, while Taroh would
purify the mutant Gs protein. Neil agreed. We were ready to go.

As scientists often do, Taroh and I pinned our hopes on something
we already understood. We would explain the boys' precocious
puberty by invoking the functional defect the lab had discovered
in pituitary giantism, four years earlier (described in the preceding
chapter). Gs mutations in that disease abolish the built-in timer that
controls the rate at which Gs turns itself off. We resurrected our old
metaphor, based on the man-made timer that used to control turn-off
of corridor lights in French hotels. (To refresh your memory, look
back at Figure 6-1.) For the hotelkeeper, the timer was designed
to save energy and francs. In the case of Gs, the delayed turnoff

furnishes a molecular memory, lasting less than a dozen seconds, of the momentary hormonal stimulus that turned it on. Such a memory means that a momentary stimulus with hormone elicits a more prolonged activation of Gs, as if a quick jab at your doorbell were to trigger ringing for a full 10 seconds—a sound likely to grab your attention. Similarly, cells probably also use the prolonged cyclic AMP signal to enhance their sensitivity to external signals.)

In the pituitary giants, the Gs mutations inactivated the timer altogether, so that the corridor light stayed on . . . and on and on. The result was elevated cyclic AMP in pituitary tumors, which caused them to secrete too much growth hormone. The analogy with excess testosterone secreted by the boys' testes was too obvious to ignore. True, the specific amino acid replaced by the boys' mutation was located at a position in Gs far from either of the amino acids affected in the mutant Gs of pituitary giants. But we strongly suspected that both sets of mutations inactivated the timer.

To test this suspicion before attempting to purify wild-type and mutant Gs proteins, Taroh planned an easier experiment: he would compare cyclic AMP responses triggered by the boys' mutant Gs to responses triggered by the mutant Gs found in a pituitary tumor or by wild-type Gs. Rather than literally inject the respective proteins into cells, Taroh would repeat a trick we had borrowed from others earlier in the recombinant DNA revolution—that is, he would induce the cells to make the mutant or wild-type proteins by introducing DNAs for the respective mutant or wild-type genes into separate sets of monkey cells in culture.

The results titillated us, but were also puzzling. As we knew it would, the pituitary mutant impressively elevated cyclic AMP—the corridor light stayed on. Gs with the boys' alanine-to-serine mutation elevated cyclic AMP also, but very weakly—indeed, to a degree only modestly greater than we saw in cells expressing recombinant wild-type Gs. Why should the boys' Gs generate dimmer light than the pituitary mutant? We made up a provisional story—perhaps for some reason the light shines more brightly in testis cells than in the monkey cells Taroh used. Not very convincing, but for now we would leave it at that.

The next result was more unsettling. Using an antibody, we measured recombinant Gs in the cells. Those expressing wild-type Gs or the pituitary mutant contained equally large amounts of Gs protein. Cells with DNA encoding the boys' mutant Gs, however, contained little or no mutant protein. Because this mutant Gs was invisible but nonetheless mysteriously able to trigger a modest increase in cyclic AMP, Taroh dubbed it the "stealth mutant". After two months of experiments, we were not much closer to answering our questions. Cyclic AMP measurements would not tell the tale, we decided. Instead, to show that the stealth and pituitary mutations altered Gs function in similar ways would require hard-core biochemistry.

Clearly, Taroh's next task would be to compare the rates at which the stealth mutant and wild-type Gs turn themselves off—that is, to compare how often their respective magic-removing activities convert the magic totem to a dummy totem (GTP to GDP, for the cognoscenti). We imagined that the stealth mutant, emulating the pituitary mutant, would exorcise the magic at a vanishingly slow rate, too slow to measure.

————

As research partners, Taroh and I were an odd match. Taroh, in his early thirties, was slight, round-faced, and politely reserved. Always clad in a button-down shirt and neatly pressed trousers, he spoke slowly, carefully choosing precise words in a language he was rapidly mastering. In contrast, I was voluble, enthusiastic, and more emphatic than precise. I was also 20 years older, bearded, given to episodic corpulence, and scruffily attired. (Most students, and postdocs—like the Principal Investigators, or PIs—in our labs wear jeans, sneakers, and wrinkled T-shirts. In experimental biology labs, it's almost a uniform.)

Another difference between us was the cultural gulf between the USA and Japan. Not used to constant deference or polite indirection in postdocs, I slowly began to realize that Taroh was pulling his punches in conversation. He never contradicted me, the PI, even when he was sure my idea for an experiment was wrong. Instead, he would respectfully agree and blithely do the experiment his way. Sometimes I would insist, and occasionally I was even right. More often, Taroh would tell me the result of the experiment he had chosen to do, subtly hinting gratitude for my astute (and sometimes imaginary) suggestion that he do it. As I tried to coax Taroh to be more direct, I learned one source of his indirection: astonishingly, on several occasions in Japan his comments had offended senior scientists, who had warned him that he spoke too frankly and should mend his ways. He was determined not to fall into the same predicament again.

At the lab bench, Taroh was meticulous and exact, with the fabled work ethic of Japanese scientists. Often he worked straight through the night, and was found dozing at his desk the next morning. One unusual behavior mystified his labmates. Taroh would sometimes spend hours carefully *watching* a kind of experiment everyone else allowed to proceed without close supervision. In gel electrophoresis, a routine procedure in many labs, an electric field induces proteins to migrate slowly through small pores in a gel. Because small proteins migrate faster than big ones, we often use this procedure to separate proteins of different sizes from one another. By occasionally checking the migration of a blue dye that moves rapidly through the gel, the experimenter knows when to turn off the electric field and stop the experiment. Lab members swore that Taroh watched every minute of the dye's progress. More amusing than watching paint dry, I suppose, but still bizarre. Nonetheless, Taroh's strategy seemed to work: proteins in his gels separated more cleanly than in anyone else's.

More amazing, though, was Taroh's serene disregard for a serious physical disability. Accidental damage to his hip in infancy had left him with an awkward lurching gait, which was slow and, when first encountered, painful to watch. Taroh went about his business so unperturbed that we soon forgot his disability. He met experimental obstacles with similarly brave serenity. If one approach failed, he simply planned another, insisting, with a seraphic smile, that the right experiment would soon explain the disease we found so mysterious.

I was not so sure. Fretting about every puzzling result, I would ask: Are we over-interpreting a trivial finding? Or are we ignoring an important one? I knew my most useful skill as a researcher intertwined closely with my most grievous flaw. My forte was the ability to combine disparate pieces of a puzzle into a convincing story. Sometimes, to my delight, the stories proved true. More than once, however, I had been burned by a lovely scenario that explained everything—until it didn't. So I kept recalling the Red Queen's extravagant boast in *Alice in Wonderland*: "Why, sometimes I've believed as many as six impossible things before breakfast." I might not match her productivity, but often managed to believe at least one impossible thing before dinner. Teaching students not to fall in love with their hypotheses, I remained a pushover for elegant ideas. The corrective, of course, was to test such ideas more rigorously. A disagreeable purgative, yes—but it worked, at least when I took it.

I should mention one more difference between Taroh and me. He knew much more real biochemistry. I understood the principles, but he knew how to do the experiments. Taroh's biochemical skills were to prove essential.

———

Taroh set out to purify the mutant and wild-type Gs molecules, so that he could put them through their paces in test tubes. Al Gilman's lab had worked out procedures for purifying Gs, in the course of work that would soon earn him a Nobel. Compared to these pioneers, we had two huge advantages. First, they had already shown how to perform the trick. Second, in the meantime the recombinant DNA revolution had made it much easier to obtain proteins in large amounts, often greater than could be extracted from normal tissues. By now it was almost routine to incorporate DNA from a mammalian gene into *Escherichia coli*, a common gut bacterium, to grow up scads of bacteria making the protein of interest, and then to harvest it for purification. In Taroh's hands, the bacteria made Gs in fair amounts, but the protein was hard to purify. Months of painstaking work produced minuscule amounts of partially pure protein, barely enough for our first experiments. The hard work renewed our respect for the Gilman lab's prowess.

Right at the outset, Taroh's Gs preparations told us that the stealth mutant was less stealthy in bacteria than in animal cells. To determine Gs abundance precisely, Taroh used a super-magic totem, which was a chemical analog of the magic totem designed to fit tightly into its binding pocket in Gs but resist conversion to a dummy totem. A radioactive version of this totem whose magic could not be dispelled made it possible to "count" G protein molecules in a test tube by measuring radioactivity bound to protein. The bacteria did accumulate a smaller number of stealth molecules than wild-type Gs molecules, but the difference was far less than predicted by the mutant's stealth in monkey cells.

The ability to count Gs molecules in an extract set the stage for a huge surprise. Measuring the rate at which a known number of Gs molecules converted magic to dummy totems, Taroh found that, on the average, one stealth mutant molecule performed this conversion every 17 seconds—almost 20 times *more* often than wild-type Gs, which accomplished the de-magicking act every five minutes or so. This behavior was opposite to that of the pituitary mutants, with their locked-on switch. The half-life of magic totem molecules bound to the latter mutants was too long to measure, but certainly greater than 30 min. (As I described previously, this "half-life" is the time taken for half the magic molecules bound to a population of Gs molecules to be converted to dummies.) How could both the pituitary mutants and the stealth mutant elevate cyclic AMP, when the first could not turn off at all, and the stealth mutant turned itself off more frequently than normal? Curiouser and curiouser.

We began to entertain an intriguing explanation for the stealth mutant's apparently faster rate of converting GTP to GDP. Perhaps the mutant's timing device turned it off quite normally, but the stealth switch merrily turned itself on again—almost immediately, every time. It would be as if an indefatigable bellhop were to flip the corridor light back on as soon as the timer turned it off: guests could take their time searching for the right room, because the corridor would be illuminated most of the time. The stimulated hormone receptor behaves rather like such a bellhop, of course, turning Gs on over and over until the hormone disappears. In this case, however, the bellhop was invisible—suggesting that Gs might turn on all by itself.

The idea was new to us, and it took some time for Taroh and me to get our heads around it. The diagram in Figure 11-1, combined with the accompanying Table, may help to make the timing clearer.

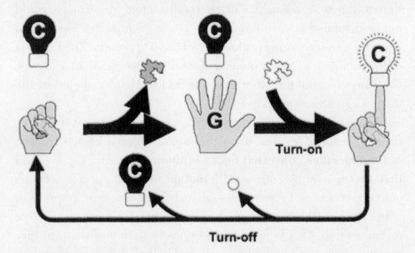

Figure 11-1. Gs defect in precocious puberty. Mutant Gs binds the magic totem weakly and releases it rapidly (thick arrows, left). The magic totem is present in large concentrations, however, so that the mutant remains in the inactive, dummy totem-bound state (fist, extreme left) for a very short time—6 seconds, perhaps, in each cycle—and transits much more often (heavy arrows, right) into its active state, with magic totem bound (hand with finger extended. Consequently, it spends almost two thirds of its time in the active state (see Table).

In our Gs activation/inactivation scheme, normal Gs spends most of its time in an inactive state (the fist-shaped hand in the Figure), which is maintained by the dummy totem occupying a binding pocket in the Gs molecule. In the absence of input from the hormone receptor, the dummy key falls spontaneously out of the pocket quite rarely, perhaps once every 5 minutes or so. With the dummy gone, another magic totem molecule can enter the newly empty pocket (that is, the open hand in the center of the diagram). The new magic causes the hand to form a fist again, with index finger extended to activate adenylyl cyclase (symbolized by the light bulb in the diagram). The finger is extended until the timer removes the magic, whereupon Gs returns to the inactive (fist) state.[1]

Table. Normal and mutant Gs proteins spend different amounts of time in the three states that comprise the activation/inactivation cycle.

		State of Gs		Turnover rate
	Fist (inactive, dummy totem)	Open hand (binding pocket empty)	Pointing finger (Active, magic totem)	(Magic converted to Dummy, per hour)
Normal Gs	5 minutes	<1 second	10 seconds	11.4
Normal Gs + hormone	1-2 seconds*	<1 second	10 seconds	300*
Pituitary Giants	5 minutes	<1 second	>30 minutes	<2
Precocious Puberty	6 seconds	<1 second	10 seconds	225

*For normal Gs responding to stimulation by a hormone receptor, duration of the "fist" state (bound to the dummy totem) is variable, because activation occurs at a rate that depends on the receptor and the hormone.

Mutations could increase the activity of Gs in either of two ways. First, as we found in tumors of pituitary giants, the mutant protein may not be able to flip its switch off, so that the magic totem maintains its magic for many minutes, while cyclic AMP continues to accumulate (see the previous chapter). We were now imagining a very different possibility (Figure 11-1): the boys' mutation might have rendered

Gs unable to hold the dummy totem firmly in its pocket (or fist, in the metaphor) for more than a few seconds. As a result, a new magic totem molecule would enter the site much more frequently, just as it does when hormone receptors stimulate normal Gs. Thus magic totems would be converted to dummies more frequently—perhaps as often as once every 17 seconds, as Taroh's initial experiments suggested. Of those 17 seconds, less than one was needed for the magic totem to enter the empty pocket, and 10-12 to remove its magic,[1] leaving the dummy to enjoy an extremely short sojourn, of perhaps 5-7 seconds, in the pocket. If so, a mutant Gs molecule would be active almost two thirds of the time, rather than the brief 10 seconds enjoyed, every five minutes or so, by normal Gs.

We liked this idea because it generated clear predictions, of a kind we could test. First, in test tubes the stealth mutant would not need hormone receptors to stimulate cyclic AMP production; instead, cyclic AMP would increase in the presence of magic totem alone. In contrast, wild-type Gs would increase cyclic AMP accumulation only in the presence of an activated hormone receptor. Second, we could measure rapid release of the dummy totem by using a radioactive super-magic totem (that is, a chemical analog of the magic totem designed to fit tightly into its binding pocket in Gs but resist conversion to a dummy totem, as described above). The radioactive compound would presumably enter the stealth mutant's binding pocket more frequently than the wild-type pocket, which grasps the dummy so tightly. Taroh's data hinted that this second prediction might be correct, but rigorous tests would require larger amounts of the stealth mutant and wild-type Gs.

Why were we were so eager to identify rapid release of dummy totems as a critical clue to the puzzle? To be sure, it neatly tied the increase in magic-to-dummy converting activity—otherwise quite paradoxical—to elevated cyclic AMP in the testis and to precocious puberty. Still, the idea had serious weaknesses. First, the whole story might reflect flawed experiments rather than genuine biology. This was because Taroh had been able to get only small amounts of purified protein, which made the totem conversion measurements variable and possibly inaccurate. Second, we had measured conversion activity without directly assessing dummy totem release. The third weakness was crucial. Rapid release of dummies failed utterly to explain the boys' resistance to hormones, and thus did nothing to resolve the paradox at the heart of the whole project. Were we beginning to succumb to the Red Queen's tempting advice? Why dally with an explanation that ignored half the paradox?

As a good biochemist, Taroh was surer than I that his results were "real." The idea appealed to me for a different reason, at once theoretical and esthetic. Rapid dummy release from the stealth mutant's binding pocket "clicked" enticingly with recently published 3D images of transducin,[2] the relative of Gs that transmits light signals in the retina. I was beginning to fall under the spell of 3D models of tiny proteins, which I loved for their cold, lambent beauty. My fascination with protein structures first flared 30 years earlier, in medical school, when I constructed a crude 3D model of hemoglobin, the red protein in red blood cells. I didn't begin to understand the math required to translate spots on an X-ray film into a 3D structure,[3] but was thrilled to learn that a protein had a real shape. Then the rigors of medical school stole my attention away, and I didn't think about protein structures again until 1985, when the structure of an Elongation Factor told us what the GTP/GDP binding pocket of G proteins must look like. But then we didn't have a structure of transducin or Gs, so we satisfied ourselves with imagining how Gs might resemble other GTP-binding proteins, and creating an imaginary Gs structure as a basis for designing experiments.

Now, in 1993, Joe Noel in Paul Sigler's lab had solved the structure of transducin,[2] and I fell head over heels in love with it. With the help of a computer, I could twirl scale models of transducin, an elongation factor, or Ras in any direction. I could ask the computer to color each shiny amino acid according to any scheme I chose, and use 3D glasses to watch it and its individual atoms dance in concert with all the amino acids. This dance revealed how each protein's unique amino acid chain folds together and allowed me to explore the surface protuberances and clefts that allow a protein to recognize and embrace another molecule. The cold beauty of a 3D model revealed tantalizing glimpses of libidinous molecular rites that keep us warm and alive. (See Figure 11-2 for the structure of Gs itself, which was solved later, and turned out to be very similar to that of transducin.)

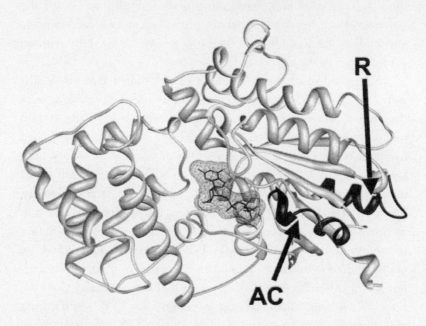

Figure 11-2. Model of 3D structure of Gs. The magic totem, GTP (chicken-wire structure), is bound in a pocket in the middle of the structure, with the "extra region" (see chapter 8) on the left and the Ras-like region on the right. The structure (spirals, arrows, and loops, all in gray or black) shown represents the main chain of the chain of amino acids, and does not show the side chains that distinguish each of the 20 possible amino acids. The black parts of the structure are those that interact with receptor and adenylyl cyclase, as indicated by arrows drawn from R and AC, respectively. Image prepared by Elaine Meng, Department of Pharmaceutical Chemistry, UCSF, from the reported 3D structure of Gsα [RK Sunahara, JJ Tesmer, AG Gilman, SR Sprang (1997) Crystal structure of the adenylyl cyclase activator Gsalpha. Science 278: 1943-1947].

One intermolecular embrace deeply entranced both Taroh and me. In the 3D model of transducin, the protein wrapped itself tightly around a chemical analog of the magic totem, which nestled snugly into a binding pocket lined by about two dozen amino acids.

One of these, Taroh and I thought, corresponded to the amino acid affected by the Gs mutation described in Neil Van Dop's abstract. We knew that similarities in amino acid sequence predict similar 3D structures, but it still felt like something of a leap to assume such a close resemblance between the 3D structures of transducin and Gs, for which a 3D structure was not yet available.

Once the leap was made, though, it was easy to see that adding an oxygen atom to the relevant amino acid would displace the magic totem molecule from its normal position. The displacement would be minuscule, a distance of about 0.7 angstrom (Figure 11-3).

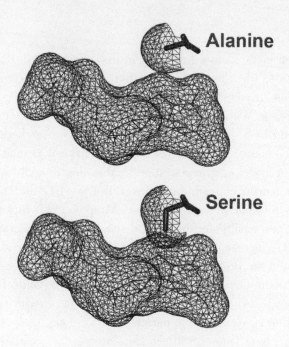

Figure 11-3. The 0.7 Å nudge. Views of the part of the magic totem (that is, GTP, on the left) that would touch alanine (top panel) or that would be overlapped by serine in the precocious puberty mutant (bottom panel). The serine's extra bulge represents its oxygen atom, which is not present in alanine. In a real Gs protein this oxygen would "nudge" GTP about 0.7 Å downward (rather than overlap it, as shown in this virtual image). Images prepared by Elaine Meng, using the 3D structure of Gsα, as indicated in the legend to Figure 11-2.

This was small even in relation to the long axis of a G-protein itself (70 angstroms) or to the depth of the GTP-binding pocket (15 angstroms). If our idea was right, evolution must machine proteins to remarkably close tolerances. By way of reference, a human hair is one million angstroms thick. (Does Rabbit Angstrom, John Updike's big-as-life creation, owe his name to this unimaginably small unit?) Still, we imagined that this small displacement might be enough to nudge dummy totems out of the binding pocket—just as gluing a big marble into the pocket of his mitt could make the catcher more likely to drop a pitched ball.

———

Seven months after Taroh began his experiments, we still had no good idea why the stealth mutation caused hormone resistance. Even when I tried to focus on other projects, I couldn't stop worrying about this one. Without harder evidence, even the precocious puberty story hung by a gossamer thread. It seemed far-fetched, at best. Using a computer, we could insert an extra oxygen atom at the right place in a model of transducin and guess that it would nudge the dummy totem out of its binding pocket. But, since Gs and transducin were not the same protein, could we extrapolate this hint to the Gs mutation responsible for the boys' disease? Even if we allowed that notion to seduce us, it failed utterly to explain hormone resistance. I presented the problem to fellow PIs, students, postdocs, friends at other institutions, and just about anybody who would listen. No matter how we twisted the data, we could not come up with a plausible explanation for resistance to parathyroid hormone.

Over a long Thursday afternoon, Taroh and I wrestled with our ignorance. Why was this a "stealth" mutant, present in much lower amounts than normal Gs? We knew that cells replace every one of their proteins at fairly frequent intervals, so that each individual protein molecule exists for a finite lifetime before the cell dumps in into a cellular garbage grinder to be chewed up. And after all, if an amino acid sequence directs the precise folding pattern of each new protein, a mistake in that sequence can prevent it from folding properly. In fact, mutations responsible for other diseases often make proteins unstable, sending them to the grinder before their appointed time—so the boys' mutation could make Gs unstable also, accelerating its travel to the garbage. By reducing the mutant protein's activity outside the testis, this would account for hormone resistance. But we needed something more: perhaps something special about testis cells made the mutant protein more stable, allowing it to release GDP more frequently, and thereby to stimulate itself. This would account for elevated cyclic AMP and precocious puberty.

Taroh and I sensed that we should have raised this idea much earlier, but even now we couldn't come up with a satisfying way to explain why the testis should stabilize a protein that was unstable everywhere else. It felt like we were stumbling our way to some kind of answer, but we had an uneasy feeling we were ignoring an obvious clue. Such mistakes are common, unfortunately—scientists do ignore obvious clues in the lab, time and again.

The next day, Friday, was my turn to present the lab's research to the Faculty Signaling Club, an informal monthly meeting of colleagues interested in cell signaling. The small audience—half a dozen or so—offered a welcome opportunity to seek advice about a devilishly unsolved puzzle. I outlined the quandary of hormone resistance in boys with the stealth mutation and precocious puberty, and then asked: "So, what is different about the testes?"

The answer came in a flash: "The testes are cooler," said a colleague, Shaun Coughlin. Shaun went on to explain why. It is not only that the testes hang in a sac separate from the body, he pointed out. In addition, a uniquely engineered arrangement of blood vessels assures that testis temperature stays 5° (centigrade) cooler than the rest of the body. Sheepishly recollecting a medical school lecture on cool testes, I spluttered that he might have a good idea. I should have remembered that male fertility requires cool testes: at body temperature, precursor cells don't develop into sperm. If testis temperature were higher, none of us would be here.

Recovering from my embarrassment, I realized how neatly the temperature difference might solve our conundrum. If the stealth mutant protein were to unfold at 37°, cells in the body would destroy it. In the testis, at 32°, the mutant might be stable and highly active.

Taroh was out of town, so I had the weekend to ponder. I had seen the key to a puzzle come out of the blue before. After months or years of pushing, pulling, and prodding a problem, a new fact suddenly makes everything clear. The new fact may come from an experiment in the lab, a finding by others, or, as in this case, from the insight of a scientist not directly involved in the experiments. On the other hand, elegant ideas are often wrong. Many mutant proteins are sensitive to changes in temperature, but could a mere 5° decrease prevent the stealth mutant from unfolding? Afraid to embrace the new idea, I vacillated between elation and doubt.

On Monday morning, Taroh shared none of my doubts. Instead, he politely reminded me of another relevant fact. The stealth mutant was much less stealthy in bacteria, perhaps because we grew bacteria at 30°, rather than the 37° used for tissue culture cells. He couldn't wait to set up the decisive experiment in mammalian cells.

Taroh finished the experiment two days later, just before we set off for sushi. To savor the result a while longer he had resolved to delay telling me, but finally the revelation was too beautiful to keep to himself. (My personality, in contrast, always makes me want to blurt out the good news immediately, perhaps because I'm afraid that if I wait it might not be true. Many scientists hang on to their discoveries for a while, however, in order to savor them as Taroh did.)

In any case, what a revelation the new results turned out to be! We were beside ourselves with joy. Rapture is not easy to reconstruct, but I do remember a lot of hand shaking and backslapping—plus, probably, more sake.

The results were crystal-clear. Wild-type Gs behaved exactly as expected: its abundance in mammalian cells was identical at 37° and 32°. The stealth mutant, of course, was almost undetectable in cells grown at 37°, but—much to our delight—abundant in cells grown at the lower temperature. Two hours after Taroh cranked the temperature back up to 37°, the stealth mutant protein disappeared. Yes, the mutant was unstable at body temperature, but splendidly stable at testis temperature.

In our new mood we were sure the dummy totem release experiments would come out exactly as we hoped, revealing a novel mechanism for G protein activation by mutation. Even the shaky inferences we made from looking at transducin's totem binding pocket now seemed likely to be correct. A few months confirmed all our backslapping bravado. The Red Queen be damned: intuition was right on all counts! By tweaking the purification protocol, Taroh obtained much larger amounts of normal and mutant Gs and showed that the stealth mutant *did* release dummy totems much more frequently than wild-type did (see the accompanying Table). Later, when the 3D structure of Gs was published, the binding pocket of Gs proved a perfect replica of the pocket in transducin—the amino acid mutated in the stealth mutant rubbed against the bound dummy totem in Gs just as it did in transducin.

As an extra bonus, abundant pure protein and a bit of nifty biochemistry gave us a precise molecular explanation for the stealth mutant's stealth and hormone resistance in the body. Taroh showed that the stealth mutant and wild-type Gs were equally stable in both their inactive and active states. Neither unfolds when its pocket is filled with dummy totem or magic totem, but both are more likely to unfold when their binding pockets are empty, because the unbound state is not stable. This empty period, between releasing the dummy and its replacement by the magic molecule (that is, the open hand shown in Figure 11-1), is equally unstable in both the wild-type and the mutant protein. As the Table indicates, the difference between the two proteins is how often they pass through the empty state. In fact, the extra oxygen atom sticking into the pocket of the stealth mutant causes it to empty that pocket 225 times every hour, vs. 11 times per hour for wild-type Gs. This gives the mutant protein 20 opportunities to unfold for every one opportunity afforded the normal protein. Because unstable proteins always degrade faster at higher temperatures, this difference made the boys' Gs disappear in the body, but their Gs was stable enough in the testis to drive production of testosterone. In this way, nudging the dummy totem, GDP, 0.7 angstroms from its normal location is directly responsible for both precocious puberty and hormone resistance.

———

For years I remembered—and told—the story in just this way. But memory is often mistaken, as I discovered from re-reading notes I had taken at the time. Twice a week, I would jot down telegraphic accounts of what I was thinking about findings in the lab and ideas for future experiments. Among these, I found an account of Taroh's and my Thursday discussion, the day before Shaun came up with his revelation. The notes describe our asking why the stealth mutant should survive in the testis, but not the body. Apparently, we came up with three conjectures—all of which I found equally unappealing. First, gonadotropin receptors, present in the testis but absent in body cells, might associate with the stealth mutant and protect it from degradation. Alternatively, persistent activation of the stealth mutant by repeated encounters with magic totems might unmoor it from protective docking sites at the periphery of the cell, as the lab had recently found with a quite different (and man-made) Gs mutant.

The third idea was just as sketchy and tentative, indicating that I didn't quite believe or even understand it. Beginning with a lame tautology, the relevant passage went on to ask an almost throw-away question: "Different rates of degradation might be expected if testis cells are postulated to degrade the mutant more slowly . . . . Is the degradation faster at 37° than at a slightly lower temperature in the testis?" Finally, the notes ask whether the stealth mutant's stealth would diminish if cells were grown at a temperature lower than the 37° used in routine tissue culture.

For many years after that time, I remembered a sudden dramatic revelation that resolved the paradox of hormone resistance and precocious puberty. But that was not the real story. Instead, we followed a meandering, hesitant path, glimpsing the solution indistinctly one moment, discounting it the next, and eventually stumbling over it when a friend reminded me of something I already knew. Whatever I may have told myself, real clicks rarely come right out of the blue. But the click was real nonetheless, and we relished it! We had a novel, internally consistent explanation for a bizarre, unprecedented genetic disease. (Later, we read that the striking pigmentation of Siamese cats constitutes a kind of precedent. A mutated component of the pigment-making machinery produces dark hairs in the feet and tips of these cats' ears, where skin temperature is low.)

Now that the rapture has receded, what difference did it make to explain the molecular basis of a syndrome that combines hormone resistance with precocious puberty? Unfortunately, knowing the consequences of a 0.7-angstrom jiggle in Gs did nothing to help the two afflicted boys. We did suggest a maneuver that might have mitigated one of their two diseases: wrapping the testes in knitted wool might warm them enough to destroy the stealth mutant and reverse precocious puberty. (A parallel approach induces reversible sterility in animals.) The boys' families elected not to try this untested approach, which in any case would have done nothing for the boys' other symptoms.

In contrast, Taroh and I reaped huge but intangible benefits: the fun and excitement of pursuing the mystery, the satisfaction of the click at the end, and the opportunity to re-live the experience by telling the story.

That said, however, I have to admit that different people get their clicks in different ways. For instance, consider this real-life response to the story I have told here.

A young woman called me from London, saying she worked for the scientific journal that would soon publish our paper.[4] Her telephone voice—in an English accent that mixed clipped precision with a sexy drawl—got my immediate attention. "Dr. Bourne, I see you say testicles are cool. Tell me what you mean?"

I launched into an eloquent three-minute disquisition on blood vessels to the testis, male fertility, and testis temperature. But I sensed I was losing her attention when she repeated the question in a different way: "Do you mean to tell me that testicles are cooler than the rest of the body?" I confidently assured her the answer was yes.

Her instant reply: "I must say, Dr. Bourne, that has not been at all my own experience!"

CHAPTER 12

The Fulcrum

WORKING TOGETHER

I've already stressed, over and over, that discovery almost always depends on more than one person, because two minds working together are much more powerful than one. One example, a pervading theme of this book, is the interaction between two researchers, one senior and one junior. Early on, I played the junior role, supervised by successive lab directors. Later I became the senior party, advising postdocs and graduate students in my own lab. Regardless of which role I took, the interaction has always felt direct, personal, and intense. In academic experimental biology labs, such interactions serve as the essential fulcrum for harnessing the energy that makes virtually everything happen.

"Mentoring," the current academic buzzword for this relation between senior and junior researchers, conjures up a tweedy advisor and a whiff of pomposity. "Apprenticing" emphasizes the junior partner, but I like it better, because it smacks of the shop and is rooted in a verb that means "to learn." But I want to talk about both partners in this chapter, and so will refer more generally to the "interaction" between the student (or postdoc), on the one hand, and the research supervisor or Principal Investigator (PI), on the other.

The core of this interaction is economic. Like an attending physician at a university hospital or a partner in a law firm, a PI mentor in a lab takes responsibility for teaching smart young people how to do the job, in exchange for their willingness to work hard, many hours of day and night, at relatively low pay. At my institution, graduate students and postdoctoral fellows enter the lab about 10 a.m., five days a week, and return home 10-14 hours later. Often they work long hours on weekends or holidays, as well. At a beginning salary of about $27,000 per year, the graduate student obtains a PhD degree after about five years, and devotes the following five or six years to working as a postdoc, usually at a different institution, with a beginning yearly salary of around $37,000. Finally she or he will be ready to take an independent research position (at a higher salary) in academia or in a biotech company.

The interaction is not an equal one. In an academic lab, the PI sets research priorities for everyone who works in the lab, determines their salaries, confers raises and promotions, and approves award of the PhD. The PI's most critical power stems from writing the crucial recommendations that often decide what kind of job the student or postdoc will get on leaving the lab. Fortunately, this power is not absolute, but is instead buffered by ineluctable necessity—that is, by the lab's nearly absolute dependence on the cheap, highly skilled labor of students and postdocs. I am not sure whether the economic survival of partners in law firms and professors of medicine depends so strongly on their supervisees. Certainly, however, most labs at my institution could not survive without their young people.

I have the impression that the apprenticeship arrangement in biology labs is more personal and intense than analogous arrangements in most medical training programs or law firms.[1] A PhD's learning experience is supervised by a very small number of primary mentors—usually one for the PhD and one for the postdoctoral fellowship—compared to the many partners in a law firm or clinical professors in medical academia. Consequently, doctors and lawyers proudly cite the hospital or law firm where they were trained, while PhDs trace their scientific lineages and research styles back through generations of individual mentors. In addition, PIs in our labs probably exert greater efforts to "place" young people in the best possible slot at the next level of training or in a permanent position.

My own apprenticeships followed different courses with each of my three main mentors. Gordon Tomkins was a magnificent mentor, whose style and substance I try to mimic even today. In multiple ways, Bernard Brodie taught me how not to run a lab. Ken Melmon taught me a great deal, some of which I would have preferred to avoid learning. One out of three doesn't sound like a very good score, but that one made a huge difference.

How does the scorecard look with me as mentor, rather than apprentice? Pondering this question, I reviewed my interactions with the 59 young people who worked in my lab from 1977 to 2007. It seemed presumptuous and even a tad crazy for me to grade these interactions, I thought, but at the least I should propose a criterion for judging their success or failure. To do so, I had to think about what worked, what did not, and why.

Here's what I think I figured out.

First, what happens when the interaction with a student works well? Earlier chapters described many examples of such interactions, including those with Zvi Farfel or Taroh Iiri as postdocs, and me as mentor. Chapter 5, with Gordon Tomkins in the mentor role, furnishes a third example. Rather than re-tell the stories, let me point out what they share. In two cases, both parties entered the interaction with a strongly felt need and something real to offer on their own. Gordon needed an energetic person who knew how to measure cyclic AMP, and I needed to learn from his capacity for delight in asking and answering questions. In Taroh's case, I needed a superb biochemist, and he needed to work with someone who looked at the world in a different way from his previous mentors, and was more willing to take his ideas seriously.

Zvi and I began working together under different circumstances. At first neither of us had a clear idea of what we needed from the other, or even what was on offer. As a result, I showed little interest in his repeated suggestions about the possible basis of a hormone resistance disease. Eventually, as I told the story in chapter 7, I realized that Zvi's idea was right. Until that point I, as the titular mentor, was not doing my job.

I should have known better from working with Gordon. The core value of our interaction was not his lightning brilliance, his wit and imagination, or his penetrating intuition. And it was not that he had all these qualities in much greater abundance than I, although he did. The real core was simple. Once we got to know one another, Gordon and I were engaged *together* in asking exciting questions. To me that mutual engagement made an enormous difference, revealing nuances I had not suspected and making every question more exciting, but also showing me that I could contribute to finding answers. In a negative way, my interaction with Brodie supports the same point. Both he and I began our interaction with the assumption that the Mentor (capital M, in this case!) would impart wise advice, the Student would follow it, and Success would inevitably accrue. That didn't happen, of course, nor did Brodie and I ever work and think together. (Earlier in his career, he and his colleagues certainly did so, and Success did accrue.)

These examples, and many more from my experience as a PI, prompt me to propose that core value, mutual engagement, as the principal criterion for "grading" the interaction between me and the young people who passed through my lab. Every example of such an interaction is necessarily idiosyncratic, because we all bring to it needs and personal qualities in fantastic varieties and contradictory mixtures. Given that immense variety, I judge that the interaction truly works if I have the sense that the student or postdoc and I engage our minds to tackle a problem together, and that the mutual engagement sustains itself over time—for months, at least, and in some cases for years. If so, the interaction should be awarded an "A" grade. Most of the interactions I reviewed met this criterion.

As I expected, their successes correlated, if only roughly, with those of the corresponding research project in my lab and with the student's or postdoc's subsequent success in science. For our purposes it is important, I think, to assess the interaction rather than the student, postdoc, or mentor. Crucially, a successful interaction depends equally on both parties, because both must contribute to answering a question or resolving a problem. At the same time, nothing about the criterion of mutual engagement implies that the parties begin with equal knowledge and expertise and finish by contributing equally to every discovery. In all 59 cases, I had the advantage of age, as well as experience in thinking about experiments and how to evaluate evidence. Almost always, I knew more about the question and the field, as the director of a lab certainly should. My asymmetric interaction with Gordon allowed me to learn valuable lessons and later to teach them and other lessons to my own students and postdocs, as I describe below. In every case, though, it bears emphasizing that both participants in the interaction bear equal responsibility for making mutual engagement work. If it is successful, both will learn and both will teach, in the end learning together more than either thought possible at the outset.

One characteristic is common to every successful interaction I have had with students—that is, I look forward to renewing each of them. I have warm memories of each person, and am curious to know what she or he is doing, thinking, feeling, and planning. Most of them, I suspect, feel the same way about me.

What about less successful examples of this interaction? One way or another, in these cases "mutual engagement" was stunted or lacking. Most of these students or postdocs published good papers based on work in my lab, and several became distinguished and successful scientists. But for one reason or another, the two of us failed to "reach" one another in a consistent, sustained fashion. I can't be certain where the problem really lay in any case. Although my natural inclination would to trace the problem to the student or postdoc, rather than to myself, this cannot be a correct judgment in every instance—after all, Brodie would probably have judged me in one or more of these same ways, and many students or postdocs have surely detected my own faults, as I did his.

The interactions I assess as outright failures are fortunately few. In one case the postdoc (Julian, in chapter 8) turned out—after he left the lab—to be mentally ill, and another postdoc erroneously accused two labmates of fabricating their data (a story not touched on in this book). One or two others presented problems—laziness and incompetence at the lab bench—that consumed a great deal of everyone's time, and made mutual engagement impossible. In all these cases, my principal mistake was in hiring the individual to begin with. The warning signs were there, but I was not smart enough to read them.

Before proceeding to describe further examples, I should say that my views are not shared by every PI. Many feel that terms like "mentoring" and "mutual engagement" are at best beside the point and at worst hypocritical prating, too touchy-feely for real scientists. Like many of our predecessors in the first half of the 20th century, these no-nonsense PIs rely on the idea of research training as an essentially Darwinian struggle, in which the fittest learn how to do it right, while the rest fail. I think they are wrong, even in assessing their own behavior. Instead, it appears to me that many of these individuals preach Darwinian survival but in practice get things done by following the principle of mutual engagement. Most successful scientists, now as in the past, engage young people to collaborate as valued colleagues in their labs.

In this connection, let me cite the testimony of a friend and colleague, Roger Nicoll. Roger is a highly respected senior neuroscientist at UCSF, whose research lab stands out for its productivity and originality. His experiments and ideas, along with those of his former students and postdocs, have led the way in understanding behavior of synapses in the brain. I asked Roger to tell me the secret of good mentoring. The trick, he said, is to "make the students and postdocs think they are your colleagues, as smart and committed as you are." Because it is nearly impossible to pull off such a fake successfully, the mentor has to believe it himself. Roger's Rule goes like this: "Trust, respect, and like the people in your lab. Talk with them about everything and anything. Treat them like colleagues, and they will be."

In terms of Roger's Rule, think for a minute about my conversation with Zvi Farfel, many years ago. I came into that conversation assuming that Zvi was wrong, and therefore not a real colleague. Fortunately, Zvi was stiff-necked enough to pay no attention to my arguments. By refusing to stop pushing, he finally showed me he was definitely a colleague, regardless of what I might have thought. At that point Roger had not yet enunciated his Rule, so I had to learn it the hard way.

In practice, Roger's Rule is eminently practical, even essential, rather than touchy-feely romanticism. But it isn't always easy to follow, as we'll see.

———

As I have tried to emphasize, this interaction is different for every PI, every student, and every postdoc, because we all differ from one another. Still, certain issues come up over and over, in almost every case. I can succinctly summarize one of these with this edict, which I would display in huge red letters over the entrance to every laboratory:

Don't just do something. Think!

Can a highfaluting intellectual endeavor like experimental biology attract a student who has trouble thinking? Or a faculty member with the same trouble? The answer is yes, on both counts. Let me first describe the problem, and then talk about why it happens.

My first example is a third-year graduate student I shall call James. I was not his advisor, but served as a member of his thesis committee. At our most recent committee meeting, James had justly taken pride in telling us about how he overcame formidable technical difficulties in "constructing" transgenic mice expressing a gene with a precisely designed defect. The protein encoded by this gene carried a very specific functional defect and useful tags that would allow him to do a series of exciting experiments.

Now, three months later, James had done some of those experiments, and came to my office seeking advice. The first experiment had produced precisely the result he expected, fulfilling one of the hopes that had persuaded him to spend 18 months making the mutant mouse. But the unexpected result of his second experiment disappointed him terribly. To James's dismay, this second result seemed to contradict the explanation he (and everyone else) would have proposed to explain the earlier result. James had carefully double-checked both experiments, confirming that both results were correct. The paradox was "real," which left him grumpy and discouraged.

Listening, I too found the paradox disturbing. At first I praised James for accomplishing so much already, and proffered a liberal dose of hortatory wisdom—Cheer up! Paradox and contradiction are just what we should be looking for! I tried to get him to tell me more about experiments in other labs that might be relevant to the issues he faced, but those results also seemed mixed at best, and perhaps as contradictory as his two experiments were. Convinced that the past two years' work had brought him to a terrible impasse, James felt terrible. I was tempted to shift into drill-sergeant mode, but fortunately had enough sense to stifle the impulse.

Driving home that night, I reflected that James was bamboozled by a confusing array of contradictory facts, which didn't seem to fit a manageable pattern. My own lab had often faced similar difficulties. (One example was the paradoxical disease Taroh Iiri and I tried to solve.) The next day, following Roger's Rule, I sought James out to chew over the questions he faced. We came up with tentative thoughts that might resolve some of the paradoxical results.

I heard myself emphasizing another Rule I had learned from Gordon, about how to deal with an overwhelming set of complicated, confusing facts. The trick, Gordon used to say, is first to gather together all the information you can assimilate, and then do your damnedest to simplify it. Will removing any fact from the mix allow an explanation that fits all the other facts? Is there a different fact whose omission would allow you to formulate a different explanation? "Yes" answers to such questions identify possible facts that require re-testing, as well as potential explanations to be explored with experiments.[2] Any explanation we come up with (or even all of them) may be proved wrong—but so what? At worst, that just means you have to keep on looking. It's not a sin to be wrong. Keep at it.

James and I didn't get it all figured out that day, but he realized that more experiments might resolve the paradox. At this point, he took over and did exactly that, with little or no further input from me. The next time I heard the story, he had cobbled together more than one plausible explanation to account for his experimental results so far. Several months later, James's further experiments revealed that one of these explanations was correct, and would form the basis of an excellent PhD thesis.

The story represents triumphs for Gordon's Rules, but the most important lesson from James's story is that he overcame the paradox himself, thinking about it hard, on his own. For me it was one of the best possible rewards a mentor can have—that is, after pointing in the right direction, to watch the student figure out the solution on his own. The interaction had done its job.

A sad counter-example was the case of Frank, the young faculty member I had to ask to leave UCSF during my stint as chair of a department (chapter 9). Frank, remember, couldn't pay attention to my pointing out an internal contradiction in one of his grant requests. When the NIH review panel found the same contradiction, they turned the grant down. His basic problem was that he somehow didn't realize how crucial real thinking can be.

Frank told me he thought about experiments "all the time, but especially when I'm actually doing them—pipetting, putting samples into the scintillation counter, that sort of thing." He did not, significantly, set aside a time for thinking, in a situation where he could write down his ideas. (In addition to encouraging young people to keep painstaking records of all experiments and results, I try to teach them to record in writing the thoughts behind every experiment, as well. Why this experiment and not a different one? What exactly do they predict will happen? Reviewing the notes makes it easier to think more clearly the next time.)

Frank's second critical defect was his unwillingness or inability to seek and profit from advice. This problem is not rare among young biologists (or, I suspect, in any other group!). Perhaps Frank had been so inundated with advice that he never had to ask for it. For many students, the problem is simply fear of being revealed as ignorant or inadequate in some way. They keep their findings and ideas to themselves. Laughing, I tell them that the lab's most essential equipment is either the telephone (to call someone who knows more than you do) or their feet (to propel them to another office or lab bench to ask a question). More fundamentally, they need reassurance that ignorance is not a "sin," but is inevitable whenever you try to do something new. The true sin is allowing ignorance to persist. I reveal my own ignorance all the time. Students delight in discovering that I know less than they do about lots of things, and that I am eager to learn.

Why should young scientists, superbly educated and very smart, find it too hard to put aside time to think? One reason is that experimental biology inevitably requires lots of rushing about. Animals and cultured cells need care and feeding. Chemicals and fluids need to be weighed and pipetted. Microscopes require careful watching and meticulous recording of results in photomicrographs and movies. Numbers require calculating. Sometimes it seems as if the amount of energy and time devoted to these activities directly determines whether they will succeed. In addition, smart people who have always done well in courses have a skewed notion of what thinking really is. They imagine that the whole swirling broth of imagining, planning, reasoning, and judging is a spontaneous natural function, which should take place instantaneously, without conscious effort. Except for the odd genius, however, most of us find thinking fiendishly difficult, and rarely spontaneous. If I don't set aside a specific thinking time, weeks may pass without my tackling any difficult question I can avoid by honoring a more urgent demand.

A third reason can be laid squarely at the door of mentors. A mentor may think too well and too fast, as Frank's postdoctoral adviser seemed to have done, or focus too strongly on getting the apparently crucial experiments done, at the expense of time and effort devoted to thinking about them. Although I have yielded to that temptation, I usually got much better results—as I described in the story of the 0.7-angstrom click—by puzzling over the problem with someone else, often a student or postdoc.

———

Every mentor has a short list of problems that recur in interactions with students, along with her or his own prescription for dealing with them. "Thinking" is not the only problem. I'll mention three more.

Confidence. A few years ago I was advising a brilliant, extraordinarily competent young scientist, whom I'll call Martha. As a graduate student, and in the four years of her postdoc, she had shown an amazing knack for identifying the right experiment and executing it superbly, even (or perhaps especially) when the experiment itself was hard to pull off successfully. Now she was getting ready to find a faculty position and run her own lab. Along with everyone who knew her, I felt sure that she would land a position in a very good place, and that she would soon become a leader in her field.

As Martha prepared her application, she began to express doubts and worries, mild at first and (I thought) almost trivial. I teased her a bit—obviously, I said, she just loved to worry, but it was time for her to stop ignoring her accomplishments and the well-deserved praise she had already received. This approach seemed to work, at least in the sense that she stopped talking about her worries. Finally, however, Martha had to put together a job talk, describing her accomplishments. Knowing that faculty at first-rate institutions would use this talk to judge her ability, she was afraid it wouldn't be good enough. The day before her practice talk, delivered to me and a room full of labmates, she came down with a bad case of influenza. She soldiered on anyhow, and the talk was terrible—disjointed, limping, much too detailed, and even a bit boring.

Two days later, when the flu had cleared, Martha asked me to go over her slides for the talk. She felt terrible about her performance, which made her fear she just wasn't good enough to land a good job and become an effective independent scientist. Surprised, I asked what had become of all the certainty and self-assurance Martha had shown in her work, not just at UCSF but also during her PhD training earlier. "I was just pretending," she replied. "Other people always think I'm confident and capable, because I act that way. But really I'm always doubting, worrying, fretting. I know my defects better than they do. Maybe I'm really a fraud."

It had taken a while, but I finally caught on. Martha was suffering from the crippling sense of doubleness and inner fraudulence so many high-achieving people feel, off and on, all their lives. I feel it often, but manage most of the time to convince my colleagues that I am confident and competent instead. I told Martha that what she called "pretending" has proved for me an essential coping mechanism, because donning a cloak of confident competence eventually helps a person to believe it himself. Pretending is not very useful, by itself, but in combination with real achievement it can often carry the day.

Martha got the message. With a few adjustments her talk became truly exciting, in keeping with the work she had done. She found an excellent position and her career is already taking off.

The mentor himself can easily crush the confidence of some students. Indeed, in my youth I was sometimes given to arrogant and derisive comment, like the "Laughable" I wrote on Gary Johnson's manuscript (see chapter 7). Since then, I have realized that derision and scorn are useless and dangerous, even when their object seems richly to deserve it. The obverse truth is that praise and encouragement can do wonders, even for people who seem ultra-confident and almost invulnerable. Like me, they need to know that someone else sees their worth. The mentor can't fake regard for a student's worth, which has to feel real to both parties. This is the real linchpin of Roger's Rule. As my own confidence has grown, I have gotten better at supporting the confidence of others.

Focus. Bright young scientists often have a hard time learning that it's better to ask and clearly answer one question than to ask many and answer none. Choosing that one question is always *the* pivotal decision we make.

It often seems to me that this problem is greater for the exceedingly bright and capable young scientist than for his less brilliant contemporaries. I remember a pivotal conversation with one extremely smart student, Brian, just at the point when he was writing a paper about a very nice finding. Asked what he should do next, he launched into a detailed description of possible directions, all imaginative and all fascinating.

I couldn't convince Brian that no one could finish all these projects in three short years, but he did agree that it would be best to begin by working on only one. All the questions he had identified seemed equally plausible and intrinsically interesting to both of us, so I suggested he choose one by applying a very simple criterion. Which question is least likely to be asked in other labs? By that criterion, one question stood out. Brian chose it, and made it into the basis of a long and productive career.

I once watched Bruce Alberts,[3] a faculty colleague at UCSF, propose a different criterion, for a similar reason. Bill, a bright graduate student, was presenting results of the last six months' work to his faculty thesis committee. Bruce arrived, a few minutes late as always, disheveled and with his shirt hanging out. He listened as Bill outlined multiple questions, each to be answered by complex genetic experiments using yeast cells.

Eventually Bruce broke in: "Tell me, which one of your questions could produce the equivalent of a home run?"

Bill made a choice. When Bruce asked him to defend his choice by explaining what he hoped to find, he did an excellent job. "Maybe you should tackle that question first," Bruce gently suggested.

Communication. It is not surprising that I've cited so many examples that arose in the most common advice-giving context in any academic lab. Frank's grant application, Martha's job talk, Gary's manuscript, and Bill's thesis committee presentation were all attempts to communicate complicated ideas. Advice about communication is practical and crucially important, but students and postdocs often find it difficult to follow.

Part of the reason is a common misconception: that communicating a new explanation for a natural phenomenon is much less valuable than doing experiments and establishing new facts. One of my postdocs furnished a sad but comical caricature of this point of view. Joan (not her actual name) focused with laser intensity of the task at hand, to the point of creating an invisible but nearly impermeable barrier around her lab bench. When she was engaged in an experiment, reading a paper, or assessing data, everyone around her learned to stay as far away as possible. Joan did lots of experiments, but never discussed them with others in the lab, because they might steal her ideas. Even with me she would reveal what was going on only when she was absolutely sure how to interpret it. When she finally wrote a paper, it was always "just the facts" and certainly correct—but, sadly, not very interesting. While she was in my lab, I could always add spice to the manuscripts, so they got published. Afterward, she landed a good assistant professorship, but didn't publish much, and her career has languished.

Although Joan behaved like a caricature, many students share her inability to understand that imparting new knowledge to others is intrinsically worthwhile, in and of itself. They don't quite believe that communication benefits not only the recipients of new knowledge, but also the communicator, who almost always clarifies her own understanding as she puts the story together. It often takes such students a long time to learn the enormous practical value of communication—for attracting help and collaborators, getting a job, and obtaining grant support.

Even when students realize the importance of communicating their ideas, teaching them how to do so is a demanding but often rewarding task. I have devoted many hours to taking notes and giving advice at students' oral presentations, practice talks before job interviews, and manuscripts. With enough hard work, fortunately, the talk's next version inevitably improves, or the manuscript becomes clearer.

———

Perhaps the biggest problem with not communicating science to others is that it impairs transfer of information in the other direction as well. For researchers like Joan, when the transmitter goes on the fritz, the receiver often follows. Without either, the entire scientific enterprise would grind to a halt. (The metaphor is similar for marriage. Certainly Nancy is my most important mentor/collaborator, and we work hard to keep our transmitters and receivers in working order.)

I have met a few experimental biologists whose internal mental dialogues generate ideas, corollaries, and fertile criticisms as well as any dialogue between two "ordinary" smart scientists. These are geniuses, but even they often benefit from advice and collaboration, as exemplified by Watson and Crick. For lesser intellects, the benefits are proportionately much greater, in fact essential.

Soon after Gordon died, I realized that I could be a vastly better scientist, and enjoy it more, by enlisting the help of others. Some of those others were the students and postdocs in my lab, who appear elsewhere in this book. But I also went out of my way to learn from any biologist smarter than I. In my early years on the faculty, Phil Coffino and I talked about experiments almost every day. Lubert Stryer and (later) Elliott Ross and Al Gilman gave me invaluable advice about

G-proteins. Peter Seeburg and other people at Genentech taught my lab how to work with DNA. Harold Varmus taught Kathleen Sullivan and me how to use retroviruses to express proteins in cyc^- cells. Ira Herskowitz and I lunched together every week to talk about signaling and G-proteins (every week, that is, until I foolishly wrote the self-righteous letter described in chapter 9). People like Bob Stroud, Bob Fletterick, and Fred Cohen helped me to learn to cope with 3D structures of G-proteins and receptors. Almost every paper published from my lab was reviewed by two or three other faculty colleagues, who were not co-authors. My continuing need for input from smarter colleagues was one reason I helped to found UCSF's informal Faculty Signaling Club, at one of whose meetings Shaun Coughlin reminded me that testicles are cool.

When young people are interviewing for jobs, I always urge them to think hard about whether institution X vs. institution Y is more likely to offer good opportunities for forging connections like those I have enjoyed. I say that such connections can make them better scientists, but I also have to add that such connections require hard work. Some fraction of potential mentor/collaborators—I would guess 25% or so—simply will not or cannot find the necessary time, generosity, or skill to play such a role. Once the right person is found, of course, it is always necessary to reciprocate in kind, by offering advice, reviewing papers, etc.—but this in itself should be fun, and scientifically stimulating, providing one has chosen the right person as a mentor/collaborator.

A much subtler problem, for some people, is lack of trust—in essence, fear that one or another adviser/collaborator may take ideas or information and use it himself, to their detriment. Sometimes this fear is ill-founded, as it clearly was for Joan, my postdoc. In the rare cases where such a fear is justified, it is usually possible to detect strong hints beforehand, from a senior person's reputation or even the behavior of his colleagues. (I once interviewed a young faculty member at another institution, who told me he could trust no senior faculty in his department because "They hate each other so much that if B helps me out, A will do his best to screw me." Science too has its petty villains, and often they congregate in a single department or institution.)

For me both the hard work and the risk of trust have reaped
an inestimable harvest of good things. With the exception of Ken's
machinations when he left UCSF, in 40 years of research I can
remember only one instance where a questionable act of another
scientist caused me any damage whatever. (In that case, a journal's
review of one of my papers was delayed for five months, because one
reviewer wanted to give extra time to a former protégé engaged in
similar experiments.) My lab has been "scooped" plenty of times, but
always because the other team got the answer first. I have suffered lots
of negative reviews of submitted manuscripts and grant requests, but
in every case the reviewer was either correct or honestly mistaken,
but never malevolent (or at least that's what I think). This record
may represent unusually good luck, working in a field peopled by
unusually collegial and helpful scientists, or my inability to think of
experiments others want to do. Instead, I suspect it represents the
normal experience of most experimental biologists in the second half
of the 20th century.

Let us hope so. In any case, I continue to counsel my young
colleagues that trust and open communication are not just effective,
but absolutely necessary. If we continue to act as if that advice is
correct, it will be.

CHAPTER 13

Where Now?

CAN THE FUN LAST FOREVER?

In 1999, just before I turned 60, I began to change the focus of my lab, because G-proteins and receptors were getting a little old. For the next eight years or so, I asked how white blood cells home in on their targets, attracted by chemical signals produced by bacteria or sites of inflammation. How do these cells know where the signals are coming from, and decide to crawl in that direction? Switching into a field I knew little about was a risk, but it paid off. I had fun, and contributed new findings and ideas to the field.

Then, almost three years ago, I undertook a second and more delicate negotiation with my psychic needs. That is, I began to retire. Now I am an emeritus professor, the lab is closed, and my last postdoc moved to a new job at the end of 2007. I no longer have to write grant proposals, serve on promotion committees, keep up with the pell-mell progress of other labs, get approvals from lab safety committees, or persuade journals to publish my papers. What a relief!

I planned carefully, to retain as many sources of fun as possible. Now I attend meetings of three or more labs every week, and help a few students and postdocs as they write papers and make career decisions. At the lab meetings I occasionally contribute a question or suggestion, but always enjoy the vicarious pleasure of watching the birth and growth of new findings and new ideas. In the meantime, Nancy and I travel and read everything we can get our hands on. These are activities I always enjoyed, and I enjoy them still. The fun side of the ledger consistently shows a profit.

Still, I am sorry to have lost the buzz and striving excitement of direct involvement in research. Disengaged from the fray, I must be content to wait for the eventual dénouement to be worked out by someone else.

So I have devoted much of my free time to writing, beginning with this memoir. Making a complex scientific story intelligible to non-scientists has offered new challenges, and revisiting the past has proved a real adventure. Writing also turns out to be a difficult and often discouraging task, to the point that I flirt occasionally with the idea of dropping it altogether. But the pleasure remains greater than the pain, and I plan to write another and rather different book when this one is done.

Looking back, I see that I have led a truly charmed life, lucky beyond anything I could have imagined. I lived in a fortunate time in the richest country in the world, and was even more fortunate in choosing the right parents and the right partner for life. Educated in first-rate schools and by superb mentors, I then managed to hitch a ride on one of the greatest voyages of discovery in human history, the unprecedented biological revolution of the decades after 1970. I received more recognition, praise, and reward than I deserved—though never as much as I wanted, because my ambition far exceeded my energy and ability. Nonetheless, for me the delight, excitement, and fun of those years exceeded anything I could have anticipated.

Enough about me. What about the wondrous world of experimental biology? Where is it going?

———

One damp, gray San Francisco morning, two years ago, I sat looking out my office window, in a reverie about this memoir, then unwritten. The reverie was interrupted by a loud knock at the door, followed by a gawky young woman with bright gray eyes and a wide, toothy smile. Almost six feet tall, she towered above me.

After wondering for a moment who she was, I realized that this was Sharon, a 19-year-old sophomore at UC Berkeley. At her parents' request, a friend of mine had asked me to talk with her about a possible career in experimental biology.

I asked the usual questions. Yes, she's taken science courses, and learned to cut and splice DNA in high school. Her grades were good, especially in medieval history, music, and chemistry. She plays guitar and sings in a pick-up band, plays tennis, and swims. Besides biology, Sharon is also thinking about medicine and law. "Really, I'm interested in lots of options. I need to know what questions I should ask."

"So what questions are you already asking?"

"Here's one," Sharon said. "What are experimental biologists after? Why do they come to work in the morning?"

A good question, hard to answer in a few sentences. Sometimes I don't know exactly what I think until I say it, so I plunged ahead.

"We want to discover something that will dazzle us and our friends. We hope other scientists will congratulate us, saying that's an elegant experiment, or a question we should have asked long ago. We're hungry for praise.

"But that's only part of it." I went on. "What we really want is to keep the fun coming—as fast as last year, or last week."

"What's this about fun?" Sharon asked. "Do you mean the thrill of discovery—something romantic like that?"

"Sure, sometimes—but real discovery doesn't happen every day or even every year. It's more the thrill of understanding, like clicking a piece into a puzzle."

I gave her an example. Stan, a second-year grad student, had told his lab the day before about his efforts to purify a protein. For six months nothing had worked, but he finally figured out a clever way to do it, opening doors to all the experiments he needed to do. I never saw anybody more thrilled.

Sharon smiled, intrigued. Then she brought me back to earth.

"Maybe, but that's not what I hear from a senior who works in a lab at Berkeley." Sharon frowned and looked me in the eye. "He says it's a very competitive world, graduate students are afraid they won't make it, and nobody is brilliant enough or ruthless enough to compete with people like the Berkeley faculty."

Realizing that Sharon wants real answers, I suddenly saw kaleidoscope of my own insecurities, complete with images of

Brodie, Gopal, Melmon, Elliott and Al. Perhaps I had better go with the truth.

"We're human, Sharon. Competition is the way the world works, a lot of the time. Without competition, ambition loses its force, and most of us don't get much done.

"Sure, I've seen cut-throat competition. And I knew at least one scientist who was a practiced deceiver. But doctors or lawyers aren't all saints. Neither are scientists.

"Still, cooperation, advice, and help are much more common—or at least they have been, in my world." I shrug my shoulders and add, "In fact, joining with others to solve a puzzle is a pleasure in itself. Especially when they are smarter than I am."

Before Sharon leaves, I think I've persuaded her to try a stint in a lab to see how she likes it. We talk about Berkeley professors whose labs might be fun to work in. In fact, I suggest she try more than one lab, if possible—but I don't tell her how long it took me to find the kind of mentor I needed.

(Today, two years later, Sharon remains an undergraduate, still undecided about her future. But she is doing a trial run in a lab. We'll see.)

———

Today I feel just as evangelical about experimental biology as I did when Sharon visited my office, two years ago. If she does become a scientist, I predict that when she is close to my present age, 40 years from now, Sharon will be able to answer questions like these: What happens, in brain neurons and their molecules, to create addiction to cocaine? Or to nicotine, or to alcohol? Which genes act together to cause maturity-onset diabetes, and how do they do it? Ditto for schizophrenia, or bipolar disorders? Which genes allow malarial parasites to live and prosper in a mosquito? In a person? Which gene products in the parasite are the best targets for effective new anti-malarial drugs? Which genes, which brain cells, and which molecules control learning and memory? Or mouse and human behaviors like mating, aggression, and nurturing young?

The past 40 years of experimental biology suggests that answers to such questions are pretty sure bets. Could I, entering medical school just as the genetic code was solved, have foreseen the consequences? No one knew that the DNA revolution and the code would illuminate hundreds of new protein families and the causes and treatment of myriad diseases. And no one knew—and here's the most certain prediction of all—that biology would answer myriad questions we couldn't even imagine asking! For example, Acquired Immunodeficiency Syndrome, or AIDS, was unknown in the 1970s but can now be controlled by drugs. Without tools furnished by the DNA revolution, we would know little about the pathogenesis of AIDS, and would have no way to treat it.

But let me ask a different question—if Sharon becomes an experimental biologist, will she and her generation reap as rich a reward in sheer fun as my generation and I did over the past 40 years? Evangelical fervor prevented me from raising the question with Sharon, but I privately worry that the answer may be no. The essential worry is that academic experimental biology may already be falling victim to its own success. Over my lifetime in science, the whole enterprise has grown vastly bigger and richer. Its size and its ability to explain diseases and accelerate discovery of new treatments have created economic and social pressures unimaginable in the simpler days of the 1970s and 1980s. When lab research was a cottage industry, I could write a grant proposal aimed at solving a question that interested me, and if it interested the reviewers I would get the money. I could do with that money more or less whatever experiments I chose, and respond to new findings by changing research direction, without asking anybody's permission.

Now the situation is different. Every decision is dramatically more "monetized" than ever before. Grants are rarely rewarded to first-time applicants. Successful applicants are older than they used to be, and more likely to have enjoyed continuing support for a decade or more. Competition is tougher, because the population of smart, well-trained applicants is much greater, and total funds have stopped increasing. As a result, limited funds are distributed disproportionately to projects whose outcomes appear sure bets, even when they are not very exciting. I have watched young investigators being pressured, prematurely, to re-direct a grant proposal toward a clinical application, or an NIH committee urging recipients of a large cooperative grant to change the goal of their project in midstream, even before the grant supporting it is due for renewal.

The problem is not that emphasis is shifting away from basic questions toward more "applied" questions related to disease. Rather, I worry that rigid rules and bureaucrats will discourage scientists from taking risks, and so decrease not only the fun and creativity of experimental biology, but also its ability to make new discoveries.

I used to joke to my colleagues about what a disaster it would be if the U.S. Congress were to discover how much fun lab research really is. They wouldn't be satisfied with reducing federal funding for research. Instead, because fun is dangerous, they would probably outlaw it altogether. In reality, of course, fun is absolutely essential for real discovery, and its disappearance would bring disaster. Without fun, desires for power, fame, and money would become by default the principal motives of biologists. Such desires are fine and necessary, but we are most creative when driven by our own curiosity and imagination, rather than by dreams of riches and renown.

So I am not pleading for vastly increased public expenditure on biological research, whether "pure" or "applied." To be sure, almost any amount of money would be better spent on the NIH than on foolish wars and a vast military establishment. But government must meet a host of (non-military) public needs, many just as critical as biological research. Right now, fortunately, many of my colleagues are trying to meet the challenge by working to change the NIH, their universities, and their local research environments. Instead of more money, we need to spend biological research dollars in ways that foster, rather than curtail, the fun and delight of understanding nature.

Most of the time, though, I realize that these fears are over-wrought. The truth is that the tantalizing questions will keep on coming, and human curiosity is hard to suppress. So it is my fondest hope—and my firm expectation—that experimental biology in the new century will furnish as much delight to coming generations as it did to mine.

NOTES

PROLOGUE:
WHY READ THIS BOOK (AND HOW)

[1]My favorite examples include HF Judson, *The Eighth Day of Creation: Makers of the Revolution in Biology* (Simon and Schuster, 1979), on the origins of molecular biology and the scientists who made it happen; JD Watson, *The Double Helix: A Personal Account of the Discovery of the Structure of DNA* (1968); and EO Wilson, *Naturalist* (Shearwater Books, 1979), the superb memoir of a great evolutionary biologist.

[2]One of the most cited examples is the race to discover the three-dimensional structure of DNA. The team of James Watson and Francis Crick won, while the lonely effort of Rosalind Franklin failed. Watson's book, cited in footnote 1, tells the story from his and Crick's point of view. The difficulties of trying to solve a difficult problem on one's own are beautifully described in B Maddox, *Rosalind Franklin: the Dark Lady of DNA* (Harper Collins, 2002).

[3]It is confusing that signaling pathways like these look very much like chemical pathways, which preceded them historically but mean something quite different. A chemical pathway in cell metabolism, for instance, describes conversions of molecules (A into B, B into C, etc.) into other molecules by a series of reactions, indicated by arrows. In this book, unless I note otherwise, pathways depict signal transmission (arrows) between molecules, represented by letters.

[4]Literary types will see the parallel with a quality John Keats called "negative capability, . . . which Shakespeare possessed so enormously, . . . that is when man is capable of being in uncertainties, mysteries, doubts without any irritable reaching after fact and reason." I think Keats meant that poets must make themselves open-minded on purpose, accepting that real uncertainties often cannot be readily (or perhaps ever) resolved by logic, even when they point ultimately to a deeper romantic truth. Readers trying to plumb poems by poets like Wallace Stevens will have felt a pressing need for negative capability. This kind of capability is also useful, in a real sense, for scientists faced with nature's puzzles. Unlike Keats, however, we expect that the uncertainty *will* be resolved by a new fact or a new way of looking at the old facts. Sometimes we are right.

CHAPTER 1. UNCONSCIOUS DECISIONS: GROWING UP

[1]The line's striking brevity contributes much of its poignance, but scholars don't agree on exactly what Virgil meant. In context, he seems to have been saying that tears are an inevitable, central fact of human experience.

CHAPTER 2. ASKING QUESTIONS: MEDICINE, THE TUTOR OF BIOLOGY

[1]William Harvey, discoverer of the circulation of blood, is often quoted as saying that "Medicine is the great tutor of biology." I have not found the actual source in Harvey's writings.

[2]Daddy's admission to medical school at U.Va., back in 1926, was difficult in a different way. In those days, a student could start medical school without finishing college. After two years of college, Daddy had his medical school interview. In a short conversation, the interviewer told him his grades were not good enough for admission, so he would have to try again later. "I just broke out crying," Daddy told me. "I sort of bawled. The old guy felt sorry

for me and said the school would give me a chance." Every week afterward, for the first two years of medical school, the interviewer would seek him out, put his hand on his shoulder, and say: "Now don't let me down, Bourne." A scenario unimaginable today, or in 1961.

[3]Mountcastle discovered that the cerebral cortex is organized into columns of neurons. Later he was to do landmark work in the field of sensory perception. Today's neuroscientists revere his penetrating insight and experimental rigor.

[4]Max Perutz reported hemoglobin's three-dimensional structure in 1959, after 17 years of painstaking work [MF Perutz (1964) The hemoglobin molecule. Scientific American 211:64-76]. Perutz was awarded a Nobel Prize for this work, along with his colleague, John Kendrew, in 1962.

[5]O Avery, C MacLeod, M McCarty (1944) Studies on the chemical nature of the substance inducing transformation of pneumococcal types: Induction of transformation by a desoxyribonucleic acid fraction isolated from Pneumococcus Type III. J Exp Med 79: 137-158.

[6]HR Bourne, HN Wagner, M Iio, JR Jude, GG Knickerbocker (1964) Cerebral blood flow during external cardiac massage. J Nucl Med 5: 738-745.

CHAPTER 3. A NOT SO ARTFUL DODGER: TWO YEARS AT THE NIH

[1]If the radioactive tracer was not distributed in exactly the same fashion under the two circumstances, its rate of washout from the brain might depend on local variations between one region of the brain and another, rather than upon the actual rate of blood flow through the whole brain. I'm certain that my co-authors knew this very well, but I had not asked them. Now I know that the accuracy of *every* experimental procedure is based on many assumptions, and it's essential for the experimenter to know what they are and make certain they are correct.

[2]The first transmitter (left side of the board) is called noradrenaline, which is close chemical relative of adrenaline. The second transmitter was serotonin, and the blood pressure drug Brodie said released it from brain neurons was reserpine. The same drug also triggers depletion of the adrenaline-like transmitter from neurons. Brodie contended that reserpine induces depression and sedation by increasing release of "free" serotonin from neuronal stores. His opponents were certain that reserpine-induced depression reflected loss of the adrenaline-like transmitter. Both may have been right, but Brodie's view can be bent to accord with the action of "selective serotonin reuptake inhibitors" (SSRIs). SSRIs, of which the best known is Prozac, are thought to relieve depression by preventing neurons from taking up serotonin again after they have released it onto the neuron downstream. If reserpine *causes* depression by increasing "free" serotonin's effect on downstream neurons, as Brodie thought, then an SSRI should induce depression, rather than alleviate it. To fix this apparent contradiction, we would have to add a codicil, to the effect that an SSRI reduces the amount of serotonin available for normal release from the upstream neuron. If so, the SSRI would reduce the amount of serotonin that reaches the downstream neuron. The prevailing explanation for the action of SSRIs, however, is that they *increase* the size of the serotonin signal at brain synapses—a contention directly opposite to the codicil. As a non-expert, I lean toward the prevailing view, but am not qualified to argue very strongly for or against it.

[3]The book focuses on three remarkable scientists: Brodie, Julius Axelrod, and Solomon Snyder. As indicated by the full title of his book—*Apprentice to Genius: The Making of a Scientific Dynasty* (Macmillan, 1986)—Kanigel describes transmission, by precept and example, of lessons, attitudes, and scientific styles from each mentor to the next. Brodie comes off as a flawed genius, and Axelrod as a brilliant disciple who eventually outgrew and rebelled against his teacher. Snyder, equally brilliant, continues to revere and consciously emulate his mentor, Axelrod. Young people who wonder how scientists learn from their mentors should read this book.

[4]The antimalarial agent, atabrine, was ineffective because doctors gave it in doses that were infrequent and too small. Brodie's group recommended

changes in the dosing regimen that made the drug much more effective. In addition to acetaminophen, Brodie and his colleagues invented procainamide, which served as a valuable anti-arrhythmic for the next 25 years, although it is little used today.

[5]Axelrod's experiments discovered these drug-metabolizing enzymes, and showed they were located in liver microsomes (a discrete membrane fraction, distinct from the cell's outer membrane, that can be extracted from broken cells). The story has it that Brodie announced to the lab that the list of authors would be alphabetical—with a single exception: he, Brodie, would appear first.

[6]The precursor, ATP, or adenosine triphosphate, serves as the energy currency of every cell. Made by releasing energy from nutrients, ATP then drives the energy-requiring processes that keep us alive. Evolution, ever thrifty, has recruited ATP for other purposes in addition, exemplified by its role as a cyclic AMP precursor.

[7]To do so, Sutherland's colleagues had to reconstitute the adrenaline response from component parts of liver cells. First they first placed liver fragments in a homogenizer, which broke up the cells. Then they separated the homogenate into two fractions: membranes of the cell and the fluid inside, called "cytosol." Then they reserved the cytosol on ice, treated the membranes with adrenaline to elicit production of a "second messenger," and terminated the action of adrenaline by boiling the membrane fraction to kill its enzymes. Because the messenger itself was unaffected by boiling, it could be detected by the ability of the fluid (after boiling) to induce the cytosolic machinery to release sugar from a starch-like precursor. They went on to purify the substance that transmitted the message from membranes to cytosol; it was cyclic AMP (cyclic adenosine-3',5'-monophosphate).

[8]Axelrod and his colleagues were trying to determine how noradrenaline is metabolized. After injecting a radioactive version of the amine, they found that it left the blood rapidly, but was stored in certain organs, including the heart, blood vessels, and spleen. Such stores could not be detected in organs surgically disconnected from neurons of the sympathetic nervous system.

Noradrenaline turned out to be stored in the endings of these neurons, and to be released by electrical stimulation or neural reflexes that control heart rate, blood pressure, and coordinated responses to danger (fight-or-flight). Reserpine and several other drugs regulate blood pressure by their effects on neuronal storage of noradrenaline.

CHAPTER 4. VAULTING AMBITION: LEARNING A NEW GAME

[1]HR Bourne, KL Melmon, LM Lichtenstein (1971) Histamine augments leukocyte adenosine 3',5'-monophosphate and blocks antigenic histamine release. Science 173: 743-745.

[2]Unlike ISO, the effect of cholera toxin was delayed: cyclic AMP became elevated 30-60 minutes after toxin treatment. Even stranger, cells needed to "see" the toxin for only 10 minutes—an hour later, cyclic AMP rose and white cell functions were impaired, even though all the soluble toxin had been removed 50 minutes before. The toxin is composed of two parts, one of which binds to molecules on the cell's surface, allowing the second part to enter the cell and elevate cyclic AMP. This second part is an enzyme, which modifies Gs, the regulator of adenylyl cyclase described in chapters 6 and 7. More specifically, the enzyme transfers a portion of a small molecule, called NAD^+, to Gs. This is why the elevation of adenylyl cyclase activity is delayed, and why it persists after the remaining toxin outside the cell is removed. Chapter 6 describes discovery of Gs, and chapter 7 tells how the toxin's action contributed to understanding the structure and function of Gs and a family of similar proteins.

[3]I followed the plagiarism accusations from afar, with keen interest. The chapter that incorporated the borrowed material was in a textbook edited by Robert Williams, the Seattle endocrinologist I had interviewed for a job, years earlier. The principal editor of the pharmacology textbook, from which Ken borrowed, was Alfred G. Gilman, a scientist described in chapter 6. For an account, see C. Norman (1984) Melmon resigns Stanford chairmanship. *Science* 224:1324.

CHAPTER 5. LESSONS IN DELIGHT:
NEW WAYS TO THINK ABOUT EXPERIMENTS

[1]The acronym stands for *p*rotein *k*inase *A*. Protein kinases are enzymes that transfer a phosphate group from ATP to certain other proteins. ATP, the reader may remember, is the same compound that serves as a chemical precursor in the productive of cyclic AMP itself, and as the principal energy chemical of every cell. The "A" in PKA indicates that the enzyme's activity is stimulated by cyclic AMP.

[2]Fingers or toes, for example, separate from one another only if cells die in the webby tissue between them, and the body's immune system ruthlessly kills white blood cells that might otherwise attack against our own cells and tissues. In fact, excess cyclic AMP can kill normal T lymphocytes, the white cells from which the S49 lymphoma was derived, as described in chapter 4.

[3]This chapter refers to several papers we published on S49 cells in the period from 1973 to 1975. The references follow.

On PDE: HR Bourne, GM Tomkins, S Dion (1973) Regulation of phosphodiesterase synthesis: requirement for cyclic adenosine monophosphate-dependent protein kinase. Science 181: 952-954.

On PKA mutants: PA Insel, HR Bourne, P Coffino, GM Tomkins (1975) Cyclic AMP-dependent protein kinase: pivotal role in regulation of enzyme induction and growth. Science 190: 896-898; J Hochman, PA Insel, HR Bourne, P Coffino, GM Tomkins (1975) A structural gene mutation affecting the regulatory subunit of cyclic AMP-dependent protein kinase in mouse lymphoma cells. Proc Natl Acad Sci USA 72: 5051-5055.

The *cyc*⁻ mutant: HR Bourne, P Coffino, GM Tomkins (1975) Selection of a variant lymphoma cell deficient in adenylate cyclase. Science 187: 750-752.

[4]Negative feedback crudely resembles the way a thermostat controls room temperature: heat generated by the furnace damps its own intensity, just as the cyclic AMP signal damps its intensity. In fact a thermostat controls the

furnace, which is analogous to adenylyl cyclase, rather than cyclic AMP degradation in the S49 cell. In biology, negative feedback circuits may regulate either production or dissipation of a signal, and often control both.

[5]One of my colleagues, Philip Coffino, isolated an S49 mutant in which PKA was normal, but cyclic AMP still failed to kill the cell. These "deathless" cells did stop growing and did accumulate increased amounts of PDE in response to cyclic AMP. The precise mutation that created "deathless" cells is still not known, I think.

CHAPTER 6. DANCERS AND BULLDOZERS: ANATOMY OF A DISCOVERY

[1]The paper's suggestion that adenylyl cyclase is present in cyc^- membranes was supported by the ability of cyc^- extracts to make cyclic AMP under special conditions. Warming the membranes slightly (to 30° centigrade, more or less equivalent to a warm but not broiling summer's day) destroyed the activity, however. By itself, adenylyl cyclase could not be stimulated by ISO or Gpp(NH)p, although cyc^- membranes contained R. In addition to the cyclase itself, wild-type detergent extracts contained not only adenylyl cyclase (highly sensitive to temperature), but also a more heat-resistant component, which turned out to be Gs. Adding Gpp(NH)p to the wild-type extract made Gs even more resistant to heat, strongly suggesting that it contained a site for binding Gpp(NH)p and probably GTP. See EM Ross, AG Gilman (1977) Resolution of some components of adenylate cyclase necessary for catalytic activity. J Biol Chem 252: 6966-6969.

CHAPTER 7. OUT OF THE WOODS: A LAB OF MY OWN, AND TWO DISEASES

[1]Dante introduces his *Divine Comedy* with these words:

> Midway on our life's journey, I found myself
> In dark woods, the right road lost.

These are the first lines of *The Inferno of Dante*, translated by Robert Pinsky (Farrar, Straus, and Giroux, 1994).

[2]Z Farfel, AS Brickman, HR Kaslow, VM Brothers, HR Bourne (1980) Defect of receptor-cyclase coupling protein in pseudohypoparathyroidism. N Engl J Med 303: 237-242.

[3]The clue to what is really going on came from an unusual pattern of inheritance of hormone resistance—patients inherit the disease from their mothers, almost always, but rarely from their fathers. This is unexpected, because the Gs gene is not on the X-chromosome, so patients should inherit a Gs mutation from the male parent just as frequently as from the female parent.

It turned out that the expression of Gs in certain tissues, like that of a growing number of other genes, is genomically "imprinted"—an uninformative technical term meaning that some tissues selectively express the protein product of only one of a normal person's two Gs genes, each of which is inherited from a different parent. It turns out, in fact, that a child's kidney makes Gs protein from the Gs gene he or she inherited from the mother, but not from the gene that came from the father. Usually, the mother's Gs gene produces enough Gs for the kidney to function normally. But if the mother carries an inactive Gs gene on one of her chromosomes and passes that chromosome to a child, the child's kidney will resist the actions of Parathyroid Hormone, thereby triggering kidney-related effects of the disease. Who knew? There is much more to genomic imprinting, and to inheritance of the hormone resistance disorder.

The imprinting story in pseudohypoparathyroidism is described in LS Weinstein, S Yu (1999) The Role of Genomic Imprinting of Gs-alpha in the Pathogenesis of Albright Hereditary Dystrophy. Trends in Endocrinology and Metabolism, 10:81-85. For a more general discussion of genomic imprinting, see MS Bartolomei and SM Tilghman (1977) Genomic Imprinting in Animals. Annu Rev Genet 32:493-525.

[4]Both Gs and transducin, like other receptor-activated GTP-binding switches discovered later, are composed of three protein subunits: α, β,

and γ. For our purposes the α subunits are the most important, because they bind and break down GTP, stimulate responses, etc. Although β and γ subunits play important roles in transmitting signals, we shall ignore them in this book. Thus my references to Gs, transducin, or other proteins in this family sometimes involve functions really mediated by all three members of the trimeric protein, but at other times (especially when I discuss DNA sequences or 3D structure) pertain directly to the α subunits of Gs, transducin, etc. The cognoscenti will know the difference, and others will not care.

CHAPTER 8. BLISS IN THE AFTERNOON: RIDING THE DOUBLE HELIX

[1]DNA (deoxyribonucleic acid) in our chromosomes is composed of two chains, closely intertwined in a double spiral. Each chain is a long chain in which the links are nucleotides arranged in a specific order. Each nucleotide contains one of four different "bases"—adenine (A), thymidine (T), guanidine (G) and cytidine (C). Base sequences of the two chains complement one another, so that A or G in chain 1 always bind, respectively, to T or C in chain 2. Thus, for instance, a string of bases like AGCTA is always complemented by TCGAT. Dan's experiment was designed to identify a "complementary DNA" (cDNA) for transducin—meaning that he sought DNA whose nucleotides contained bases in a sequence complementary to a string of bases that encoded a specific protein, transducin. A cDNA is cloned by using enzymes to make a DNA sequence complementary to the sequence of a nucleic acid, "messenger" RNA (ribonucleic acid), which is closely related to DNA. Because messenger RNA is used to carry the "message" from DNA in the cell's nucleus to protein-making machinery outside the nucleus (see note 2, below), the order of bases in each individual messenger RNA encodes a specific protein. Once the cDNA has been made, it is "cloned" to produce many stable copies for later use. To do so, molecular biologists take advantage of the primitive sex life of bacteria, which transfer genes from one organism to another in the form of circular DNA sequences called plasmids. Once a cDNA is inserted into a plasmid, the plasmid

is then incorporated into a bacterium, where it replicates along with the bacterial DNA. For non-scientists who really want to understand DNA, messenger RNA, and proteins, the best introduction is HF Judson, *The Eighth Day of Creation: Makers of the Revolution in Biology* (Simon and Schuster, 1979).

[2]DNA is sometimes referred to as the "blueprint" from which proteins are made. More properly, the sequence of bases (A, C, G, and T) in a stretch of DNA specifies the sequence of amino acids in the corresponding protein. DNA is not directly translated into protein, however. Instead, the stretch of DNA is first "transcribed" into a slightly different language, called "messenger RNA," in the cell's nucleus. Messenger RNA is then transported out of the nucleus to the cell's protein-making machinery, which "reads" or "decodes" the sequence of bases in the mRNA to construct a correctly ordered sequence of amino acids. The code is not simple, with a single base specifying a single amino acid. This is because nucleic acids are composed of only four bases, while proteins are made up of 20 amino acids. Instead, the genetic code uses three bases as a "codon" to specify each amino acid. Thus, for instance, CAG is a codon that specifies the amino acid glutamine at position 227 in Gs, and CGG specifies arginine, the amino acid substituted for it in certain pituitary tumors. A three-base codon can be made up of any three of the four bases, in any order. Consequently, such a code could in principle specify 64 different amino acids. But 64 is greater than 20, so that many amino acids are specified by more than one codon—that is, the code is redundant. Just as the cell's machinery reads the mRNA code to make a unique protein, knowing the code allows scientists to read a cDNA sequence and predict the sequence of amino acids that will make up the corresponding protein. Again, non-scientists will learn more about the code and how cells read it in Judson's *The Eighth Day of Creation*, cited in note 1, above.

[3]The Halliday paper is KR Halliday (1983) Regional homology in GTP-binding proto-oncogene products and elongation factors. J Cyclic Nucleotide Protein Phosphor Res 9: 435-448. The Jurnak paper is F Jurnak (1985) Structure of the GDP domain of EF-Tu and location of the amino acids homologous to Ras oncogene proteins. Science 230: 32-36.

Chapter 9. A Gamble Pays Off: Department Chair

None

Chapter 10. All in the Timing: Switches, Timers, and Pituitary Giants

[1]For the Halliday and Jurnak references, see footnote 3 to chapter 8, above.

[2]This chapter refers to several papers on timer mutations in Gs. First come the back-to-back papers by Susan Masters and Michael Graziano on Gs mutations that alter the turnoff reaction: SB Masters, RT Miller, MH Chi, F-H Chang, B Beiderman et al. (1989) Mutations in the GTP-binding site of $G_{s\alpha}$ alter stimulation of adenylyl cyclase. J Biol Chem 264: 15467-15474; MP Graziano, AG Gilman (1989) Synthesis in Escherichia coli of GTPase-deficient mutants of $G_{s\alpha}$. J Biol Chem 264: 15475-15482.

　　The paper by Lucia Vallar is L Vallar, A Spada, G Giannattasio (1987) Altered G_s and adenylate cyclase activity in human GH-secreting pituitary adenomas. Nature 330: 566-568. The blurb I wrote about it is HR Bourne (1987) G proteins and cAMP. Discovery of a new oncogene in pituitary tumours? Nature 330: 517-518.

　　Finally, Claudia's paper on pituitary mutations in acromegaly is CA Landis, SB Masters, A Spada, AM Pace, HR Bourne, L Vallar. (1989) GTPase inhibiting mutations activate the α chain of G_s and stimulate adenylyl cyclase in human pituitary tumours. Nature 340: 692-696.

[3]To do so, David Markby in my lab used enzymes to remove the extra region, along with sequence that contains the key arginine, out of the DNA encoding Gs and spliced the remaining Gs sequence back together at the site of excision. For convenience, we called the protein encoded by the respliced cDNA remnant "Ralph," to indicate its "Ras-like" length and putative turnoff properties. The fragment encoded by the piece of cDNA that David

removed was called "Gail," to indicate its putative role as a "GAP-like" domain. The fanciful monikers turned out to be correct predictions: Ralph by itself could bind GTP and stimulate adenylyl cyclase, but was unable to convert GTP to GDP; Gail by itself did neither; mixing pure Gail with pure Ralph, however, allowed the two to associate in an embrace that could convert GTP to GDP at a rate similar to the rate measured with intact Gs. If we replaced the arginine of Gail with another amino acid (as the pituitary mutations did), Ralph embraced Gail quite nicely, but the GTPase turnoff rate was vanishingly slow. Thus David showed that the Gail region, which ordinarily acts as an intrinsic GAP, can also serve as an extrinsic GAP. (See DW Markby, R Onrust, HR Bourne (1993) Separate GTP binding and GTPase activating domains of a Gα subunit. Science 262: 1895-1901.) Just as the Ralph-Gail story was published, Paul Sigler's lab reported the first 3D structure of Gt: exactly as we predicted, the Gail domain snuggles tightly next to one side of the GTP-binding pocket, pointing the arginine side chain toward the GTP. (See JP Noel, HE Hamm, PB Sigler (1993) The 2.2 Å crystal structure of transducin-α complexed with GTPγS. Nature 366: 654-663.)

[4]R Dawkins, *Climbing Mount Improbable* (WW Norton, 1996).

[5]My guess is that this particular timer began as a degenerate enzyme, distinguished by the fact that its shape changed detectably, depending on whether its binding pocket was occupied by its enzymatic target (the magic totem molecule) or by its dummy product. This shape change provided two potential identity tags (saying, in effect, "I am active" or "I am inactive"). The tags could be displayed or hidden, depending on the chemical totem that occupied the binding site. As readers will remember from chapter 1, protein molecules in every cell repeatedly rub up against one another, looking for recognizable identity tags, which tell them where to sit and what to do. We need only imagine that chance mutations in other proteins allowed them to recognize the first G-protein's identities specifically, and act upon them. Eventually, additional mutations conferred some of these other proteins the ability to regulate the G-protein's transitions from one identity to another.

CHAPTER 11. THE 0.7-ANGSTROM CLICK:
RESOLVING A PARADOX

[1]It is the extra phosphate group in guanosine-*tri*phosphate (that is, the third phosphate group in GTP) that makes it a magic totem, able to turn Gs on. This phosphate induces the Gs protein to take on a new shape that can stimulate adenylyl cyclase to make cyclic AMP production. Gs retains that shape until the pocket enzymatically removes the extra phosphate, converting the magic totem into another dummy. In normal Gs, the magic lasts an average of 10-12 seconds.

[2]JP Noel, HE Hamm, PB Sigler (1993) The 2.2 Å crystal structure of transducin-α complexed with GTPγS. Nature 366: 654-663.

[3]Although the actual mathematics remain mysterious to me, here's an impressionistic account of what the crystallographer does. After positioning a crystal containing billions of copies of the protein, she exposes it, at different angles, to a powerful X-ray beam. Because the protein's structure is repeated many times in the crystal, in the same orientation relative to the beam, X-rays "bounce" off atoms in the structure (more precisely, off electrons in those atoms) in such a way that the frequency of bounces at a particular angle correlates with the densities of electrons hit by X-rays at a particular location and angle. The deflected X-rays then collide with a X-ray detector, where they create distinctive patterns of spots. The patterns, of course, differ for every angle at which the crystal was exposed to the beam. Sophisticated mathematical tools convert the intensities and locations of spots into distances between electron densities in the crystal. As a crystallographer explained it to me, it's as if someone gives you a list of the distances between all the structural features of a house—doors, windows, doorknobs, electrical fixtures, heating ducts, etc.—but without naming the features themselves or telling you their relative locations. Your job, of course, is to build the house, but you can't do that without knowing something about where the actual structures are—that is, you need an image of the house. To create an image from the photons in visible light, microscopists and astronomers focus the light with lenses. No physical lens, however, is capable of focusing the X-rays. Accordingly, in place of a lens

crystallographers use additional tricks (e.g., insertion of heavy atoms with great electron densities) and more math to identify locations and specify intensities of the actual electron densities. These are then converted into 3D images (models) that represent relative electron densities in the structure they are studying. Then they build a model of the protein, carefully fitting the chemical structures of amino acids, arranged in the correct sequence, into the 3D pattern of electron densities. Such a model is depicted in Figure 11-2.

[4]T Iiri, P Herzmark, JM Nakamoto, C van Dop, HR Bourne (1994) Rapid GDP release from G_{sa} in patients with gain and loss of endocrine function. Nature 371: 164-168.

CHAPTER 12. THE FULCRUM: MINDS WORKING TOGETHER

[1]My knowledge of mentoring in the law is second-hand, gleaned from my wife's experience as a trainee in law firms and as mentor to "associates" after she became a partner. I know more about mentoring in medicine, by virtue of my own experiences in medical school and as a "house officer" in the somewhat distant past, but also from many friends who have served as doctors in training or as physician mentors.

[2]Long after Gordon's death, I read Sydney Brenner's funny account of a similar process [S Brenner (1997) In Theory. Current Biology 7:R202]. Brenner, a great molecular biologist, wrote that when we are too ignorant to devise an hypothesis that covers all the facts, we apply "Occam's Broom"—that is, we sweep under the carpet unpalatable facts that don't fit whatever hypothesis best accounts for most of the other facts. Gordon would have agreed, with the codicil that we must remember what's under the carpet, which may later turn out to be true and important. Occam's Broom is a pun on Occam's razor, a maximum to the effect that one should always choose the simplest hypothesis that accounts for the facts. The razor may allow us to throw away hypotheses we don't need, but in the real world we sometimes need to "throw away" facts instead, at least tentatively—hence, Occam's Broom.

[3]Bruce, an eminent molecular biologist, was at this time chair of the Department of Biochemistry at UCSF. He later served as president of the National Academy of Sciences and as editor of *Science* magazine.

Chapter 13. Where Now? Can the Fun Last Forever?

None.

CPSIA information can be obtained
at www.ICGtesting.com
Printed in the USA
BVOW10*2310251117

501182BV00002B/34/P